D1010583

Women in College

WITHDRAWN
UTSA Libraries

Books by Mirra Komarovksy

Leisure, a Suburban Study, Co-Author
(with M. A. McInerny and G. Lundberg)

The Unemployed Man and His Family

Women in the Modern World

Common Frontiers of the Social Sciences, Editor

Blue-collar Marriage

Sociology and Public Policy, Editor

Dilemmas of Masculinity

Women in College: Shaping New Feminine Identities

WOMEN IN COLLEGE

Shaping New Feminine Identities

MIRRA KOMAROVSKY

Basic Books, Inc., Publishers

NEW YORK

Library of Congress Cataloging in Publication Data

Komarovsky, Mirra.
  Women in college.

  Bibliography: p. 339.
  Includes index.
   1. Higher education of women—Social aspects—United
States—Case studies. 2. Women's colleges—Social
aspects—United States—Case studies. 3. Vocational
interests—United States—Case studies. 4. Sex
role—United States—Case studies. I. Title.
LC1756.K56 1985   376'.65'0973   84-45307
ISBN 0-465-09198-9

Copyright © 1985 by Mirra Komarovsky
Printed in the United States of America
Designed by Vincent Torre
10 9 8 7 6 5 4 3 2 1

The University of Texas
At San Antonio

To my grandnieces

Sarah, Ruth, Nora, Molly

with the hope that in their lifetime
the gap between the rhetoric of equality
and reality will disappear.

Contents

PART III

Women and Men: Roles in Flux

Acknowledgments

From the inception of this study through its completion, I have received help from many sources. Jacquelyn A. Mattfeld, formerly President of Barnard College, encouraged me to pursue the project and directed me to possible sources of funding. I received the major grant for the first two years of research from the National Institute of Education (NIE G 79-0087). Completion of the study was made possible by a grant from The Dorothy Spivack Fund of Barnard College. I received supplementary grants from the Heyman Family Fund and the Sidney S. Scheuer Foundation. It gives me pleasure to acknowledge my indebtedness to these sources of financial support.

Ellen V. Futter, President of Barnard College, and Charles S. Olton, Dean of the Faculty at Barnard, were unfailingly encouraging and generous throughout the four years of the study, and I am deeply grateful to them.

The following research assistants participated in the interviewing at one or more stages of the study: Geraldine Malter (a graduate of the School of Social Work), Ellen Mayer, Mary Phillips, Susan Christopher, Nancy Naples, and Terry Shtob. All but Ms. Malter were advanced graduate students in sociology. Terry Shtob made an important contribution both as an interviewer and in the analysis of the data on occupational decision making.

James Crawford, Grants Officer of Barnard College for the first three years of the study, facilitated its administration with enthusiasm and devotion. As he took on another assignment in the college, his successor as Grants Officer, Michael Pleters, was helpful on many occasions. Constance Boudelis typed several versions of the manuscript, and it was my fortune to profit from her patience and skill.

I am greatly indebted to Charles H. Page for his generous and skillful editing of several chapters of the manuscript. Rose Coser and Herbert Gans were kind enough to read the original manuscript and to make cogent suggestions.

Judith Greissman, Senior Editor at Basic Books, refused to indulge an impatient author, and the book greatly profited from her editorial revisions.

My greatest obligation is, of course, to the students who participated so generously in this four-year study. They gave much of their time in repeated interviews, partly, perhaps, because of their intrinsic interest, but largely, I suspect, because they shared my conviction that knowledge can lead to the greater use of reason in human life.

Women in College

Introduction

TWO intellectual quests stimulated the writing of this book. First, I sought to understand the experiences of undergraduate women who today confront such rapid transformation of their roles as women. Second, I wanted to find out what impact the college itself had on the women. Did it make a difference in their attitudes and aspirations?

The generation of undergraduate women who are the subjects of this study live in a period of transition from one social system to another. Few changes in American society during recent decades are more radical than the changes in the status of women. To cite but a few examples, in 1950 only one out of five married women was in the labor force. By 1980 slightly over one-half of married women worked. Moreover, a married woman was more likely to work if she had children at home than if she had none. In 1950 women constituted less than one-third of college undergraduates. This percentage had risen to over one-half of all college students by 1980. Other signs of this transformation are seen in the professions. Between 1971 and 1981, the proportion of lawyers and judges who were women rose from 4 to 14 percent; of doctors, from 9 to 22 percent. In 1960 only 28 percent of women aged twenty to twenty-four were unmarried compared to 50 percent in the same age group in 1980 (Woloch 1984:526).

For all the wider opportunities to participate in the public spheres and the more egalitarian values now enjoyed by women, female undergraduates face many dilemmas, inconsistencies, and outright contradictions. They are inspired to reach toward new (for women) levels of achievement in a society that fails to provide the means necessary for the realization of these goals. The problems of combining careers and motherhood is an illustration of such a dilemma. These young women often receive conflicting messages from their parents, who are proud of their daughters' high professional aspirations even as they keep reminding them about the probable costs of such choices. Added to parental ambivalence are the frequently conflicting pressures from male and female friends, the college, and mass media. I shall attempt to identify the varieties of these conflicts and to discover what enabled some college undergraduates to cope with the current confusion while others floundered under cross-pressures of their social world. The fact that some students coped and others failed to cope may suggest to readers that it all depends on the individual. Nothing could be further from the author's position. Whatever the makeshift arrangements some individuals succeed in making today, the roots of the current problems are social. The concluding chapter of this book outlines the institutional and cultural changes required to resolve the current disorganization adequately.

The existing literature on the second problem—the impact of college—is so voluminous as to raise the question: Why another study? What remains to be discovered? A single reference, an assessment of four decades of research on the impact of college on students (Feldman and Newcomb 1969) contains a seventy-five-page bibliography of past studies. Moreover, numerous studies since 1969 are listed in the bibliography of this book.

Vast as this literature is, the reader will not escape one repeated lament. This is explicit in Feldman and Newcomb's conclusion, where they state that inferences from freshman-senior differences on tests, the predominant method of such research, tells us little of the "actual processes by which different students adapt in different ways to their college environments" (p. 48).

More recent studies that report the high achievement record of graduates of women's colleges also underscore the need for studying the processes at work (Tidball and Kistiakowsky 1976; Oates and Williamson 1978). "The 1980 Profile of Women's Colleges" is very explicit in its conclusion: "What occurs at these colleges to encourage the development of leadership and aspiration? Further research on the most salient characteristics of academic environments and their effects on students is needed" (The Women's College Coalition, p. 8). Another study, by Brown (1982), concludes on the same note:

> This is a descriptive study of differences in the outcomes for women with different college experiences and different initial career plans. These data do not show a causal relationship between college environments and women's career plans—women in selective women's colleges, regardless of their initial plans, seem more likely to

express the Ph.D/Professional career plans at the end of college. . . . The lack of stability in college effects on women's career outcomes is somewhat disconcerting. Future research should focus on identifying the characteristics of women's colleges that facilitate women's career plans (p. 327).

Taking up the challenges suggested by these cited researchers, the present study and this book asks: What are the processes by which students (in this case, women) react in similar or different ways to their college experience? What predispositions and which features of the college account for the similarities and differences? Of course, no single study can encompass the full range of college influences. This study focuses on what might be termed the gender perspective of female undergraduates: their lifestyle aspirations—that is, the relative importance of marriage, children, and work in their plans for the future— and attitudes, beliefs, and values related to their feminine identities.

The selection of the women's college (one of the so-called Seven Sisters) as the site of research was deliberate. The graduates of this college, part of a major university located in a metropolis, have an exceptionally high record of professional achievement, a fact noted in the literature but not conclusively accounted for. A fuller profile of the college is included in the appendix.

Obviously, the results of this investigation will not be representative of female undergraduates at other colleges. My review of the literature will serve, to some extent, to place the findings in relation to other recent studies.[1]

The purpose of this research, however, is not to compare

---

[1] Some of the major studies of peer influence, teacher-student interaction, and related topics were done in secondary schools rather than in colleges. These studies are not included in the literature review.

educational institutions. The crucial comparisons are those among the various subgroups of the college. The research strategy focused on identifying the various patterns of persistence and change and on attempting to account for the observed difference. By way of illustration, at entrance to college in 1979, some students had no interest in lifelong careers and remained in this sense "traditional" until the end of their senior year. Others equally traditional at entrance became committed to careers. Which factors in their backgrounds and which aspects of the college experience contributed to these different outcomes?

THE FOUR-YEAR RESEARCH

The study began in the fall of 1979 when 630 freshmen entered college. A random sample, stratified by race and religion, was selected out of the total. It consisted of 241 students who each received a set of questionnaires, scales, and tests. By my and my assistants' deadline, two weeks later, the rate of return was 96 percent of the original number approached, giving us a sample of 232 students, including both residents and commuters.

This unusually high rate of return may be explained by the fact that the study had been announced at the orientation meeting of the entire freshman class and by several mail and telephone follow-up requests for student cooperation.

In addition to the quantitative data contained in 232 sets of questionnaires and scales, 201 students were interviewed for about an hour, to clarify and supplement their completed forms. The intended choice of major and of occupation and the Life-Style Index (career and family aspirations for the future) were the primary topics probed in these interviews. For example, a student who checked several occupational options was asked to specify the perceived advantages and disadvantages of alternatives and, hence, was very apt to reveal some of her values, uncertainties, and conflicts.

In the spring semester, nine freshmen kept diaries, following an outline I prepared, and were interviewed every two weeks. (They received a modest honorarium for this work.) The purpose of the diaries was to generate hypotheses regarding the impact of college on the study's dependent variables for the interviews in the fall of 1980.

The second phase of the research took place in the beginning of the sophomore year, September 1980. Fourteen of the students in the original sample had withdrawn from the college. The others received replications of all the research instruments measuring dependent variables—for example, life-style preferences, attitudes toward sex roles, choice of major and of occupation, attitudes toward the women's movement, and the preferred age of marriage. Ninety percent of the sophomores returned this second wave of questionnaires, giving us a sophomore sample of 196 students. The major research procedure at this time consisted of interviewing a subsample of these respondents. Five students refused to be interviewed; seventy agreed to two two-hour interviews. Three interviewers assisted the author. They followed a twenty-two-page guide prepared by the author. Each taped interview was summarized by the interviewer, and the transcribed two-part interviews averaged about forty typewritten pages each.

The final phase of the study took place in the academic year 1982–1983, the students' senior year. (There were no tests or interviews in the junior year.) In the fall of 1982, all of the 175 members of the original sample still in college received questionnaires replicating those sent to them in their sophomore year. The rate of response was 88 percent, yielding a sample of 154 seniors.

In addition to the quantitative measures, two-hour interviews with sixty-five seniors were held in the spring of 1983. Three research associates assisted the author in conducting the senior interviews.

Our methods, consequently, combined quantitative measures (questionnaires and scales) and qualitative data (interviews and diaries). Although the interview was the major research tool, the interplay of both methods was a distinct feature of the study. The techniques of interviewing are described in the appendix.

The interview process produced rich descriptions of experiences. The limitation of such in-depth case studies is of necessity their small numbers and, hence, the statistical unreliability of intrasample comparisons. But many hypotheses of this study are buttressed by the internal evidence of the interviews—the expressed attitudes of the respondents related to the sequences of events. A statistical correlation that is a mere accident of sampling would not be supported by such further evidence. For example, we found an association between strained parental marriages (or divorce) on the one hand and the daughter's career commitment on the other. Although the sample was relatively small, supporting evidence for this association was forthcoming in several interviews. To illustrate, daughters of divorced parents often attributed their determination to pursue a career to the failure of their mothers' traditional role. In the words of one such student:

> We lived in the suburbs, my father had a business, my mother was a perfect American housewife. Then my father left us high and dry, and my mother had no education and a mortgage to pay. So we had to be

uprooted to this miserable place where no one understood me. I've learned that that's not a good plan to follow.

The procedure of discerning causal links in a single case is discussed further in the appendix. There is another compensating advantage of in-depth interviews compared to surveys using large and statistically more reliable samples. The abundant excerpts herein from interviews do more than "illustrate" a concept or a generalization—they convey additional knowledge, the kind that captures in richer detail the flavor of life experience of women undergraduates. The reader catches the idiom and the tone, the intensity of feeling, the indignation and the humor, the association of ideas, the overtones of pride or embarrassment. Here, for example, are the words of a student from a tight ethnic community who, after an initial rebellion against her family, returned to the fold in her senior year.

> I was so determined to break away from my family and the entire community that I drove to the college with a vengeance. The more they told me not to go out, the more I'd go out. . . . I told them this: "If you told me to go left, I'd go right." Now I realize I can't keep making decisions based on what my parents don't want to do. I have to think of what I really want. I've had my escape for four years and it's time to return to reality. . . . In my freshman year, when I used to think about a career it was kind of exotic: It was like I'd see something in a movie. I would see a picture of myself out there. Now I know I don't belong in that movie. I would feel ostracized from my community.

The use of excerpts from the interviews throughout this book is intended, in a kind of fusion of scientific and "literary" functions, to convey the immediacy of an experience even as it seeks to communicate some of the major theoretical concerns of this study. The variety of ways in which the college operates as an agent of socialization for women's roles, the forces that shield some students from the influences that change others, the social mechanisms of coping with cross-pressures exerted by competing demands or conflicting values of significant others in the lives of students—these and other sociological concepts acquire fuller meaning and come to life as the interviews unfold.

The choice of the interview as the dominant method was dictated by one other, related consideration. It is the author's hope that this book will be useful to students, professors, and college personnel; to parents; and to others concerned with women's education. To anticipate some value that students may derive from reading these personal accounts, the introductory chapters on the transition to college are a case in point. The helpless bewilderment of a freshman who imagines that her difficulties are unique may give way to a greater degree of rational detachment as she discovers the near-universality of some problems. Equally valuable is the confrontation with the diversity of other problems and adaptations. Personal growth comes about as the student, previously limited by preconceptions of her social and psychological identity, is exposed to new regional, class, and ethnic subcultures, as well as diverse personalities. Experience, in and of itself, does not always suffice to ensure intellectual awareness and conceptual ordering of the chaotic flow of events.

If this is true of interaction with classmates, it is more true in relationships between professors and students, contacts that are of necessity circumscribed. But whatever new insights the teacher can acquire into the world of undergraduates are bound to enhance her or his performance as teacher. Information provided by the interviews should contribute to this end.

So much for the possible uses of the vivid descriptions the students themselves provided of their varied experiences. As for the study as a whole, it is the author's hope that, in identifying the characteristics of this college that served so admirably to develop the student's potential, the book can point the way to some educational policies that would serve this goal even more effectively.

PART I

The Transition

to College

This book is based on interviews with women undergraduates. The names I have used of all the individuals are not real names and some locales and identifying details have been altered, while preserving the integrity of the case studies.

1

Integration into the College Community

WHETHER they approached it with idealized expectations or apprehension, freshmen regarded the transition to college as a major step toward adulthood. They saw their tasks clearly: to wean themselves from dependence on their parents; to establish relationships with a variety of classmates and others; and to develop self-discipline for demanding college study without the supportive supervision of secondary schools.

The reality of the first months of college—"knowledge by experience"—brought many unexpected challenges, disappointments, and satisfactions. Overall, each freshman had to discover the "shoulds" and "should nots" of the new social milieu—the norms for relating to roommates, classmates, faculty and administration, and male friends. Novel situations are bound to require some improvisation

15

of roles since familiar social scripts seldom fit perfectly. Put most generally, social interaction is a balancing act because one is unlikely to maximize all valued goals simultaneously. How much more difficult this balance becomes when the freshman college student is uncertain of existing norms and consequently of risks inherent in alternative decisions.

Moving into college residences frequently presented problems ranging from noise, standards of cleanliness, and taste in furnishings to conflict in moral values. Such differences raised dilemmas of choice. What frustrations should one tolerate in order not to alienate potential friends? How, for example, does one strike a balance between the wish for privacy and the desire for sociability? Does one keep the door to one's room open, can a visitor come in at any time after knocking, or does one set limits to protect sleep and study? The norms governing relationships between roommates had to be learned. One freshman wanted to spend the night at her boyfriend's but her roommate was sick. Should she return early to attend to the sick friend? If she didn't, would she—*should* she—feel guilty?

In another case, when her boyfriend from another college came to visit, a freshman expected her roommate to accommodate her by moving out for the night. The indignant roommate refused, only to wonder subsequently whether such a request was generally deemed to be legitimate. Incidentally, this particular situation remained troublesome even when roommates shared the same values, as reported by one student in her freshman journal:

If the two are good friends, they both feel guilty: the one who imposes this problem and the one who has the option of thwarting her friend's love life. In a case like this, it usually goes on for as long as the person who is alone can tolerate it or until the couple starts to feel uncomfortable. The person who is alone usually gives in to the boyfriend spending the night because if she says "no," she will either (a) seem jealous or (b) seem to have sexual hangups of her own. So she says nothing. But then the couple begins to feel guilty for imposing on the girl. Having been on both sides of the fence, I find this a situation to be avoided like the plague.

Another first-year student in a coed dormitory was disturbed by the loud rock music played late into the night by freshman males. The latter, in turn, were indignant at her request for quiet. Now that they were liberated from parental nagging, wasn't a degree of rowdy freedom, they remonstrated, exactly "what college life was all about"?

One student found her two suitemates casual about paying bills and doing housekeeping chores. Made uncomfortable by this disorder, she was prepared to assume more than her fair share of responsibilities. But would she thereby acquire the reputation of being a "heavy," a reputation that her suitemates would certainly convey to the male friends frequenting the apartment?

One final illustration from a freshman journal:

> I had always taken it for granted that a girlfriend would forgive you if you broke a plan in order to see a guy. An evening with a guy is a change of pace, whereas you can see your girlfriend any time. But my roommate was furious when I broke our date for a guy. She said that I was disloyal and lacked respect for women.

This student's background had apparently insulated her from the new cultural value of the solidarity of "sisterhood."

Beyond the general problem of learning new norms,

there are four specific problem areas in making the transition to college: forming social ties with classmates and, to a lesser extent with professors and college counselors—that is, the task of integration into the college community; the vicissitudes of academic self-esteem; the impact of culture shock upon the student's self-concept; and separation from the family. Each of these problem areas is the subject, in turn, of this and the next two chapters.

FORMATION OF SOCIAL TIES

The site of this study was a women's college. An editorial in the student newspaper of the affiliated men's college, published during freshman orientation week, sought to prepare incoming students for the impersonality of the new environment:

> You're all out in the wilderness now, away from your homes and your roots, wandering around trying to spot where you can settle down—you are trying to fit in. But there is no "in" at [this university]. The first thing you're going to have to learn about student life after orientation is that there isn't any. No, you are not going to die, but a lot of the time you're going to feel that no one at this school would really care if you did.
>
> The basic attitude . . . is that, if you are a student at this school, you know how to handle yourself . . . how to select your courses, find your way around the [city], handle all the emotional traumas that come with being a student.

How prophetic was this warning for the students entering

the women's college of the university? I estimate that some 43 percent of the freshmen did not resonate to the dismal tone of the editorial.[1] In the words of one seemingly well-adjusted student:

> I felt comfortable in the college from the very start. Everyone on my dorm floor got along really well. We all ate together. Until we got to make other friends, we could always find company with people on the floor. My two best friends now are girls I met on the floor in the first month of college.

For a significant proportion—57 percent of the sample—however, feelings of alienation and loneliness did color their introduction to college. These feelings varied in intensity from extreme to moderate and transitory. Among the lonely students, the phrases "I found college cold and impersonal" and "No one knew my name" became a familiar refrain in the interviews. One such student recollects: "I went for days without talking to anyone, and it was depressing to walk across the campus and not even see a familiar face. I felt lonely and intimidated, as if I didn't really belong at the college."

Such isolation in the midst of dense collective activity in packed elevators, classrooms, libraries, and cafeterias resulted not only in loneliness but in a disorienting loss of identity. Lack of communication results in pluralistic ignorance of the extent to which this emotion is shared by others. This, in turn, explains the recurrent complaint of cold indifference on the part of classmates. "I was surprised," remarked a freshman, "how cold people were. No one

---

[1] The percentages based on the total sample are not to be taken as representing the class of 1983 as a whole. Our random sample was stratified by race and religion. Certain minority groups were more numerous in the sample than in the class as a whole. Offsetting this disadvantage was the opportunity the procedure provided to compare racial and religious groups.

reached out to me, no one stopped me after class to talk, no one on this campus wanted to form a friendship." Again: "People just come in and out of class and that's it. You don't even see them on the campus." "I used to walk into the lunchroom," said another puzzled freshman, "and see people sitting there by themselves eating, looking down into their plates as if they didn't want to meet another's eye." And another freshman admitted that when she did have lunch in the college cafeteria, she ate quickly, looking down at her plate in order not to appear as lonely and insecure as she felt.

It is against this background that we can understand the warm appreciation so frequently expressed for a teacher who "knows my name!" It is as if this recognition reestablishes the lost identity.

Even a freshman who had no difficulty in making friends admitted: "You have to be outgoing and friendly and not afraid to reach out to people. People who are shy probably have a lot of trouble making friends here *because no one is likely to walk right up to you and start a conversation.*" (Italics added.)

An interesting nuance in norms governing the initiation of social interaction was reported by several students. The first few days of freshman orientation are characterized by friendly gregariousness. Reminisced one freshman:

> People assume that they are all strangers in the same boat and they approach each other freely. But this cools down very fast. After a while no one knows what's accepted or not accepted and I was afraid to give the impression of being lost and stupid. Everyone except me appeared to be walking briskly and knowing where they were going. This added to my sense of insecurity.

Another freshman expressed a similar opinion: "At first it

was still respectable to go up to somebody and introduce yourself because everybody was new. Later this would be considered rather forward; you might be barging in when little groups have already formed."

The overtones of desperate loneliness are evident in the sacrifices some students made in the interests of "belonging." One freshman entered college with a high-school friend and clung to a clique that soon formed around her friend, though she strongly disapproved of their values. She found the group superficial, materialistic, not interested in studies or in careers, and concerned only with finding husbands. She had nothing in common with their Gucci outfits. But she needed to be able to say "hello" to someone and to be with some familiar people. In order to preserve some sort of identity, she used to show up looking very unkempt and be criticized for her appearance. Apparently this role of a rebel was the best compromise she could make between her self-esteem on the one hand and the need to "belong" on the other.

And another excerpt from an interview: "I had envisioned college experience as running all over campus, bumping all the time into people you know—a total social environment. But it turned out to be quite different and I felt very lonely. You get so overwhelmed here that you don't want to stick out and start a conversation." This was all the more surprising for this student because she had been very social in high school.

We had expected the commuter-resident status to be a major determinant among the alienating social factors, but no significant difference was found between the two groups. The explanation of this surprising result lies in the need to distinguish between integration into the college community (or some segment of it) on the one hand and the subjective experience of alienation and loneliness on the other. The commuters complained that leaving the campus in the late afternoon and being away over the weekend made participation in campus activities virtually impossible. For some going to college turned out to be merely attending classes—a disappointing continuation of high school.

In comparison with the residents, the commuters were indeed handicapped in forging new social ties. Yet despite this peripheral relationship with the college community, they failed to report a stronger sense of loneliness. The explanation is likely to lie in the fact that they continued to enjoy the familiar supports of their families and frequently of their high-school friends as well. The residents, although they did have an advantage in establishing campus social relationships, missed these former supports.

If continued association with high-school friends mitigated the commuters' loneliness at the start of the freshman year, this advantage weakened over the course of the year. The high-school friends who were still accessible in home communities generally attended public colleges. The differences between them and the freshmen attending this Ivy League college soon generated a reciprocal process of alienation. The freshmen, full of new experiences, sometimes irritated their local friends, several of whom complained, "All you talk about is your college." On their part, the Ivy League freshmen also experienced a sense of estrangement from the local crowd. In the words of one student:

Sometimes when I am out for the weekend with my high-school friends, I feel like I no longer belong. They are exposed to the same people and the same things as in high school. I, on the other hand, am living in a completely different atmosphere. My college classmates are more intelligent and more cultured. I think I am gaining maturity and poise, and it often makes me feel superior and even further removed from my friends. This tends to make me feel mad and a little guilty because I would like to maintain my friendships.

Campus residence facilitated social interaction, but it did not ensure it when roommates or floormates proved uncongenial. One freshman described her head-on collision with a roommate: "We were complete opposites. I was neat; she was messy. I was studious and she was social and wanted to party in our room on the expressed conviction that the appropriate place for study was the library, not one's room. She went out with men a lot and would stay over and I didn't believe in that." Another student complained: "No two people on my floor were alike. Some were eggheads, others druggies or punks. They weren't well-rounded people with whom I could associate."

Apart from residential-commuter status, other social factors affected both the degree of social integration into the college milieu and the experience of alienation. Entering college with a friend or friends was a significant factor in early adjustment both for commuters and residents. A student who moved into the dormitory with two old friends was exultant: "I was so lucky! I didn't have to make the adjustment of living in a little box with total strangers; I didn't have to enter the dining room alone and face all those unfriendly faces. I am not one to go to a pickup bar and be part of the meat market." Her two friends not only spared her these experiences, but the threesome ventured out to attract other classmates and soon became the active center of a larger group of female and male friends.

Besides the commuters and residents, a small group of students stood in a rather different relationship to the college community. These students remained on the periphery of the college social life by choice. Their significant social ties were with neither high-school friends nor college classmates, but with other circles in the metropolis to which they were linked through relatives, boyfriends, or some special interests.

Racial, ethnic, and religious minorities, however alienated some may have felt from the dominant community, enjoyed an advantage from an administrative decision to set aside some freshman orientation events that put members of these minorities in touch with one another, and the religious clubs on campus served a similar function. These social affiliations bound students into segregated groups. One Hispanic student appreciated this arrangement as a source of support in a predominantly white school. "A lot of Hispanics are not wealthy," she said. "And it was important to have other Hispanics guide us around. It did not make me feel segregated. It was a help to know that there were others like me here."

Some members of minority groups, even while enjoying the support this provided, felt, however, that they paid a price for it. Confessed one freshman: "I have always opposed segregation along racial and ethnic lines. After all, one of the major advantages of college is supposedly to break down such divisions. But here I am: having joined my own group at the outset, I now feel bound to it."

Not every member of a minority could take advantage of such opportunity for ready-made affiliation. The most isolated freshmen were members of Black, Hispanic, Asian, and other minority groups who resented this "imposed" identification because class, cultural, or religious differences estranged them from their minority classmates. Our interviews have provided half a dozen poignant accounts of these marginal women who spent their freshman year in conflict over their identity and on the periphery of both their own ethnic and other groups.

Among other social factors affecting the transition to

college, the student's place of origin—such as size of community, region of the country, and a foreign birthplace—played an important part. This situation is discussed in chapter 2 in the section on culture shock.

So far we have considered peer relationships of the entering freshmen. Teachers and counselors, by and large, did not seem to provide sufficient channels of integration into the college community. Freshmen confessed feeling too intimidated by faculty members to initiate contacts. They felt that only "a specific question" or a "good reason" would justify making use of a professor's office hours. Some students attributed this social distance to their own shyness; others projected the blame upon the faculty who, they felt certain, would find a visit to the office an unwelcome interruption unless a specific problem justified it. As for freshman advisers, the students generally reported that their contacts with them were limited to getting required signatures at registration.

Yet a number of students found their place in the college community almost from the outset. For some, strong intellectual interests, combined with purposeful self-direction, served to overcome the social distance between students and faculty. These students participated in class discussions and often initiated conferences with their teachers, setting up a rewarding cycle of instructor interest in them that increased their intellectual engagement.

A few students who had felt themselves to be somewhat deviant during high school, because of their strong intellectual interests or feminist values or both, found the climate of the college particularly exhilarating. They were now rewarded for qualities penalized by their high-school peers, and this enhanced their self-esteem and motivation.

Still another mode of integration into the college community was exemplified when students with strong artistic, athletic, religious, or political interests were lucky or energetic enough to find on the campus extracurricular activities representing these concerns.

Skillful and enterprising manipulation of the "impersonal" environment served to provide warm reassurance to some students who craved personal relationships with adults. Equally dependent students, lacking such skills, felt deprived. An example of this enterprising approach was reported by a freshman who, with a classmate, decided to take the chance of inviting a female professor to dinner. Their initiative paid off. The professor accepted, and other social gatherings of several students and two faculty members of their department followed.

A few students reaped some advantage from the impersonality of the campus, testifying to its maturational effect. The very frequency with which classmates were seen walking, eating, or studying alone tended to remove the stigma attached to such isolation. This in turn meant that when individuals preferred solitude, they could choose it without feeling deviant.

The greater freedom to follow one's preference without humiliation is illustrated by the following excerpt from an interview: "I was surprised to see so many people sitting by themselves in the college cafeteria. Some were eating with their face in a book, signaling that they didn't want to be bothered." The student explained that eventually she herself was no longer afraid of having lunch by herself. Her schedule was so busy that it was restful to have a little time to be alone. Nevertheless, she still wouldn't eat alone in a restaurant, for she would imagine people thinking: "Oh, that poor person. She has nobody to eat with."

In a similar vein, another student remarked:

When I came to this campus, I had a lot of growing up to do. In high school I had six close friends and I was very happy that way. But now I learned to deal with some people casually, on a superficial level. Before coming to college, I didn't see this as being a valuable asset. But now I've learned that this is important not only in order to survive on this campus but in jobs and in life in general. And I have learned to do it.

The problems of estrangement described throughout this chapter characterize the initial stage of transition to college. A small minority of students continued to feel alienated from classmates throughout the freshman year. In some cases, the very severity of the difficulties suggests psychic conflicts; other problems point to a poor fit between class, cultural, and general social characteristics of the student on the one hand and the dominant climate of the institution on the other.

One such psychic strain is described by a white student, a daughter of educated parents:

I have never lived through such depression, such isolation, and such loneliness. I had pinned a lot of hopes on college. When coming here, I thought I would meet a lot of really incredible people, people who were truly intellectuals but who also had heart. All I found were phony people who had neither heart nor real intellect. Working this summer was a startling experience because I found that these working-class people were much stronger, and were also just more giving, more understanding, more caring, and more accepting. I don't have anything good to say about the people at this college or anything good to say about my experiences with them. All I can say is that the women I've met here are a bunch of assholes. The people here made me feel afraid of my emotional makeup, but I don't want to become cold like them and distant, and I don't want to become like my mother. She would fit in better here because she's got something bad to say about everybody and she is also cold and controlled. The people here were not willing to open up to me and therefore I wasn't willing to open up to them.

This student dropped out of college in her sophomore year.

Another student, a daughter of foreign-born, middle-class, Catholic parents, also had an unhappy freshman year. Hers was a problem of disappointment with herself on all fronts. Despite her conscientious study, her grades fell below her expectations. But what most depressed her was her social life:

It's the people-meeting part of college life that is driving me crazy. Most of my high-school friends have boyfriends and I feel left out. The people in college who don't interest me are the ones who always try to be friendly. The people who lead more interesting lives than I do, and whom I would like to associate with, so intimidate me that I don't know what to say when I meet them.

Such isolated students were a small minority, however. The great majority did form social ties. As will be discussed in chapters 2 and 3, the most striking findings are the changes students felt they have undergone by the end of the freshman year and the primary influence of the peer group as the source of these changes.

In summary, a considerable proportion of the students either felt integrated into the social and intellectual life of the college from the outset or possessed personal resources to overcome some institutional obstacles and became all the more mature and independent in the process. Others, with few social contacts on the campus, enjoyed a year of vigorous intellectual awakening.

The debit side of the ledger, however, is important. Limited interaction with their teachers outside the classroom deprived freshmen of the intellectual engagement such contacts might have generated. Feelings of isolation depleted energies available for academic work. Peer groups emerged in this study as a major factor in the students' development, even if they occasionally demanded excessive conformity.

The recognition of these problems was undoubtedly the impetus for significant institutional changes that happened to coincide with the study. The number of freshman advisers was substantially increased, from nine to thirty-one. In an effort to create a heightened sense of community, the college adopted certain features of the "house system" to link professors and administrators to particular college residences. This, in turn, involved faculty participation in some social activities of the students (dinners, teas, and the like) as well as occasional lectures, discussions, or musical events.

Perhaps the major change was a curricular reform requiring every entering freshman to register for a freshman seminar with a maximum of eighteen students. The seminars, led by mature teacher-scholars, center on broad-ranging intellectual issues and aim at stimulating student participation and developing abilities in oral discourse and in writing. In the large introductory lecture classes, the passive or shy student can avoid interaction with professors. The small seminars might lead to more active participation and intellectual engagement of the freshman at the very outset of her college career.

2

Changing
Self-Concepts

THE TRANSITION to college takes place in late adolescence—a period characterized by the insistent press of two questions: "What kind of person am I: bright, shy, warm, sexy, selfish, moody, ambitious . . . ?," and "What kind of person do I want to be?"

In the search for answers, the freshman scrutinizes her peers and professors for clues about both her own personality and her ideals. In the words of one freshman: "What is this girl with her head in the books all the time up to? Should I be like her?" This watchful scrutiny may be disturbing both in the new insights into oneself and in the confusion about ideals.

This section is concerned with academic performance. Other changes in self-concept are the subject of the next part of this chapter, "Culture Shock."

VICISSITUDES OF ACADEMIC SELF-ESTEEM

A handful of freshmen found college work less difficult than the reputation of the college had led them to expect. The overwhelming majority, however, found the transition from high school to college a severe challenge.

One general aspect of this challenge was the college's expectation that the student is mature enough to assume full responsibility for meeting academic requirements. As one freshman put it: "In high school we were treated as unruly children who must be constantly supervised on the assumption that, otherwise, we would do everything wrong. In college you are suddenly on your own, and expected to do everything right." The proper allocation of time was one such new responsibility: How much to study? What to do with an hour between classes? How to review for exams? As indicated in the following text, the manner in which individual students coped with these particular questions was one of the determinants of academic success.

Challenging though college courses generally were, the level of academic achievement during the freshman year did not constitute a problem for 45 percent of the sample who performed well and whose grades were high, in a few cases higher, than they had anticipated. By contrast, 49 percent suffered some crisis of self-confidence, varying from severe to relatively moderate. (The remaining 6 percent of the cases were ambiguous.) This chapter is principally concerned with the second group.

It was to be expected that in a highly selective college students at the top of their high schools academically, now in competition with equally able peers, would be likely to face a change in their ranking on the local totem pole. One freshman who did not receive a single A on her first set of college examinations was shaken:

I was having trouble adjusting to the idea that I was just average. I had never been average in my life. I wanted straight A's. I was raised with the idea that if you try hard enough, you can do whatever you want. So when I didn't get the better grades I felt that I just blew my whole future.

Another freshman reported:

I came to college feeling very confident because I was at the top of my high-school class, a member of a small group of elites. But the very first day of classes, it hit me when students would raise their hands and give these really brilliant comments and I felt that they were a lot smarter than I. It was a very deflating experience.

"Being a big shot in high school spoiled me," admitted another freshman: "I didn't do very well here. I wasn't special and that was a big comedown." And similar voices:

I always knew that I would face greater competition once I got to college, but I thought I would still come out on top. I was wrong and I have trouble dealing with it. If I get a B− on a paper, I think that I will always be a B− student *and a B− person.* I know this is a fallacy, but I can't help feeling dragged down by my grades.

Again: "I was used to being the outstanding female, and now I'm in a school with a lot of outstanding women. This college makes me feel very insecure. I regressed."

Among those disappointed with their academic performance, the intensity of the stress varied with two circumstances. The sense of failure was linked less to the objective level of accomplishment than to the gap between aspiration and results. One freshman who received B's in all her courses was so depressed to have fallen below her customary high-school A record that she considered seeking therapy.

The degree of stress varied also with the salience of academic achievement for the freshman's self-esteem. For members of groups in which popularity with men was the basis of prestige, and for students with family or other problems, disappointment with grades was mitigated or overshadowed by these other concerns.

What were the responses to a damaged self-concept? Some students' initial reactions were clearly maladaptive in the sense that they resulted in a still deeper sense of failure. A freshman who entered college aspiring to be a writer tells her story:

> I had the reputation of being an excellent writer in my high school. My English teacher thought so and took a personal interest in my writing. So I was shocked when in my first college English course my professor wrote a note saying that I was intelligent but needed help with my writing. She offered to work with me. I was so let down by this note that I never bothered to go to see her. I didn't feel close to her and didn't want to discuss coldly something that was so important to me.

A similar cycle of disappointment, withdrawal, and still lower achievement is described by a freshman who was so "depressed" by poor grades at midterm that she "lost all motivation to study. I began to neglect my studies and, feeling guilty, I would nevertheless often go to a play or a party before an exam. This didn't help my grades." "It kills me," said another freshman, "to get a B− and, when I do, I turn to other things, like partying with guys."

An insightful student described her angry reaction to the competition encountered in college:

> I did absolutely nothing all year. I got by because of my

superior high-school background. I wrote the required papers but I put absolutely nothing into them. It was a ridiculous attitude. I know what it is to be motivated but this was my way of reacting to the competition. I figured I would show them that I can still pass my courses without studying.

Another reaction to disappointment in academic achievement was to question the system of rewards, more specifically to stress the irrationality of grading, which allegedly rewards and penalizes in fortuitous ways, reflecting neither student ability nor effort. "It's not that I don't study," explained an earnest student, "it's that I don't have the intuitive knack some people have of knowing what to give the teacher on exams." A peevish classification of students was given by this disappointed freshman:

> There are, of course, some students who cut classes and drift through four years of college, clinging by a hair to minimal requirements. But I am immensely jealous of the fortunate people who do some work, without being workaholics, and do very well on exams, fooling their professors into thinking they are studying very hard. Finally come the most unfortunate souls: those who study hard and conscientiously and then come across as lazy and dumb *because they don't have the knack to do well on tests.* I guess I fit into the last category. (Italics added.)

Insofar as the disappointed students appeared to displace the blame from self to others, the faculty fared much better than fellow students. Only a handful of the interviewees attributed their failure to a "batch of rotten teachers who oversaturate you with dry nuts and bolts, without conveying the deeper implications of their subjects." Much more pervasive was the attribution of "cutthroat" competitiveness to classmates. The recurrent and bitter accounts of competitiveness sometimes had the ring of a mythology fed by anxiety and rivalry.

The accepted norm, at least in this college, prohibited direct inquiries about grades as an infringement of privacy. Curiosity had to be satisfied by a general question: "How did you do?" and an equally general response: "Not so well" or "Pretty good." Close friends, of course, gave fuller information.

This convention of semiconfidentiality alleviated but did not eliminate the strain of competition. For one thing, the norm was sometimes violated. "They would boast about their grades," complained a student, "and ask you what you got on this test or that paper. You could tell that they were glad if they did better than you."

Moreover, competitiveness impinged upon students in other ways—for example, in the reluctance of a classmate to lend notes or in the difficulty of organizing study groups before exams. References to the ruthless competitiveness of premed students, fueled by anxiety over admission to medical schools, were commonplace. So were stories, generally based on hearsay, detailing incidents of foul play and including also the male premeds of the affiliated college: buying term papers, destroying a rival's experiment in the laboratory, making a deal with the teaching assistant, a female undergraduate offering sex to a male teaching assistant in exchange for a copy of a forthcoming exam. However trustworthy these accounts, they clearly reflected both anxiety and rivalry.

This competitive atmosphere was praised by a few students, though the benefits attributed to it were not always in the service of the ideals of a liberal education. One student, proud of her insight, noted:

I used to see academics as an end in themselves. But I

suddenly realized that the greatest value of the college is in training you for the competitive world outside the classroom. College is just a microcosm of what it's like to be in any competitive situation. You feel good if you overcome the barriers, which is really what life is like.

These maladaptive reactions to the initial blow to self-esteem appeared to undermine academic performance. Some sense of the failure to cope is conveyed by a student struggling to keep afloat:

After staying up very late to type a paper, I missed my alarm and didn't make class. I decided to skip the rest of my classes because I had a midterm the next day. . . . I had also missed a few classes before the winter break because I had been studying for other midterms.

. . . I had my suitemate's boyfriend wake me early so I could study some more. He woke me at 8:30, but between showering and talking to my suitemates, I didn't start studying until 10:00. I skipped my first two classes in order to keep studying for another test.

This student had three incompletes at the end of the first semester.

In sharp contrast with such defeated students were others, equally disappointed in their initial grades, who took steps to analyze and improve their academic performance and who succeeded in regaining their self-esteem. The major factor associated with improvement was a change in study habits. As reported in the interviews, only rarely was this change brought about with faculty assistance. One freshman was so discouraged by her initial poor performance that she felt "very close to quitting college." One of her teachers, however, had developed a technique of helping students with their research, studying, and writing in special conferences. She attributes to him her renewed confidence and enthusiasm about college.

The influence of classmates in improved habits of study was mentioned much more frequently. For example, one interviewed student testified that she was "shocked" to receive all C's on her first set of midterms.

> She was depressed to let her parents down, all the more so because they were spending so much money to send her to an Ivy League school. She kept phoning her parents to apologize for her poor grades, but they urged her not to take the first grades so to heart.
>
> This student decided to observe and talk to classmates about their study methods. She realized that she "screwed up" her studying by following her customary high-school pattern of cramming for exams the night before. At home everything was slow and laid back and she hadn't realized how fast-paced the college classes would be. The women in her dorm were "high-speed" women who got their work done quickly and on time, and she tried to follow their example. She stopped reading novels and studied daily instead of waiting till the tests. She was delighted to end up with a B+ average for the first semester, and her parents teased her: "See, we told you that you could do it."

Another student recouped her self-esteem not only by more work but by a deliberate decision to participate in class discussions, an action that, in turn, increased her self-confidence:

> "I got really frightened at first. In high school I felt that most students were less intelligent than I." But, in the first weeks of college, she was shocked to hear students talk intelligently in class about books she'd never even heard of. "This shook my self-confidence and I never volunteered in class." After the first set of

exams, she decided to talk to a lot of students, people she didn't even know, about the test and as a result decided that, brilliant as some students were, if she worked hard she could measure up. Moreover, she understood the importance of discussing issues in class even if "one wasn't so completely certain of one's views."

The following excerpts also testify to the importance of classmates for those students who improved their performance.

Another freshman, disappointed in her early grades, began "to watch the studying of my friends." She soon realized that the pattern of studying that worked for her in high school would not do in college. She was in the habit of letting the less interesting work slide and then cramming as hard as she could before exams. Her more successful college friends, on the other hand, kept up with all their courses throughout the semester and then were relaxed before exams. She watched them organize their work and tried to emulate them.

One academically successful student tried to provide tutelage to a friend:

Try to keep up a steady pace of three to four hours of studying every day. I do. I had heard stories about people pulling allnighters a couple of times a week. I don't think that's the proper way to study, even for an exam. I work hard, but I don't go crazy and overprepare. One example, for our geology exam we had to answer four essay-type questions. I prepared my four questions and concentrated on being able to give good answers to those four questions. One woman in the class studied for a week and knew all of the material that had been covered in the first half of the semester. She was so overprepared that she couldn't answer the specific essay questions and thus did poorly on the exam. I got an A. In comparison to the other women, I think I've worked hard, as hard as they did, but I was more focused in my work.

Another student credits her roommate with helping her, by example, to understand how to "get things done": "I really had no idea of how to study. My model became my roommate. She was compulsive and worried too much, but she was very important to me in making me see how people get their work done."

This section has depicted the patterns of response to the initial disappointment in the level of academic achievement. Students dealt with their disappointment in a number of ways. As discussed, some had a maladaptive reaction of withdrawal and depletion of effort, whether or not accompanied by projection of blame upon others or the environment. Other students searched for the causes of unsatisfactory performance and were able to mobilize resources to improve their records.

Still another type of response to initial disappointment was shown by students who made some peace with a changed self-image. Several elements were involved in this reevaluation and adjustment, as illustrated in the following case:

A student with a straight-A high-school record was upset with her first set of college grades. "What's going on here?" she asked herself. "I am working as hard as I can and still I'm getting only B's." Some of her friends were doing better. She finally came to the conclusion that, though she will no longer be the "brain" of the class, she was working to her full capacity and if she was getting B's, then she was a B student in college.

But this acceptance did not come automatically or easily. She took the trouble to seek out her college adviser to inquire how she rated among all the members of the freshman class. Her adviser was encouraging and she left reassured that she wasn't slipping behind the others.

Additional support was provided by her boyfriend, who repeatedly assured her that to do one's best was all anyone should expect of oneself. When she explained to her parents how much more demanding college was in comparison with her notoriously easy parochial school, they understood that she wasn't fooling around. Indeed, they too kept assuring her that they were satisfied with a B record.

In contrast to this student who made some peace with her disappointing record through conscious reflection and support of significant others, rationalization and denial were the psychic mechanisms of a few failing students. "I came to the conclusion that grades are not important, college is for learning," said one student. And another, with several D's and incompletes, presented, at least in the interview, an unconcerned stance, dismissing her poor performance as a temporary phase.

This discussion has dealt with the impact of the freshman year upon the academic aspect of self-concept and self-esteem. The next section traces influences of the early encounter with college life on other aspects of personality.

CULTURE SHOCK

In the literature received from the college, the entering freshmen could not have missed the proud claim to the exceptional diversity of the student body. Even when the cosmopolitan character of the college was viewed as one of its chief attractions, some students could not fully anticipate the impact of such diversity. Coping with the initial jolts of "culture shock" was a continuous process.

Our study of culture shock began with a general question: "As you think back to the first months of college, can you recall any differences between you and your classmates in attitudes or behavior that surprised, interested, shocked, or intrigued you?"

Slightly over a third of the students denied any such reactions. Some explained that the student body of their high schools had been more heterogeneous and therefore they were accustomed to cultural diversity. Others spent the first year of college in self-contained, homogeneous religious or ethnic cliques with only superficial encounters with outsiders. Finally, as brought out earlier, a few students were too isolated from college classmates to experience any culture shock. But this sheltered group constituted a minority of the sample. Nearly two-thirds of the students cited illustrations of culture shock.

Examination of the effects of these encounters with cultural diversity reveals certain overall patterns, as well as more complex and subtle processes. Generally speaking, the initial impact was in some cases disturbing and disorienting; in others, it was neutralized by an impenetrable defensiveness. Still other students felt that contacts with the different values of diverse people helped them to transcend their past parochialism and to attain a broader and more realistic understanding of society—the influences aided the students' intellectual and emotional development.

Among the most sensitive areas were differences in attitudes toward religion, sex, feminism, drug use, study versus social life, manners, and appearance. Apart from, but occasionally intertwined with, these specific attitudes were more general encounters with racial, religious, ethnic, and social class differences.

Attitudes toward women's roles varied sufficiently to generate debate and self-questioning. The strongly traditional freshmen who looked forward to full-time home-making soon found themselves on the defensive. The spectrum of attitudes nevertheless was wide enough so that most students found differences to the right and to the left of their own positions, as seen in the following excerpts:

> If you are so intent on looking for a husband, why did you come to such a demanding and competitive college?
>
> I wouldn't let a guy pay for a movie or a dinner. I believe that a liberated woman must pay her own way.
>
> I wouldn't think of going Dutch with a guy unless I wanted to let him understand there is no romantic involvement.
>
> I hate girls who giggle, and mince, and get dumb as soon as there are guys around.
>
> Some girls are so militant and hostile that I don't blame men for calling them "castrating bitches."

The transforming impact of the college on attitudes toward male-female relationships is illuminated in the following case:

> The student was on the honor roll in her provincial high school but, in conformity with the values of the

ruling high-school clique, popularity with boys was the most highly desired goal. Accordingly, she derived greatest self-esteem from being sexually attractive to men and had had intercourse with several partners in high school.

The freshman year at college produced changes in her self-concept and ego-ideal. From her new perspective, she now considers her high-school social world culturally impoverished. In that "partying set" it was deemed inappropriate to raise any political or intellectual topic at a mixed gathering. As she observed with growing admiration her college classmates, she noticed that their reading was not limited to books assigned in class. More significantly, male approval was not their main goal in life. They felt free to disagree with men and their whole manner did not change as soon as men appeared on the scene. Her roommate said: "Well, I am prelaw and let guys think what they will."

This appreciation of her more liberated classmates came gradually. In the first months of college, she was shocked to realize that the guys she met in bars and through friends, rather than accord her recognition for attending an Ivy League School, thought that at her college the "girls are bitchy." Her first reaction was to conceal, at these casual encounters, her affiliation with her college. Gradually, however, she began to resent their attitudes and began to wonder whether she had attracted the "wrong sort of man." She felt a new longing for a boyfriend who would want to talk to her and not just go disco-dancing and have sex.

She had a brief illusion that she had met such a college guy who, at their first meeting, talked a lot about politics and thus enhanced her self-esteem as an intellectual companion. At the end of the evening he asked her whether she would come to his room. She spent that night with him. Her newly found pride was short-lived. His complete indifference to her in subsequent chance meetings on the campus was a blow. This incident crystallized both her longing for male companionship and her new values. Lonely as she was, she realized that she was no longer interested in visiting college guys who smoked grass or in associating with guys in bars who made passes without wanting to talk to her.

This student felt that her attitudes toward men changed in the course of her freshman year under the influence of her classmates. She no longer wanted to be a "chick" to the guys. Puzzled at first, she finally understood the contempt her feminist roommate expressed for women who were satisfied to be merely sex objects to a man.

A different change in attitudes toward men was experienced by a Latin-American student.

At home we were taught to be wary of men. Men were irresponsible; they would get girls pregnant if we didn't watch out. The big message was "Don't trust men; they'll take advantage of you." When I came to college I saw that my new friends didn't see men like that. It is not that they are so trusting, they just feel more self-confident about their ability to avoid being victimized by men.

At the time of the interview, in the fall of her sophomore year, this student felt that she too became "less paranoid because I now have the confidence that I can cope on my own terms with any man who would try to victimize me."

Sexual attitudes and behavior were another key source of stress. As will be apparent in chapter 9, the college included a predictably wide variety of types: virgins, freshmen who had already had a number of lovers, those involved in an exclusive affair, lesbians, women for whom the topic of sex was too sensitive for discussion, and others who reported their sexual experiences in explicit detail. Exposure to such variety of both principles and behavior disturbed, reinforced, or transformed the attitudes freshmen brought with them at entrance to college.

Some students were shocked by the naiveté of classmates, just as some were shocked by others' sexual permissiveness: "My roommate didn't know what masturbation meant, or oral sex. When I explained oral sex, her response was 'Oh, gross!' She was kind of childish. She was into sports and I was more into decadence."

Another student was surprised when, early in her freshman year, she heard a group of classmates talking about how disgusting premarital sex was and what little self-respect women who sleep with their boyfriends must have. This astonished her because she had gathered from her suitemates that women at the college were somewhat liberated and at least not so hung up about sex.

By contrast, another freshman was very upset because in the first week of college her roommate slept with several different guys. She met someone at a beer party and slept with him that night. At a party the next night, she met somebody else and slept with him. "I guess girls who engage in casual sex imagine that they are popular with men," the interviewee remarked, "but one of the guys my roommate slept with told me later that she was a 'slut,' that he had little respect for her and would use her for what he could get."

Differences in sexual norms are more disturbing when encountered in a person who otherwise belongs to the student's in-group. Dissimilarity in an out-group—religious, ethnic, or class—is more expected and therefore less disquieting. An example of such an in-group difference was reported by a sheltered, only daughter of a devoutly religious family.

This student adhered to the ideal of premarital chastity. Of all the classmates she met in the first weeks of college, the most congenial was another student of the same religion. They shared the same taste in clothes and a disdain for girls who came to class looking like slobs. They had similar academic interests. To convey the propriety of her new friend, our respondent summed up: "She was the kind of girl my mother would have liked if I brought her home."

The shock came when her new friend informed her that she was about to leave on a week's holiday with a man, many years her senior, who, as it turned out, was not her first lover. "But what do your parents say?" Our student was bewildered. "They wished me a good trip" was the response. Our respondent summed up: "If I left on such a vacation, I would have no home to return to." The friend came back from her holiday and resumed sexual relations with her young lover.

This friendship did not endure. "We were just too far apart," explained our interviewee. "I could hardly impress her if I felt overjoyed to be finally allowed to stay out till 1:30 A.M. on Saturday nights." All the same, she was somewhat amused at her mother's horror ("A heathen!") when she recounted her friend's adventures.

Such estrangement between students was not an inevitable consequence of differences in sexual experience. Another freshman, also a virgin, was "shocked" to learn that her roommate had been sexually active since she was thirteen and had had many lovers. The most surprising thing was that "It didn't faze her somehow, it seemed so natural to her to get into bed with whomever she chose." This friend, so unlike our respondent, had taken amphetamines and LSD, and still smoked marijuana two or three times a week. The two students discussed how ironic it was that they could be so different and yet so close: "We could talk for hours in our room. There was a lot of good communication between us."

Several factors distinguish the two cases of virgins who came to know sexually experienced classmates and account for the estrangement of the first and the continued friendship of the second couple. For the first student, virginity was a matter of religious principle and the acceptance of a strong parental vigilance. Perhaps this docility was tolerable given her exceptional attractiveness and popularity with men, despite the limits she set on physical contact. She appeared to view herself as a desirable woman who will have sex and marriage whenever she is ready and meets the right man.

For the second student, more rebellious and intellectually involved and more feminist, the contact with the new friend was a glimpse into a world that both shocked and intrigued her. She had had little social life in high school, which she attributed in part to having been overweight. She had very few moral scruples about premarital sex. Her new sexually experienced friend may have been regarded as someone who might facilitate her own development in this sphere. At the same time, her own self-esteem in this friendship was assured by her involvement with intellectual issues and with causes, which impressed and found a responsive audience in her roommate.

Another case illustrates the liberating effect of classmates upon a Catholic student who did not wholly approve of them, but was able to profit from her new friends while remaining true to her basic values.

"My family was very religious. And we had very strict standards. I was under my parents' thumb and did mainly what they said. Now I know that there are different ways of living your life. Being with women here at college has been an eye-opening experience for me. They are not quite so uptight, so religious, and they don't have such strict moral values. I still believe in the moral values of my parents, but I think that they should be moderated a bit. It's more fun being a little bit looser than it was at home. At home I never dated. Here I go out with guys and I enjoy myself. I still hold on to my basic moral values, but I have a good time. The girls on my floor are moderately into drugs. On Friday and Saturday nights everyone sits around and gets high smoking pot. I don't do drugs and I often go off and sit in my room until they've finished smoking."

The thing that surprised her most about the group was how emotionally and sexually expressive they were. "At the beginning, I was really surprised to hear people talking about themselves and talking about their sexual experience. It scared me, and I would walk out and go to my room and do my studies. But the more I hung out with the group the looser I became. I talk myself now. I'm not as sexually explicit as they are, but I talk about my emotions and my problems. I've come to a better recognition of myself through that process. I feel more comfortable with myself, and I've also learned to accept some of my imperfections. Listening to other people's problems, I began to realize that it's okay to have problems and to talk about them, that I didn't have to be perfect and I didn't have to hide my imperfections. I now recognize that I have imperfections and I'm not afraid to talk about them. I feel that I'm a better person for it."

This "group therapy" was not the sole liberating factor of new friendships. Another revelation was the recognition that one had been mistaken in an earlier belief that a certain surface human characteristic was inevitably a symbol of traits one despised.

A student reported that her new friends taught her not

to judge people by appearance. "I used to judge people by the way they looked. I never thought I could be friendly with someone who was very fashion-conscious. I used to think that they were shallow because that was all that was on their mind. My best friend here on campus is very fashion-conscious, and I've come to realize that she's not a shallow person, that she's intelligent and sensitive, and that she likes to develop her own personal style as an extension of her personality."

For some students, the racial, religious, ethnic, and class diversity of the college provided them with their first contact with members of other racial and ethnic groups in the shared status of a classmate. One Catholic freshman who attended a parochial high school in a small town explained that she "never had a conversation with a member of a different race." She was "dazed" all through the freshman orientation to meet "all those Asians, Blacks, Latins, Greeks, Jews, Koreans, etc., etc." She thought that was a "great experience." To be sure, her closest friends during the first semester were a group of white Catholic girls. But whereas they "stuck together," she "ventured out." She had a Jewish male friend and some Protestant and Jewish female acquaintances. Her parents did not allow her to date this Jewish man and she did not; a phone call was all right, but certainly not a movie or a dinner together.

However superficial, contact with diverse groups was bound to increase the knowledge of cultural differences. "Last year, just before Christmas," reported a freshman, "I was telling a girl in one of my classes about my family's Christmas plans and asked her about her own plans." She replied that she was an Orthodox Jew and, of course, her family didn't celebrate Christmas. "I was really surprised and embarrassed," and she concluded, "I was so used to a

Catholic neighborhood that it never struck me that some people just weren't Christian." Another student reported: "I had a roommate from Sri Lanka," adding, "I thought, wow, that's great. I love talking to people from all over, hearing about different cultures."

A Black freshman entered her room on the first day of college to find a middle-aged Black woman arranging the roommate's belongings. The freshman said, "I am going to room with your daughter." "Imagine my surprise," the student reported to us, "when the lady said: 'I am her maid, not her mother.'"

Her white roommate turned out to be a wealthy Jewish girl, and, after some initial awkwardness, they got along well, exchanging home visits and presents on their respective holidays.

One religious Protestant student became friendly with an Orthodox Jewish classmate, and both learned a good deal about each other's cultural and religious backgrounds.

The most profound change in stereotypes occurred when personal congeniality criss-crossed ethnic or religious identity. Thus a Catholic freshman reported her experiences with a roommate upon entrance to college:

> In spite of her roommate's knowledge that she would find some sexually promiscuous women at college, she was shocked "in a way" when she encountered that kind of behavior in her roommate. "She was Catholic and *very* conservative and the first thing she did when I walked in the room was to lay down the rules: no alcohol in the room, no drugs, and no men in the room after 8 P.M., including my brother. Then, not long after that, she staggered into the room with a man at 3 A.M. one night, drunk." The two women didn't get along and our interviewee switched roommates.
>
> "I moved in with an Orthodox Jew and got along with her much better. We had interesting conversations

on intermarriage, and I was intrigued with her different perspective on religion. It was very interesting to me that she was just as dogmatically against intermarriage as most Catholics are. I knew how to argue against her point of view, but then I thought, 'If she's wrong about intermarriage, then maybe the Catholic position is wrong too.' "

Intergroup contact did not always contribute to increased acceptance of the out-group. Some minority students expressed anger at the prejudice they felt they encountered. More direct evidence came from students who admitted that increased familiarity with this or that group led to antipathy. An upper-class Protestant student, for example, found the Orthodox Jews on her floor pushy and hypocritical in asking her to turn off lights on Saturdays. A few students confessed that they were put off by the religious dogmatism of Catholic students.

Regional and class differences also disturbed some students. A freshman who came to this metropolis from Southern California found the city "decadent":

My friends in California were into healthy activities—outdoor exercises, surfing, health foods, etc. Here I met the punk culture, something with which I could hardly identify. I saw all of these people dressed in outrageous costumes and outfits. On campus there's a whole clique that belongs to the Punk Generation—people who have really angry, unhealthy attitudes and who are somewhat decadent. They were really blasé about the environment, about [the city], and they were really sloppy. I saw people throwing paper into the elevators, or throwing litter onto the streets.

Concerning class differences, most of the testimony came from students of lower socioeconomic backgrounds. It is possible that such contacts as upper-class students happened to have with classmates from humbler origins were not as problematic for them and hence not reported in interviews. On the other hand, to the poorer students, affluence was visible and occasionally intimidating.

Students who were the first members of their families to attend college knew very well which classmates had college-educated parents. Some were impressed with the foreign travel of the rich students to "all those exotic places" or, on a smaller scale, with their ability to buy the hard-cover editions of assigned books, which the poorer students had to read in the library.

A more serious problem of adjustment to class differences was described by an Italian freshman, daughter of blue-collar parents and the first in her family to enter an Ivy League college. The case is noteworthy both for the problems the student experienced and for the resourceful manner in which she resolved them.

This sensitive and able student felt upon entering college that she "stepped outside her background." She felt intimidated by the intellectual background of her class-mates and their college-educated parents. They, in their turn, were aware of her working-class origins. She seriously considered transferring to a public college.

Her family did not provide any support for what was her real desire—to overcome her initial anxiety and remain at college. She asked her mother about transfer-ring and her mother said: "Well, maybe you should." This was not what she wanted to hear. Her family even complained that she was losing the local accent. Her boyfriend, who didn't go to college, kept telling her that she was out of her element in this exclusive college. The conflict led her to see a psychologist who, she felt, wasn't very helpful. What did help (apart from what she termed her "stubbornness" and determination) was her involvement in several campus cultural and political extracurricular activities. She treasured the intellectual community she encountered at college. Gradually she became more involved in the college and less dependent on the very ambivalent messages of her family and her boyfriend.

The culture shock just illustrated involved a reaction to an unaccustomed heterogeneity of the campus population. Some half a dozen students with exceptionally liberal or cosmopolitan backgrounds were, by contrast, shocked by the "suburban innocence" or class snobbishness of their classmates. One student, daughter of a college professor, had been exposed in school to a racially varied group and felt quite at ease with the "strutting of a Black boys' clique." She was amused to see the white males glare at the way she could fall right in when meeting Black classmates.

Apart from the principal reactions just described, the exposure to cultural differences upon entrance to college took some idiosyncratic forms. For example, one student who had been the only Jew in her class in an exclusive boarding school was exhilarated to find Jewish classmates in college, an "escape," as she puts it, from the "WASP enclave" of her boarding school.

Another Jewish graduate of a metropolitan high school with a large Jewish population was welcomed at college by a group of male and female students involved in partying. They were Gentiles, and her intense desire to "belong" led her to conceal the fact that she was Jewish. When a roommate suggested to her and another friend that they go to church on Sunday, the friend observed that "M. is Jewish," leading to the interviewee's admission that "I was very upset that she found out."

Still another unique experience was reported by a Hispanic student. She could not identify herself with Puerto Ricans, Chicanos, or other Hispanics, but neither was she accepted by the white majority.

> Prior to entering college, this student had always thought of herself "as an American, not as particularly Spanish." At college she was the only Hispanic on her dormitory floor. "People here are so aware of color and I wasn't prepared for that. They were always asking me, 'Are you Spanish or what?' This really upset and depressed me." Even more disturbing were the derogatory remarks made in her presence about the Hispanics. She recalled a particularly hurtful remark by a non-Hispanic classmate when she attempted to argue: "Of course, you would disagree, you're a Spic." She had never before encountered such prejudice.
>
> Estranged from the non-Hispanic classmates on her floor, she couldn't identify with the Hispanic group at college. They seemed to be too different from her, "sort of like typical señoritas with long skirts and fans."

Whereas the students just discussed found the culture of the college disorienting in some particular respect, in the following case the family background and the college were so dramatically different that the student, as she aptly put it, "lived a double life, in two separate worlds." A more unusual aspect of this case than the contrast is the skill with which this young woman bridged the "two worlds" and, while pursuing her own goals, avoided potential clashes between the demands of her family and of the college.

> L. was a daughter of Latin-American parents who had only a grade-school education; her father was an unskilled worker. L. was valedictorian in her Catholic parochial school and the only child in her family to go to college.

Ethnicity, low socioeconomic class, and low educational level combined to fashion the values of her family.

She continued to live at home and commuted to college. Even if she had been able to afford the dorm fees, living away from home would have been out of the question. "My family doesn't let their daughters go," she remarked, as she explained how foreign she found the notion of her college classmates that college signals some emancipation from parental control.

Her father, even more than her mother, illustrates the manifold contradictions and ambivalences in his attitudes toward his daughter. L. heard him, "all puffed up," telling relatives and friends that she entered an Ivy League college. At the same time, he knows enough about American society and college life to realize that he was exposing her to danger by allowing her to attend college. L. was aware of his constant watchfulness and anxiety that every religious, political, and moral belief he held dear might be questioned at college.

The father also illustrates another conflict we found typical of working-class fathers with traditional ethnic origins. On the one hand, they idealize a soft, docile, "feminine" girl who marries young. On the other hand, and especially if they have no sons (or no sons who distinguish themselves in school), the lure of vicarious achievement through the upward mobility of an able daughter is very potent. And this upward mobility requires traits incongruent with the traditional feminine ideal.

L. coped with such cultural differences by not sharing new ideas with her parents. She explained that she was brought up to respect them and knew how much they sacrificed for her. There was no "back talk." She wouldn't dream of questioning their ideal of virginity of an unmarried girl or, indeed, any Catholic belief. Her father was so anti-Castro that she would never express any sympathy with socialism. Her mother's image of a homosexual man was one with earrings, dressed in skirts. L. knew it would be futile to tell her mother that a successful, "manly"-looking businessman could be homosexual.

> L. worked hard in her courses and was relatively isolated from college classmates. All the same, college changed some of her attitudes without causing any apparent culture shock. The secret of her relative serenity appears to be her self-confidence and her ability to get what she wants through interpersonal skills. "My mother may scream, but I don't argue. Even she says, 'With your soft words, you get your way.' "

If interpersonal skills helped this young woman to reassure her traditional family, her adjustment at college remains to be interpreted. Two factors would seem to account for it. To have been admitted, especially as the only person among her neighborhood friends, to an Ivy League school was a triumph in itself. She was "shocked" by the amount of college work, but "considering my competitors, I have done well enough. I know my limits and feel content to have gotten all B's."

The second factor to recognize was her relative isolation at college. "I think I passed the whole first semester not talking to anyone. I don't initiate conversation." Yet the freshman year, she concluded, broadened her outlook. She became much less moralistic—instead of saying "how awful!" she began to ask "why?" If lesbians still made her uncomfortable, she now knew that it was not because she considered them perverse but because they inhibited the natural affection she felt freer to express to women when she did not fear to be mistaken for a lesbian.

A reminder is in order: The chapter is based on interviews with the students early in the fall of their sophomore year.

Since the passage of time may have erased from memory some initial problems of transition to college, the foregoing account probably understates rather than exaggerates these problems. In any event, it conveys something of the experiences that form the background, and indeed sometimes the foreground, of academic work.

3

Family and
Peer Groups

THE LAST two developmental tasks confronting the freshmen are changes in relationships with their family and establishing contacts with college peers.

CUTTING THE SILVER CORDS

There is hardly a chapter of this book that does not make some reference to the student's family, as the "cradle of personality" and as either a reinforcer of college impacts or a source of cross-pressure vis-à-vis the college. Here the discussion is limited to the single problem of separation from the family, experienced at the beginning of the freshman year.

Clearly, entering college has different implications for students who continue to live at home and commute than for residents in dormitories whose families live at a distance from college. Another circumstance, soon perceived to affect the problem of transition, is whether the first-year college student had attended boarding school—for those who did, college was not a drastic change. Finally, the character of the daughter's relationship with her parents was bound to affect her reaction to the separation.

Whatever the circumstances, the dominant note in the interviews was the conviction that college should mark an increased independence from parents as agents of control and sources of emotional support—in short, it should be a major step toward adulthood. Only a handful of students were oblivious to this ideal norm at the outset. "I was very homebound and sheltered and I did what my mother told me. I was too tightly bound to my mother to even see independence as an issue," reflected one freshman. At least initially, a few students from foreign backgrounds accepted the cultural norm that only upon marrying was a daughter accorded some independence from parents.

For the great majority, however, transition to college signaled the imperative to cut the silver cords. This was manifested in the censure and mockery of dependent daughters. In the words of a freshman:

> Girls who live at home just cannot stand on their own. One commuter asked me if she could stay with me for a few days. I agreed, but after a couple of days she said, "Gee, I really miss my home. I miss home-cooked food and a nice warm bed and people around me whom I'm familiar with." I thought that was a very childish attitude.

Equally criticized was another freshman who allowed her mother to come and clean up her dorm room and make sure she had an electric pencil sharpener and similar "necessities." "This girl just accepts this as natural and doesn't try to break away from her mother at all" was the disapproval expressed by a classmate.

The more direct testimony of the moral pressure to strive for independence came from the daughters themselves. Their ambivalence occasionally resulted in self-blame. At other times, the inner conflict led them to project the blame upon parents who, as the daughters complained, can never say "the right thing," whether in response to their daughter's college problems or her triumphs.

In addition to this dominant struggle for independence, three types of familial relationships produced other and less frequent patterns of separation. In some cases the warfare between the daughter and her parents had been so severe that the move away from the parental home was experienced as liberation, free of the ambivalences of the more typical group. In another somewhat deviant pattern, the alienation from parents had been so great that the move to college involved hardly any change. Finally, some students appeared to approach what might be considered an ideal: their parental relationships were warm and close, generating in the daughters a sense of security and a capacity to form new relationships. This pattern is marked by the absence of traumatic incidents in separation from the family, conflict-free pleasure in contacts with parents, and a successful integration into the new social milieu.

Among the majority for whom the separation from the parental home and the struggle for independence did constitute a problem, some freshmen spoke for themselves. One of them remarked in the interview: "I often speak to my parents. I wish I didn't. I feel it is time for me to stand on my own, yet I love to talk things over with my mom." Another freshman described an occasion when she felt very upset about a low grade on an exam: "My first impulse was to phone my parents for comfort. But I resisted the temptation. I am trying to establish my independence and if I keep complaining to them about every little trouble, they would hardly think of me as an adult."

And, again, in another interview:

> I vividly remember feeling desperate one day about my school work but I decided not to call home. I was trying to make them see me as a competent adult. However, when I finally did speak with my parents I felt slightly comforted. Unlike the parents of my friends, my parents believe that I should not push myself too hard, that I should relax and do the best that I can. Hearing them repeat it over the phone helped to console me and to boost my morale.

A student indicates her conscious effort to attain independence from both parents (but especially her mother) and her degree of success in attaining it early in the freshman year in the following excerpt:

> I wanted desperately a room on the campus. I wanted to demonstrate to myself and my parents that I can do things by myself—things like feeding myself, balancing the budget, but above all to do my work without someone there pushing me. My mom knew every time I had a paper due, and she'd say things like "Don't you think it's time you started on that paper that's due Friday?" That didn't help me. I mean, it was nice to have her remind me, but I was ambivalent because I also knew I'd like to get out of this pattern and to learn to do it on my own.

Once this student moved to the campus, her mother didn't intrude and her roommate became her model. Watching her, she learned how people get their work done. "That was very important to my sense of identity," she concluded.

One freshman, all too aware of her unusual dependence on her mother, complained in her journal about discontinuities in the upbringing of girls:

> It seems that I have always been encouraged by everyone to be close to my parents, especially to my mother. Now that I've left home and gone to college, there is suddenly this great emphasis on being independent and self-sufficient. I feel a great conflict in this area. I am supposed to "wean" myself but, though I am incredibly close to my friends, I feel much closer to my mother. I called her when I lost my virginity, and I generally tell her about all the things that happen with my boyfriend. If I am lonely I call her, as I do when I get a good grade. I get a very strong and clear support from her. It is she who usually says: "I'll let you go now," or "I'm sure you have things to do," and I always go: "No, Ma, I want to talk to you some more." Sometimes her words translate to me: "Maybe I shouldn't talk to my mother so much, none of my friends do. In college you are supposed to grow up and grow away." I feel kind of embarrassed. But I can't imagine what it would be like not to be in close touch with her. I know that one day she won't be around for me to talk to; but even the thought of that fills me with dread and fear of loneliness.

So far this student has not succeeded in attaining what she accepts as the cultural norm of "weaning" herself from her mother. The only forms this effort takes are "pulling back" temporarily after repeated calls home and being "sort of snippy on the phone." Her mother understands and never "crowds" her.

The student just cited made a conscious effort to reduce parental influence. But others, having turned to their parents for customary solace, felt disappointed. As one freshman put it: "They cannot say the right thing when I phone and complain because they don't know what college is like." This dissatisfaction was voiced whether parents attempted to offer some advice or sought to reassure. A freshman told the interviewer:

> During midterms I called my mom because I was feeling so tense and upset about my exams. My mother asked me if I had organized the work in such a way that I could get everything done. That really frustrated me. I didn't call for her to tell me to organize my work. I know how to organize my work. My mom doesn't really understand what college is like because she doesn't know all of the circumstances that surround my life at college.

And another "frustrated" daughter:

> My mother is a very understanding person but when I call her she just gives me sympathy and not empathy. I'd rather that she try and understand deep down what I'm telling her rather than tell me kind of surface things, things that I already know and don't need somebody to tell me. . . . I guess it's unrealistic to expect that much because she's not living at college and cannot know what college life is like.

Another freshman was less generous toward her mother. She was upset about an upcoming test and phoned home:

> My mother said: "Well, you always used to get real nervous before a test." That really got me furious. I was having serious difficulties with a course, not some childish

pre-exam jitters, but Mother was trying to comfort me as a child, not as an adult with a major problem.

Parental criticism becomes especially disturbing when it bears upon a decision about which the student herself is in conflict, as illustrated by a freshman who accused her mother not only of ignorance of college pressures but also of changing values in midstream. She complained:

> I am forced to spend long days in the library or else I won't make it through this college. It isn't easy to keep to the grind, especially on warm days when I wish I could hang around on the lawn and meet some guys. God knows there are so few chances here to enjoy social life. I got upset when my mother, who was always proud of my being a good student, suddenly told me not to spend so many hours in the library. I didn't like it and told her to let me handle my own life. The worst part of being in college is not having enough time to do the things that matter to you.

There may have been no "right" parental response to daughters struggling with conflicting feelings. Whatever the reasons, the freshmen spontaneously and increasingly described turning to classmates for support, thus confirming the familiar generalization about the role of peer groups as agents of emancipation from parents. The daughters claimed that their parents simply could not understand their problems and that, willy-nilly, they had to turn to a classmate who did understand what it was to be intimidated by a teacher, to live with a roommate whose grades were better, to try to decide which of the five courses to study for, and so on.

One student described her full awareness of the role her boyfriend played in her growing independence from her parents. But he was the one to explain to her that she was simply transferring her dependence from her parents to him. When she first had difficulties with a course, she sought comfort from him, phoning him to explain that she needed someone to take care of her in this stressful situation. While he was a comfort for a short time, he finally told her it was time she learned to stand on her own feet and to make her own decisions.

For the daughters on whose testimony this section is based, the process of separation from parents is not continuous and is fraught with ambivalence. This ambivalence, the pull and push of conflicting sentiments, is reflected in excerpts from a student's journal:

Yesterday I spoke to my father on the phone. After hanging up, I was very upset, because I was left with the feeling that my father doesn't like me any more. I called back to speak to my mother and discuss this with her. Interestingly enough, she said that he thought I didn't like him any more. He said, "I know she loves me, but for some reason, she doesn't like me." Needless to say, this upset me a great deal.

According to my mother, my lack of physical affection indicates to my father that I don't like him. In response to this, he is cold to me.

It is very hard for me to be like the affectionate young girl I used to be. In fact, it is impossible. That is no longer the person that I am. It is very hard to explain this to him. He is involved with as many personal conflicts as I am. He wants me to mature and be able to take care of myself, but he doesn't want to lose his little girl.

I want to grow up, but in times of uncertainty I still cling to them for support. None of these things is bad, they just lead to an ambiguous situation that is not easily dealt with.

Another freshman was especially satisfied because her choice of a major was her own: "Most of my life I either didn't make a decision or my parents made it for me." Her ambivalent sentiments, however, were revealed in the following incident. When she raised her grade in physics from a C− to a B, she phoned her father long distance. "He said, 'Oh, I knew you could do it,' but he didn't seem that impressed and I was a little disappointed. What the hell! I really don't care; there comes a point when his reaction shouldn't make a difference."

Another group of freshmen could be characterized as having little nostalgia for the family nest. A sense of liberation is reflected in the words of one freshman:

My mother is a very controlling person. She used to call my high-school teachers constantly to check up on my performance. Now I can set my own limits and enjoy skipping a meal, leaving my room messy, not having to account for my time—and not feeling guilty about any of it.

Some students' relationships with their parents were so strained that the warfare continued unabated after entrance to college. In one such case the ostensible conflict was over the daughter's affair with a young man of different religion and lower social status. "I harbor a lot of resentment toward my parents for all the hassle they give us," she declared. Were it not for her subterfuges and outright lies, she believes that ties with her family would have been severed completely.

A factor contributing to familial stress was the anxiety of parents about the moral climate of the youth culture to which their daughter would be exposed when leaving the sheltered home. The more conflict-ridden the prior relationships with the daughter, the less trust, the more reason for anxiety. In the words of one freshman:

> My main desire upon coming to college was to create more distance from my mother, her prying and her nagging. I was very impatient and abrupt with her. "How was your day?" she'd ask. I didn't feel like telling her. Suppose I said that I had lunch with X. She didn't know who X was. Besides, I didn't feel it was her business. I was a college student and wanted to be trusted as an equal. I am moody. Now and then I might open up. There was that incident the first semester. I went to a party and drank ten screwdrivers. I got so drunk that the guy I was with took me to his dorm room to sleep it off. I happened to have had a lunch date with my mother the next day, and my roommate explained that I had a hangover and couldn't come. Father took time off to come for me to take me home. All I needed was some sleep but they were sure I was becoming an alcoholic.

Equally turbulent was the experience of a student who chose this college because "I was running away from my parents as far as I could." This student felt that her parents, especially her father, were very strict with her. Some daughters who testified to "neutral" or distant family relationships explained that coming to college did not involve any drastic change. A few did not disguise some longing for warmer relationships; others appeared more resigned. In any case, these daughters denied strong homesickness or overt conflict with parents. Both the acceptance of the state of affairs and some thwarted longing for closer ties are reported in the following excerpts.

One student explained why coming to college hardly seemed a "separation" from her mother:

Even in high school I did not confide in my mother about my love life or my grades or other academic problems. When I moved to the dorm, I did not feel much of a change. I didn't really feel emancipated when I lived in the dorm because I went home every weekend. I usually called home only about once a week, and my mother would call me once a week. She did most of the talking, because I never confided in her. She'd say, "How's school?" and I'd say, "Fine"; and she'd say, "How's John?" [her boyfriend] and I'd say, "Fine." I do remember calling her once when I was upset and crying. I don't remember the reason now, but I was upset and lonely. Then after I talked to her I called John and I think he came up to see me because I was so upset.

Another student was prepared to share the blame for the lack of emotional intimacy with her parents:

Sometimes I felt low, my grades were disappointing or I felt lonely. I would call home and not bring up the issue that was on my mind. I would hope that they would ask but they never did. I never got what I needed from them. My parents are not that perceptive or persistent. Just hearing their voices was nice, though we just talked about the weather. But I always felt bad afterward. I have this friend who calls home and talks to her parents about anything at all. I call home and it seems that they are so out of touch with what's going on with me that the only advice they have is "Come home." That's ridiculous! But I am not good at sharing my most intimate feelings even with my good friends.

She recalls with longing that despite their reserve, before she came to college and when she felt down, she could put her head on her mother's shoulder. "You couldn't do that to my father, only on special occasions, but my mother was okay." She concluded, "It would be nice to call them and to get that kind of close contact, but they can't do that and I haven't been able to ask for it either."

A borderline case is that of a freshman who has accepted a somewhat distant relationship with her parents. She described the relationship between her parents as "very close and intimate" in the freshman questionnaire but checked "somewhat close and intimate" in labeling her own relationship with each parent. In her own words:

> I went home about once a month but I was never really homesick. It's hard to explain my relationship with my parents because it's not the kind of nurturing you would expect. I really like them as people and want to be around them. As much as we like each other we each have our own lives. My family always emphasized independence. My mother would never do our laundry, and I am amazed that my college friends go home and still get their laundry done by their mothers. They don't call me. Usually I am the one to call them from school. I'm sure that I would have very little problem moving far away.

The final type consists of freshmen who enjoyed very close and warm family ties, missed their families upon arrival at college, but appeared to be secure and autonomous enough not to experience the ambivalence or the conflicts described in the preceding cases. These students continued to maintain very close contacts with parents by frequent phone calls, correspondence, and visits when feasible. They found no difficulties (except for a degree of homesickness for those whose families lived at a distance from college) in maintaining close ties.

A commuter who described her relationship with both parents as "very close and intimate" denied any problem of dependency:

They let me do what I want so there is no problem. My mother is a strong, special woman and has been a very strong influence in my life. My father is strong too but I don't think his influence has meant as much. My mother knows where I stand on all these issues you raised because we have discussed all this before.

We have no way of judging this student's candor or insightfulness. But several others who felt nourished by the warm family relationships were also able to form other ties at college and pursue their personal goals.

As with problems of integration into the college community, issues of self-esteem and of culture shock, so do relationships with the family undergo changes. Some freshmen reported such changes before the end of the first year. Here is the testimony of one Chinese freshman:

The experience of coming to college, hearing new things, and meeting people from different cultures has made me more independent. Before coming to college I would always go to my mother when I had a problem, and she would help me figure out a solution. But now (even though I continue to live at home and commute to college) I try to figure out things on my own before going to my mother. And when I do find a solution, I feel really good inside. It's like, hey, I did this! Before I didn't give much credit to myself. I always hung on to my mother. Yes, sometimes I tried to do things on my own and failed, but I kept trying and it wasn't that bad. Like in Chinese. I should be terrific in Chinese, but in my Chinese class I was really doing horribly. I was really discouraged, but I wasn't going to run to my mother with this problem too. I said, "It's time you stopped that and tried to help yourself." So what I did was, I studied a little harder and participated in class a little more, and it was okay. I ended up with an A in the course both semesters—my only A.

Another freshman attests to her skill in establishing a measure of autonomy without rupturing her very close relationship with her mother:

> I felt torn between my desire for my mother's approval and the need to establish some independence. The conflict crystallized over my relationship with my boyfriend. I felt that my parents were too involved in everything I did and I resented that. When my boyfriend came to spend the weekend on the campus with me, they knew it. It took me awhile to be able to say this, but I finally said to Mom, "Look, it's tough on me being judged by you all the time. If I were away from home at some far-away college, you wouldn't know whom I was seeing, what I was doing. But I want to make my own decisions, and I don't want to lie to you." Finally I was able to stay very close to my mother and still act against her wishes even to the point of living with my boyfriend the summer following my freshman year.

The following final excerpt from a journal kept for us by a freshman details the process of emancipation from parents.

> I have always been very close to my parents and I love them very much. As time passes, however, I find that I have less need for their reassurance and help. I am becoming more and more able to make decisions and handle situations that had previously caused me great stress. Whereas I used to lean on them, I now lean on myself, and share with them my sense of accomplishment, in place of my former sense of reliance. I know that I am still dependent, but the dependencies have changed. I depend on them for love and support.
> One factor that made for change is the experience of living away from them. For the past year, I have had

no one to answer to, no rules to abide by, no one watching over me, and no one to take responsibility for me. Going home, and knowing that my parents are worrying about me and wondering when I will get home, can be very irritating. It isn't that they argue with me on the subject, but just knowing that they are worried, or not sleeping because of me, can cause a lot of self-imposed guilt. Wanting to get away from this guilt, I spend even less time at home.

Emotional growth and independence have been accompanied by intellectual growth. Being at this college, and being around many ambitious and intelligent women, has given me great aspirations and the feeling that I have the potential to succeed. I think I have been inspired and influenced to achieve more. . . .

With all of these forces acting on a person who has just been placed in a totally new environment, it is no wonder that the freshman year is a year of great change. Feelings of freedom, peer pressures, learning and adapting to norms, succeeding academically (especially with the expected high standards at this college) all create enormous desire and need to mature. This is why I firmly believe that the freshman year triggers and accelerates the process of "growing up."

These insightful quotations not only bear on family relationships but anticipate another aspect of the transition to college, the impact of the peer group.

THE IMPACT OF PEER GROUPS

Several challenges confronting the students in the course of the freshman year have already been identified. The students themselves tended to attribute to their college peer groups the major influence in whatever changes they underwent in both actual and ideal self-concepts, and in intellectual interests, religiosity, attitudes toward diverse class and ethnic groups, patterns of interaction with female and male friends, and other individual traits.

College courses, professors, and the stimulating environment of the metropolis were also acknowledged as factors in development. Students who came from other regions or smaller towns often referred to the excitement of the metropolis, its museums, concerts, other cultural activities, and the very diversity of city neighborhoods.

However, the students' strong emphasis upon the peer group was unmistakable. It was reflected in the nine diaries kept by the freshmen and the two two-hour interviews with seventy students in the fall of 1980, the beginning of their sophomore year. The interview covered the courses taken in the freshman year, the professors in each course, family relationships, and gender views. The most abundant flow of information came in response to the questions on social relationships with closest friends, the "crowd," and classmates in general. Toward the end of the interview, the students were asked: "Do you think you have changed in the course of the freshman year, and if so, in what respects?" The responses to this question were, again, filled with references to social relationships. On balance, whatever the disappointments, the perceived changes were positive.

The pressing search for self-definition in late adolescence led the students to a close scrutiny of and comparison with peers. Peers apparently constituted the main reference groups for personal assessment. Possibly, as in the cases to be cited, even when a course or a teacher provided the original intellectual stimulus, the reactions of the classmates remained in the forefront of attention.

Interaction with peers increased self-knowledge as by-products of encounters with different temperaments, interests, and values. ("I am more reserved or disorganized about work, or more or less tolerant or candid," and so on). Heightened self-awareness in itself occasionally activated change. Whether the processes of change were conscious or not, some peers served as negative role models, others evoked admiration and emulation.

The interviews illustrate the scope of the personal changes students attributed to relationships with peers. Students, of course, vary in the degree of psychological sophistication. Some became aware of their personality changes only in the course of upheavals in relationships with formerly close high-school friends. Others, more insightful, did not require such dramatic signals to perceive changes in specified domains of their personality and to describe the processes at work.

To begin with, even strictly intellectual development was frequently attributed as much to the impact of the peers as to courses and teachers. In the words of one sophomore:

> This may sound funny, but I have become more intellectual. In high school, I just used to study for a test. Now I study to learn. I'm more interested in current events, in history, in going to museums. The courses and professors at this college are stimulating, but I think it is the students who affected me more. They have interesting things to say, they debate current events, they are lively and intelligent.

Another student stated without equivocation:

> What I liked most about my freshman year in college was the friends I made here. Before coming to college, I was a very closed person, like my mother, finding it difficult to talk about my feelings. My two closest friends

at college were very warm and open and they contributed a great deal to my self-confidence and ability to handle situations.

This student felt so much stronger toward the end of her freshman year that she was able to confront her family about their shared emotional problems, which previously had been hidden or denied.

A student who had given up her brief career as a figure skater, upon which she had embarked right after high school, reported both emotional and intellectual changes. She felt that she changed radically during the first year of college:

> I learned to be young and silly, to laugh, to relax with people, to drink, to try drugs. I feel a lot more at ease with people. I've had to tolerate things that I wouldn't have had to tolerate if I had continued to skate. Just different points of view, different life styles, people who aren't concerned only with exercise and their bodies, but with other things. Also my courses have expanded my mind. I feel it's amazing. Everything's new to me because I didn't have very many academic subjects in high school. It's a whole new world and my mind is stretching to take in these new experiences. All of my courses stimulate me, and I work really hard because I want to master the concepts introduced in the classes. I feel that my mind has expanded amazingly since I came here to college.

As already indicated, some students became conscious of their "new selves" as they pondered the radical estrangement from close high-school friends. A sophomore describes the deterioration of past loyalties:

> When I saw Jane [her closest high-school friend] this

summer, I couldn't believe the change in her. She was like a turtle. Her thinking was so slow. She used to be a very original person with a lot of original ideas. I don't know how intelligent she was, but she used to be very creative. Now she seems very sluggish in her thinking and her actions. When Jane was in high school she wanted a career and she wanted to be an independent woman. She wasn't interested in getting married and felt that women could do better on their own. This summer the change in her was dramatic. She seems to live in a world of fear; she's afraid of being alone. I think all she wants to do now is to get married and settle down into a safe, comfortable life. I really couldn't believe the change in her. I've changed a great deal too. I feel I am more like Jane was before she went to college. I became aware of women's issues through talking to people here and getting involved in activities that are concerned with women's rights.

My friends here at college are very academically oriented. They are independent women who are concerned with their career and their intellectual life. My closest friend, Mary, and I feel the same. We're not here to get our MRS. degree, we're here to get our B.A. degree. We both want a career very badly and we're both very academically oriented. Neither of us dates at all. We're not concerned with finding men, and we don't want that to clutter up our lives at this point. Mary said, "I know some day I'll have a relationship. I'm not anxious to have one right now and I don't want it to interfere with my academics." Mary receives a lot of pressure from her parents to date. They can't understand her attitude. Her parents feel that part of college life is dating and meeting men and having social experiences. At first my mother also felt that I was not taking advantage of the social life here. But, by this time, my mother, I think, has given up on me.

The estrangement from her closest high-school friend is not the only change this case illustrates. Clearly, her college friend, Mary, if not awakened then reinforced her career salience and, at least for the time being, her subordination of social life with men to academic pursuits. Mary apparently also strengthened the interviewee's own capacity to withstand her mother's pressure to enter the dating scene. In the contest between family and peer-group influences, the steadfastness of her friend served as an example.

Another student, K., presented in her diary an especially detailed analysis of the impact of close friends upon her personality:

> One of the nicest things about being at college this year was that I met and became friends with a great variety of people that I probably would not have considered as potential friends in high school. I think that these new friendships really reflect a change in the way I view other people, but, most important, they reflect a change in how I look at myself. It seems that in each friendship a different part of myself (previously unacknowledged in relationships with others) has emerged and grown as a result of the friendship. This may be due to the fact there is such a great variety of people at this college, but I think that it also reflects that I am really seeking out and am attracted to people who seem to represent, in some sense, the different parts of my personality that I'm discovering I really like. These new facets of myself are not the ones that my family and old friends have encouraged in me.

This sophisticated analysis unveils several processes in the impact of college peers upon personality. This student has recognized that the college provided an exceptionally diverse pool of potential associates. But she also noted her own inclination to seek out friends despite—or, indeed, because of—perceived differences between them and herself. This illustrates a finding cited in several other chapters concerning differences among students in the degree to which they tended to maintain homogeneous friendships.

As this student traced the influence of friendships upon personality, she illuminates in an especially insightful manner different modes of impact. She describes her friend Alice as one who brought to consciousness and, finally, to actual expression a previously suppressed "childish and fun-loving side of my personality" that led to new sources of enjoyment of life. K. wrote in her journal:

Alice and I met at the beginning of last semester, as we lived in the same suite. It's strange, but I had a feeling from the beginning that we would be friends. I wasn't completely sure about her at first, though. She seemed a lot more carefree and concerned with "having a good time" than my high-school friends. She went dancing at the pub, drank at the [local jazz club] and did other things that seemed a little frivolous to me at the time. When I started to think about it, though, I realized that I was a little envious of the fact that Alice was so relaxed about having fun. I'd always wished that I could be more like that.

By second semester, our friendship had really evolved and grown. At this point, I think that Alice is the most "fun" friend I've ever had. My feelings about the friendship are due, in great part, to my accepting the fact that I like acting silly and rowdy, laughing and acting like a little kid. (It's a big part of me, as a matter of fact.) Alice and I do things that other people would think are dumb and a waste of time. For example, one night (when we both should have been studying) we went all the way downtown to see a movie—which was terrible—and just because we were too lazy to get up, sat through it twice. Alice is the kind of person with whom I can eat ice cream right before dinner and not feel the least bit guilty! ... We can sit for hours and gossip and laugh about our professors and the people in our classes. These are all pleasures that I thought I could never indulge in "at my age." I think that Alice and I are the female equivalent of "drinking buddies"—we thoroughly enjoy each other's immature and illogical side (and we don't always have to act like adults). We really have fun together. We value each other as serious, worthwhile people but we can also be kids together. It seems funny, but a large part of my growing experience this year has been the acceptance of this childlike, fun side of myself.

K.'s relationship with another friend, Rita, was more complex in its influence. Rita, a militant lesbian feminist, at first aroused anxiety in K.: "She was very threatening to me." But the anxiety in itself was a source of further conflict since K. prided herself upon her rationality and idealism. She was a feminist and her ideal self-concept demanded tolerance of radicalism, even when it was more extreme than her own. The successful outcome of this conflict gave K. a sense of pride and enhanced self-confidence. Not only did she overcome her anxiety, but she succeeded in making a confidante of Rita, a deviant in her dorm and, to some extent, a person at bay among the "straight" dormmates. As she described:

Another friendship that seems to me to be important in helping me to form a more flexible and *complete* sense of myself is with Rita, a person who lived in my dorm. At first, she was very threatening to me. She is a lesbian, feminist, and vocal proponent of anything radical (or so it seems). She is a leader in the radical lesbian and feminist communities at college and in the city. I did feel an immediate connection with Rita (since I am a proponent, albeit a less radical and vocal one, of many of the same causes that Rita is involved with), especially in view of the relative intolerance of the rest of the people in our suite of Rita's lesbian and feminist politics. In getting to know Rita, it really surprised me that *she* was surprised about how much we had in common despite the fact that I'm not a lesbian or a militant feminist. For example, she seemed really impressed with the fact, after looking through my record collection, that I had a lot of albums of people who traditionally have a lesbian following. (I am attracted more to the music than to the politics.) She was surprised that I knew so much about lesbian and feminist poetry and literature.

I respect Rita for her commitment and courage. I think she respects me for my quiet, yet strong, convictions and the fact that I'm able to function relatively well in the context of my value system in the straight, heterogeneous world. (She seems to be in constant, almost violent struggle with the "outside world.") . . . When Rita was having trouble handling the cruel, offhand comments of some of our dormmates about her beliefs and practices, she came to me to talk about it. I was really flattered that she saw in me enough sensitivity and understanding so that she wasn't afraid I would be judgmental or disapproving. She also saw in me the quality of thinking independently about issues such as homosexuality, abortion, and feminism, despite common opinion to the contrary (as was the case in our dorm). She shares things with me, I think, that she wouldn't tell other people outside of the feminist and lesbian movements.

Rita has never tried to make me more militant, nor have I ever tried to convince her to be less fanatic. In fact, I think that we really respect each other's very different ways of expressing our (often very similar) beliefs. Again, I feel that being friends with Rita has allowed me to explore and experience the part of myself that is an independent and flexible thinker.

None of the other journals or the interviews presented as sophisticated an analysis of the role of friendships in personality development. In a less detailed and insightful manner, however, the great majority did stress the role of peers as the significant feature of their freshman year in college. Of course, the importance of peers is not limited to the freshman year, as subsequent chapters illustrate at length. The literature on peer influence in college is voluminous, and further references will be made to it.

In one of the most recent studies (Brown University 1980), some 2,000 undergraduate women at six highly competitive colleges were asked in the study questionnaire to rate how much each of the fifteen aspects of college had "contributed to their academic growth." "Conversations with peers" topped the list as "very valuable." Since the question was limited to "academic growth" rather than general personal development, it is somewhat surprising that lectures, reading assignments, discussions with the faculty, and all other contributors trailed so far behind peers. Possibly the students took for granted the academic program, in which they took a more passive role, as contrasted with the more involving personal interaction with peers.

In the absence of comparable studies of this college over the past decades, the author can only speculate about the extent to which problems of transition to college depicted in the preceding chapters are unique to our times. I am inclined to view the vicissitudes of academic self-esteem as the one constant problem. The standards of the college were as demanding, for example, in the 1920s and 1930s as at present and were bound to generate crises of self-confidence in some freshmen. On the other hand, the greater homogeneity of the student population with regard to race, ethnicity, and religion during those decades was likely to shield the white Protestant majority against "culture shock," albeit at the cost of strengthening ethnocentric attitudes. Integration into the college community might have been facilitated by the smaller size of the college, as well as by its homogeneity.

A more complex hypothesis is required to compare the impact of separation from the family, which can be supposed to have some constant and some variable elements over time. For resident students, as contrasted with the commuters, the separation, no doubt, always entailed some anxieties and rewards of greater independence. However, in the past, the college and the parental families were more likely than at present to share common values. The college, acting *in loco parentis,* imposed discipline in social and not merely academic spheres. Moreover, the very cultural homogeneity of the student population must have reduced the occasions for cross-pressures of the new environment and the student's family.

PART II

The Great

Decisions:

Career, Marriage,

and Motherhood

4

Entering Freshmen
View Gender

Having surveyed the challenges and conflicts of the incoming freshmen, we now turn to the great issue at the heart of this book: the students' attitudes toward gender roles and what happened to those attitudes in the course of their college experience. This chapter describes the views of the incoming freshmen from whom we collected data in the fall of 1979. Chapters 5 and 6 describe the attitudes of the seniors toward career, marriage, and motherhood, tracing various patterns of persistence and change since their views at entrance. Then chapter 7 takes up the question of occupational decision making.

Attitudes toward gender include a variety of components:

Parts of this chapter and all its tables originally appeared in "Female Freshmen View Their Future," *Sex Roles* 8, no. 3 (1982): 299–314. Reprinted by permission.

beliefs about typical feminine and masculine psychological traits and the degree to which those beliefs are stereotyped; ideals of femininity and masculinity; attitudes toward sex roles in various institutional settings and in social interaction between the sexes; and above all, the young women's aspirations for their own lives as far as career, marriage, and motherhood are concerned. Attitudes toward the women's movement were also included in this inquiry. This complex of beliefs, ideals, norms, and aspirations will be referred to as the gender perspective.

THE GENDER PERSPECTIVE

Beliefs About Psychological Sex Differences

What did the freshmen believe about female-male psychological sex differences? To find out, we administered a test consisting of sixteen propositions—for example, "Women are more sympathetic than men" and "Men are more original than women." The other propositions dealt with emotionality, sensitivity, aggressiveness, ambition, high moral character, reasoning ability, artistic inclination, straightforwardness (versus deviousness), pettiness, insecurity, superficiality, artificiality, and proneness to taking offense. For each of the items, the women were asked to respond with one of five options: "agree," "agree somewhat," "uncertain," "disagree somewhat," and "disagree."[1] (See appendix for a reproduction of the test: "Masculine and Feminine Personality Traits," p. 324.)

[1] The scale, which was adapted from two earlier studies—Kammeyer (1964) and Johnson (1969)—had previously been used by the author with a male undergraduate sample (Komarovsky 1976).

When people are asked about sex differences, they tend to wonder whether the questioner is referring to inborn or learned differences. To avoid this confusion, we phrased our general direction to the women students this way: "The purpose of this page is to find out your beliefs about average feminine and masculine personality traits in contemporary society (whatever nature or nurture had to do with these traits). Please check the statement expressing most closely your opinions."

What did we find? Most dramatically, that, contrary to the findings of past research, the beliefs of the freshmen represent quite a radical denial of the stereotypical psychological sex differences. The denial was all the more significant because of our explicit instructions, generally absent from prior studies, to disregard the issue of nature versus nurture. Of the sixteen statements implying some psychological differences, only five were upheld by 10 percent or more of the respondents. Conversely, the percentage of students who believed in the existence of sex differences fell below 10 percent for eleven out of sixteen traits. Only one statement, "Women are more emotional than men," received the endorsement of over 50 percent of the sample. Nor were the freshmen in much doubt about their judgments: Of the 3,703 total responses, only 393 (10.6 percent) fell into the category of "uncertain." Male seniors who filled out an identical questionnaire in 1969–70 (Komarovsky 1976: 15) were more tentative; "uncertain" was their response 22 percent of the time.

Another method of summarizing the findings confirms the conclusion that the freshmen perceived men and women as more alike in psychological traits than past and recent studies have reported. In our analysis of the responses, subjects were given a total score by summing up the arbitrary weights assigned to response categories (1 for "agree"; 2 for "agree somewhat"; 3 for "uncertain"; 4 for "disagree somewhat"; and 5 for "disagree"). The low scorers endorsed the belief in psychological sex differences. Conversely, the high scorers rejected the tendency to stereotype each sex, either positively or negatively. Possible scores ranged from 16 to 80. Those with scores under 50 were classified as stereotypers. Only 77, or 34 percent, fell into the first category; 147, or 66 percent, were nonstereotypers.

As for the tendency to stereotype women negatively, the evidence is abundant that stereotypically masculine traits are more often perceived as socially desirable than are attributes that are stereotypically feminine (Broverman et al. 1970). In fact, a search of the literature revealed only one study, based on only fifty-two female college and senior high-school students from the University of Kansas area (Der-Karabetian and Smith 1977), whose subjects valued stereotypically feminine characteristics more positively than masculine ones. Another study shows fluctuations in relative evaluations of female and male personalities according to grade in school (Parish and Powell 1980).

In contrast to these studies, the freshmen in the current study rejected the negative stereotyping of women. The male seniors in a previous study using the same scale (Komarovsky 1976: 16) expressed a more negative view of women.

Our respondents expressed a near consensus about psychological sex differences on thirteen of the sixteen propositions; on three of the propositions, pertaining to reasoning and leadership abilities and to originality of women relative to men, respondents were divided into two groups. Some respondents (105 of them) categorically disagreed with statements implying female inferiority with respect to all three traits; the others, the 115 "negative evaluators," checked other possible responses to one or more of the three alleged weaknesses of women.

Attitudes Toward Sex Roles

Our respondents' attitudes toward sex roles were measured by the Attitude Toward Sex Roles Scale, developed and used extensively by Spence and Helmreich (1972; 1978, 237; see appendix, p. 326, for scale). This scale consists of fifteen statements regarding the roles, rights, and privileges of women; for example, "Swearing and obscenity are more repulsive in the speech of a woman than a man" and "Under modern conditions with women being active outside the home, men should share in household tasks such as washing dishes and doing the laundry." Four response options are offered: "agree strongly," "agree mildly," "disagree mildly," and "disagree strongly." High scores were taken to represent egalitarian attitudes and low scores traditional views. The scores range from 0 to 45, with those scoring 37 and over classified as egalitarians (132 respondents) and those scoring 36 or under the traditionalists (92 respondents).

Freshmen in the present study were more egalitarian than the female undergraduates studied in other comparable recent investigations.[2]

Life-Style Preferences: Career Salience

The central focus of the study of gender perspective was the degree of importance the student attached to a career—in other words, the relative salience of a career. Our measure of career salience was based on the Life-Style

[2]For example, Parelius (1975) reported that 76 percent of Douglass College freshmen in 1973 (a college she describes as being "especially sensitive to women's issues") gave feminist responses to the expectation that a husband should help with housework. The comparable figure in the present study was 98 percent. Similarly, female undergraduates at the University of Texas at Austin (predominantly freshmen) who completed the Spence and Helmreich Scale in 1980 also gave more traditional responses than students in this study. The author gratefully acknowledges permission to cite this reference to "Sex-Role Attitudes: 1979–1980," by R. L. Helmreich, J. T. Spence, and R. H. Gibson.

Index of Angrist and Almquist (1975: 238–241). The core question of the index lists seven conditions under which married women may or may not wish to work and asks the respondent to speculate about her own inclination to hold a job under each condition, with five response choices, ranging from "definitely would" to "definitely not." Some of these conditions are: "No children, husband's salary adequate"; "One child of preschool age, husband's salary not adequate"; "Two or more children of preschool age, husband's salary not adequate"; "Two or more children of school age, husband's salary adequate." (See appendix, p. 329, for the complete reproduction of the Life-Style Index.) Another question presents the student with a hypothetical situation (involving no economic necessity for working) and asks her to choose one of several alternatives, including working (part-time or full-time); concentrating on home and family; or participating in clubs, hobbies, and volunteer work. Finally, the test asks students to project themselves fifteen years into the future and state which of five life styles they would choose for themselves: a housewife with no children, a housewife with one or more children, an unmarried career woman, a married career woman without children, a married career woman with children.[3]

Whatever the elements of fantasy or of merely verbal conformity to current slogans in students' responses, however predictive these responses are of their future behavior, the changes that have taken place on this campus since the

[3] Our criteria for career-salient classification involved the following changes in the Life-Style Index. It required the answers "definitely would" work under two conditions—first, with "two or more children of school age; husband's salary adequate" and, second, with "children have grown up and left home; husband's salary adequate." Another criterion for "career" classification allowed the choice of part-time work only with one or more preschool children; the choice of part-time work at other periods of life, say, when children are older, would disqualify the case from the career-salient category.

early 1940s are striking. Forty years ago, the author surveyed a random sample of the sophomore class at the same college (Komarovsky 1943). In comparison with the 1943 survey, the 1979 freshmen professed exceptionally high career aspirations. The questions asked in the two surveys, though not identical, are comparable. In 1943, 61 percent of the students preferred not to work after marriage. This was taken to be the choice of "to concentrate on home and family" in the 1979 sample, checked by only 5 percent of the respondents. At the other extreme, students who preferred to follow a career without marriage (2 percent) or to combine family life and a career with a minimum of interruption for childbearing together constituted 12 percent in 1943, but 48 percent of the 1979 sample. Interestingly, in 1979 a career without marriage was also the choice of only 2 percent of the sample. The remaining groups in each year were students who opted for a sequential pattern of work, withdrawal for childbearing, and eventual return to work. In 1979, 14 percent chose the response of "married career woman with no children." There is no comparable figure for 1943, although among the 10 percent of that year's career-salient students who hoped to be married some may have expected, at the time of the survey, to remain childless.

As significant as the rise in career aspirations are the changes in the values underlying these preferences, as gleaned from the interviews. In 1943, benefits that the students expected to derive from the experience of paid work were general, that is, nearly independent of the nature of the job. Work experience as such was perceived to produce long-range benefits in developing self-discipline and self-reliance, and in providing insight into the world of one's future husband as the family provider. Paid employment, as insurance against some possible economic crisis, was also considered in this light, less by virtue of some acquired technical or professional skill than as a residue of discipline and self-reliance permanently accruing from having worked for pay. Occasionally other values were expressed—for example, "noblesse oblige," the obligation to repay the privilege of higher education by making some social contribution prior to the assumption of family responsibilities.

A different image of the good life was projected in 1979. It appears that, whatever their preferred future life styles, finding one's place in the world of work is becoming, for these young women—as it has been for their brothers—essential for personal dignity and autonomy. Even relatively traditional students who were prepared to withdraw from work in order to raise a family agonized over the choice of a future occupation.

Occupation, then, has become an important component of one's self-image. This became apparent, also, in the opposition to an early marriage (see chapter 5). The most frequent refrain in the interviews was: "I want first to establish myself in my occupation, to define my own individuality. I don't want to be dependent on anyone until I've had enough time to prove that I can make it on my own." Students in 1979 expressed quite explicitly the need to bring maturity and individuality to the marriage relationship. Excerpts from the interviews illustrate that at least some students were consciously striving not to fall into the trap of transferring their dependence on parents to boyfriends, without ever becoming independent. In 1943 students appeared to share the conventional wisdom that remaining malleable may facilitate the adjustment required in marriage and that marriage itself bestows an adult status.

A revealing illustration of the current pressures against early marriages was expressed in an interview with a student who wanted to get married in her senior year:

I intend to marry my boyfriend this year, but I had to do a lot of soul searching to come to this decision. I disapproved of myself because no one at college seemed to think along those lines. Society seems to expect me to be single when I graduate from college, live alone for a few years until I can prove to myself that I can make it on my own and only then is marriage sanctioned.

But I decided that I love my boyfriend and we want to get married. I am also an independent woman, serious about my career, and I know that I can make it on my own. Since I believe that I can reconcile these interests, why should I feel so defensive about our decision to get married?

The pressure comes, first of all, from some classmates who, learning about my impending marriage, immediately dumped me into the stereotype of an unliberated, dependent woman. I resented their reaction. My mother couldn't understand how I could do college work and "take care of a husband." I told her that Jim was not a child, that both of us share household duties and marriage wouldn't change this.

Even some of our male friends reacted so violently to our news that I think our unconventional decision might have made them question their own life styles.

Surveying the ambiguities of the current scene, the author is continually struck by how different are students' responses today from those of my first students, in the 1940s. When, indulging myself in the final lecture of my course on the family, I depicted my utopian society as one with much less segregation of feminine and masculine roles and some reorganization of homemaking tasks, I aroused passionate opposition from the overwhelming majority of students. "But we look forward to full-time homemaking and child rearing as our deepest fulfillment," they remonstrated, "and would hate to live in some kind of dehumanized collectivist society, crushing all individuality in taste and style." It would have been difficult to predict then that deeply felt values and sentiments could have undergone such changes in a few decades.

The career aspirations of the 1979 freshmen are higher, not only in comparison with the distant past of the 1940s, but also in comparison with those reported for the 1970s by other researchers using comparable methods (Angrist and Almquist 1975; Epstein and Bronzaft 1972). Cherlin (1980) cites the results of a National Survey of Work Experience of Young Women, conducted by the U.S. Bureau of the Census, which shows that in 1973, 28.7 percent of White and 14.8 percent of Black women, ages twenty to twenty-one, with one year of college or more, said that they wanted to be housewives at age thirty-five. In the current study, only 5 percent of the freshmen responded in this way to a comparable question.

Ideals of Femininity and Masculinity

The freshmen in this study filled out the Gough Adjective Check List (ACL; Gough and Heilbrun 1965).[4] The Adjective Check List contains 300 personality traits, both negative (e.g., "dull," "arrogant") and favorable (e.g., "considerate," "insightful") attributes. The student is asked to check traits she or he considers characteristic of self or some specified

---

[4] The scoring procedure for classification of "feminine" and "masculine" qualities was based on methods of Sherriffs and McKee (1957). Having classified the traits checked by freshmen for each of these, the score was based on the ratio of feminine to masculine traits. Thus, for "My Ideal Woman," a score of 1 would be obtained by a student who checked as many stereotypically "feminine" as "masculine" traits in depicting the feminine ideal; the higher the score, the more stereotypically "feminine" is the ideal. A score below 1 reflects the predominance of "masculine" traits as attributes of the ideal woman.

A similar procedure was followed in the scoring of "My Ideal Man." A score of 1 or higher indicates a more stereotypically "manly" ideal, while a lower score is the result of the inclusion of stereotypically "feminine" traits in the ideal man image.

other, or ideal. In this study, students were asked to check on three separate checklists the adjectives that characterize "My Real Self," "My Ideal Woman," and "My Ideal Man."

How "feminine" was the "ideal woman" among freshmen in 1979? To be sure, they admired a "feminine" woman. (For 71 percent of 227 students the score for "my ideal woman" was higher than 1; for only 29 percent did it fall below 1.) This generalization, however, requires a qualification. The more striking finding is not the excess of traditionally "feminine" traits chosen for the respondents' ideal woman, but the very narrow margin of this excess. The mean score was a low 1.11,[5] which signifies that the ideal woman, whatever her "feminine" attributes, was also expected to possess many stereotypically male traits.

The feminine traits checked by the freshmen were familiar enough: affectionate, pleasant, sentimental, artistic, kind, tactful, sociable, sensitive. Eighty-four percent of the sample checked "imaginative," 72 percent "patient" and "helpful," 66 percent "trusting," 42 percent "idealistic," 37 percent "cautious."

The more striking finding was the extent to which the feminine image includes qualities representing action, vigor, rational competence, and effectiveness. Women undergraduates in McKee and Sherriffs' (1959) study had also chosen many similar qualities for both "ideal self" and "ideal man." The difference is one of degree—the 1979 respondents accentuated the high evaluation of traits such as the following: "ambitious" (checked as an attribute of "my ideal woman" by 89 percent of the sample), "active" (89 percent), "independent" (86 percent), "adventurous" (79 percent), "determined" (77 percent), "forceful" (61 percent), "courageous" (61 percent), and "assertive" (an adjective

---

[5] Standard deviation = .27; variance = .11.

not included in the 1959 study, 73 percent). The ideal man as projected by the freshmen was "manly," but the mean score was only 1.03.[6]

Both the ideal woman (mean score 1.11) and the ideal man (mean score 1.03) represented a nearly even mix of stereotypically masculine and feminine qualities, but of the two, the image of the ideal man contained relatively more traits generally attributed to the opposite sex. More surprising than the emergence of an androgynous ideal of a human being is the feminized ideal of the male. Consider the high frequencies of the expressive traits in the profile of the ideal male. The adjective "warm" was checked by 89 percent of the freshmen, "affectionate" by 90 percent, "sensitive" by 85 percent, "cheerful" by 76 percent, and "artistic" by 59 percent. In contrast, some stereotypically masculine attributes were muted. For example, "forceful" was checked by only 25 percent of the sample, "dominant" by 19 percent, "aggressive" by 50 percent; on the other hand, "masculine" received the endorsement of 73 percent. The adjective "sexy," missing completely from attributes assigned to men by women in McKee and Sherriffs' 1957 study, was checked as a desired quality in men by 68 percent of freshmen in 1979. The change may reflect a greater expectation of sexual pleasure on the part of young women, or a greater freedom to express this expectation.

Do these results reflect a firm rejection of the "macho" ideal of masculinity? It is possible that the instrumental traits were simply taken for granted and hence not checked, whereas expressive traits were stressed because they were more problematical in a man. Measures aimed at eliciting a ranking of valued attributes are generally subject to such ambiguity. The responses are likely to reflect in some unspecified way not merely ideal values but also felt

---

[6] Standard deviation = .34; variance = .11. Fifty-seven percent of the scores fell below 1, and 43 percent were higher than 1.

deprivations. To illustrate, in a 1974 study, 77 percent of noncollege women and only 56 percent of college women listed "a good provider" as one of the "very important qualities in a man" (Yankelovitch 1974: 98). This difference stems, in all likelihood, not from the greater materialism of the less-educated women, but from a more problematic character of a secure livelihood. In other words, a valued attribute may be checked infrequently because it is felt to be attainable and therefore taken for granted.

Confirmation of this interpretation was supplied by the students themselves in several interviews. In reflecting upon their responses to the checklist, they surmised that they may have checked the adjectives against the background of gender stereotypes. Women, they claimed, needed to acquire more assertiveness and independence, whereas men should ideally possess more of the expressive qualities they now lack. Whatever the explanation, the ideal images were a far cry from traditional gender-differentiated ideals of femininity and masculinity. At least one other recent study (Freeman 1979) also reports few differences between either female or male conceptualizations of the ideal female and the ideal male.

Attitudes Toward Women's Liberation

Given the antitraditional or egalitarian gender orientations documented in the foregoing pages, the respondents' lukewarm endorsement of the women's liberation movement appeared at first to be surprising. (See table 4.1.)

This qualified approval of the women's movement remains to be explained. Possibly the phrase "Women's Liberation Movement" carried a negative connotation for many freshmen, even if they would have endorsed the particular reforms it advocated. But another explanation was strongly suggested in the interviews. The majority of

TABLE 4.1

Attitudes Toward the Women's Liberation Movement

I.	Please indicate your feelings about the "Women's Liberation Movement" in general by circling one of the choices below:	
		Percent
	Sympathize greatly, think it is certainly justified	37
	Sympathize somewhat, think it is somewhat justified	53
	Neither for nor against it	8
	Somewhat against it, think it has little, if any, justification	2
	Very much against it, think it has no justification	—
		(*n* = 232)
II.	Have you ever been active in the movement in any way?	
	Yes	15
	No	85
		(*n* = 231)

entering freshmen simply saw no need for a collective effort at social reform. Many referred to their good fortune of living at a time when women have all options open to them. The freshmen were optimistic about their chances to attain their goals once they clarified them. The main issue was to "find their identity." Once they "knew who they were," the means of fulfilling their aspirations appeared within reach. Of course, they had not as yet experienced the problems confronting women in the workplace or in marriage. Apparently neither their own observation of their families nor the mass media reports of the women's movement sufficed to offset the individualistic ethos of our society: "A woman can attain her goals not by marching in demonstrations but by proving her worth in any endeavor she chooses."

The individualistic ethos of American society is its strength and its weakness. As a weakness, the ethos leads to relative indifference to collective movements of social reform. A striking confirmation of this fact is provided by a study of unemployed men in the Great Depression of the 1930s. Knowing full well the national scope of the economic disaster, the men nevertheless deflected the blame from the social system to their own weaknesses: "I should have listened to my brother's advice to move" (or not to move), "I should have taken a vocational course," and the like (Komarovsky 1940).

Consistency of Gender Attitudes

The foregoing pages follow a traditional approach by treating each component of the gender perspective separately. Neglected in the great volume of current research is the problem of the degree of consistency among beliefs, role prescriptions, and ideals; only a few studies address this issue. (See, for example, Kammeyer [1964], Nielson and Doyle [1975], and Rapin and Cooper [1980].) On the one hand, it might be hypothesized that psychological sex stereotyping and role prescriptions are expressions of the same underlying attitudes—that, for example, students who stereotype male and female personality traits would hold more traditional views of gender roles than those who do not view the sexes as radically different in psychological traits. After all, historically, the societal support for differentiation in the social roles of the sexes was buttressed by the belief in significant psychological sex differences. But a contrary hypothesis is also plausible. Cognitive dissonance and ethical inconsistencies are too widespread to rule out their manifestation also in attitude toward gender.

The attempt to test these conflicting hypotheses has methodological and theoretical implications. Should beliefs, norms, and ideals be found to lack a high degree of consistency, this would dictate caution in using them interchangeably in comparative studies of trends in gender ideology.

In discussing our findings, I shall report first on the relationship between perceptions of psychological sex dif-

TABLE 4.2

Stereotyping Psychological Sex Differences
and Attitudes Toward Sex Roles

	Attitudes Toward Sex Roles	
Stereotyping	*Traditional (%)*	*Egalitarian (%)*
High (*n* = 77)	64	36
Low (*n* = 147)	29	71

χ^2 = 23.284; sig. = .000.

ferences and attitudes toward sex roles. Do women who
stereotype psychological sex differences tend to endorse
more traditional sex roles? Conversely, are students who
reject psychological sex differences more likely to express
egalitarian norms? The answer to these questions is affirmative and statistically significant. Of 77 freshmen who
scored high on psychological stereotyping, 64 percent
supported traditional sex roles and only 36 percent were
egalitarian. By contrast, among the 147 "low stereotypers,"
only 29 percent were traditional, while 71 percent were
egalitarian. Although this is a strong correlation in the
expected direction, the deviant cases stand out: the high
stereotypers who endorsed egalitarian norms and the freshmen with traditional sex-role attitudes despite their denial
of significant psychological differences between the sexes.
(See table 4.2.)

With respect to the relationships between sex-role attitudes and ideals of femininity and masculinity, here again
logical consistency would seem to dictate some significant
association. Traditional role segregation would appear to
require more "feminine" or "expressive" women and more
"masculine" or "instrumental" men than is the case when
the sexes are expected to play less differentiated and more
egalitarian roles.

There is a slight, but not statistically significant, rela-

TABLE 4.3
Sex-Role Attitudes and "My Ideal Woman"

	"My Ideal Woman"	
Sex-Role Attitudes	"Feminine" (%)	Androgynous (%)
Traditional (n = 91)	77	23
Egalitarian (n = 131)	67	33

$\chi^2 = 2.034$; sig. = .154.

tionship, in the expected direction for "My Ideal Woman."
As to the ideal of masculinity projected by these young
women, however, their sex-role attitudes bear no relationship to this ideal. The strong emphasis on expressive traits
in the ideal man (warm, sensitive, affectionate, and so on)
characterize both women with traditional and egalitarian
sex-role attitudes. (See tables 4.3 and 4.4.)

Examination of the relationships between beliefs about
psychological sex differences and ideals of femininity and
masculinity is also revealing. Here again the ideal of
femininity appears to be more closely related to the other
factor in the equation than the ideal of masculinity.
Women who believed in psychological sex stereotypes
described a more traditionally feminine ideal of women,
in contrast to women who rejected psychological stereotypes. (However, this association is not statistically signif-

TABLE 4.4
Sex-Role Attitudes and "My Ideal Man"

	"My Ideal Man"	
Sex-Role Attitudes	"Masculine" (%)	Androgynous (%)
Traditional (n = 92)	47	53
Egalitarian (n = 132)	41	59

$\chi^2 = .711$; sig. = .399.

icant.) Beliefs about psychological sex differences bear no relationship to the image of the ideal man.

In conclusion, these findings of considerable consistency among beliefs, sex-role prescriptions, and, to some extent, ideals of femininity are significant but do require a methodological caveat. This consistency is not so high as to justify the *interchangeable* use of these components in comparative studies of gender ideology. Moreover, the discovery of both disjunction and consistency among beliefs, prescriptions, and ideals opens up a set of theoretical issues that require further research on the social variables accounting for these varying results.

The convergence of all respondents, however traditional or egalitarian in other respects, in their preference for expressive qualities in the ideal man suggests the possibility that some traditional "manly" attributes are taken for granted and that what the young women in our sample desired in a male are the more problematic qualities of tenderness, sensitivity, warmth, and the like. These results may not only reflect shifts in cultural trends, but may be related to the stage of the life cycle. Instrumental traits in men that ensure success in the marketplace may assume greater importance as these young women marry and raise families.

CAREER SALIENCE

As noted earlier, career salience is of particular interest to this study. As used herein, "career salient" refers to those students who were so committed to having a career that they anticipated, at most, only a brief withdrawal from work after marriage, and then only to care for their preschool children. A few of the career-salient freshmen expressed no desire to marry or to have children and instead chose to dedicate themselves completely to some chosen occupation. The students designated "noncareer" were those with only low or moderate career aspirations.

Two theoretical issues are the foci of this section. The first is similar to one raised in the last section regarding what might be termed the ideological consistency of young women who, at the average age of eighteen, aspire to lifelong careers. Are they less likely to stereotype feminine and masculine personalities in general? Are they less likely to stereotype female psychological traits negatively? Are they more egalitarian with respect to norms governing male-female relationships? Are they more sympathetic to the women's liberation movement than their noncareer classmates? Do they project a more "androgynous" ideal of femininity and masculinity?

The second theoretical concern deals with background factors that may have contributed to the career commitment of some students and its absence in others. In the course of a major shift in work participation and career aspirations of college women, who are the ones "first to take up the new and last to give up the old"? Both social and psychological factors that characterize the high, as against the relatively low, career aspirations are considered in the following pages.

Career Salience and the Gender Perspective

Two major conclusions emerge as career-salient freshmen are compared with their noncareer classmates. The first is their greater egalitarianism on all but one of the components of the gender perspective. (See tables 4.5 to 4.8.) Career-salient freshmen maintain a more positive perception of

TABLE 4.5
Career Salience and Perception of
Psychological Sex Differences

	View of women (%)	
Career salience	Negative	Positive
Career students (*n* = 111)	36	64
Noncareer students (*n* = 117)	64	36

χ^2 = 16.735; sig. = .000.

the woman's personality, uphold more egalitarian sex-role norms, and are more sympathetic to the women's liberation movement than their noncareer classmates. The one attitude both groups share is the androgynous ideals of femininity and masculinity.

The second finding is a qualification of these (statistically significant) conclusions. In each comparison there is a considerable overlap between the two groups. For example, of the 117 noncareer students, 64 percent shared the familiar negative stereotype of female psychological traits, but though a minority, 36 percent of career-salient women nevertheless also expressed this image of female inferiority. Even more inconsistent is the relationship between the degree of career salience and attitudes toward sex roles. While 73 percent of career-salient students expressed egalitarian norms, only 35 percent of the noncareer students

TABLE 4.6
Career Salience and Attitudes Toward Sex Roles

	Attitudes toward sex roles (%)	
Career salience	Egalitarian (*n* = 122)	Traditional (*n* = 106)
Career students (*n* = 111)	73	27
Noncareer students (*n* = 117)	35	65

χ^2 = 32.94; sig. = .000.

TABLE 4.7
*Career Salience and Attitudes Toward
Women's Liberation Movement*

Attitudes	Career (%) (n = 111)	Noncareer (%) (n = 117)
Sympathize greatly	49.5	22.2
Sympathize somewhat	45.9	61.5
Neither for nor against it	3.6	12.8
Somewhat against it	.9	3.4

χ^2 = 21.994; sig. = .000.

were egalitarian. Yet 27 percent of freshmen, so highly committed to lifelong careers as to be classified as career salient, expressed traditional attitudes toward sex roles. This means that some young women for whom a career is a central component of a good life might still reject "going Dutch" on dates or accept the view that "there are many jobs in which men should be given preference over women."

Some of these apparent inconsistencies no doubt stem from what Kirkpatrick (1936) identified as a wish (shared by men) to enjoy a double dose of privileges, those inherent in the traditional as well as in the modern roles. The

TABLE 4.8
*Students' Career Salience and Ideals
of Femininity and Masculinity*

Ideals	Career (%)	Noncareer (%)
"Feminine"[a]	(n = 108)	(n = 115)
High +1	65.7	76.5
Low −1	34.3	23.5
"Masculine"[b]	(n = 108)	(n = 117)
High +1	39.8	45.3
Low −1	60.2	54.7

[a] χ^2 = 2.659; sig. = .103.
[b] χ^2 = .485; sig. = .486.

relative lack of consistency may also have another source. In the interviews, the students evinced a certain lack of realism about problems likely to be encountered in combining a demanding career with family life. Indeed, some career-minded students felt that their society offers women a free choice of desired life styles. Consequently, some traditional attitudes toward sex roles, whatever their source, were not put to the test of frustrating experiences that, in turn, might have led the students to question traditional definitions of male advantages. As to attitudes toward the women's liberation movement, the same pattern emerges. Fifty percent of career-salient freshmen, as contrasted with only 22 percent of noncareer freshmen, "sympathize[d] greatly" with the movement. But this means that one-half of career salients had little or no sympathy with it.

Plans for the Future

On the whole, then, career freshmen did not foresee major problems in their intention to combine family life with a career. Although this optimism appears somewhat unrealistic, the career students were ahead of noncareer students in their plans for the future. The former were surer both of their college majors and their eventual occupations.

Presented with a list of alternatives, graded according to the degree of certainty, from "I have at present no idea of what my major in college will be" to "I am quite sure I'll major in . . . ," the career students expressed greater certainty.[7] A similar relationship obtained for occupational choices, with career students indicating greater certainty and less vacillation among a number of possible occupational choices.[8] This relationship may well be a circular one.

[7] This relationship is statistically significant; $\chi^2 = 19.318$; sig. = .002.
[8] $\chi^2 = 11.938$; sig. = .018.

Some generalized career motivation is likely to stimulate a scrutiny of occupational options. A strong interest in some field, in turn, may contribute to career salience.

The career students have been characterized as relatively unaware of problems they might encounter in the future. However, in one respect, the timing of marriage, they did display some realism (see page 120). In answer to the question "What is your best guess as to the chance that you will get married within 5 years after college?"—with four response options varying from "no chance" to "very good chance"—only 25 percent of career students, but 54 percent of noncareer students, checked "very good chance."[9] In the interviews, students frequently attributed such delay in getting married to the desire to become established in a career.

Concerning expectations of academic performance, five possible responses—ranging from "B+ or higher average" to "It is possible that I may fail one or more courses" or "I cannot venture even a guess at this point"—were included in the questionnaire. Career freshmen manifested no greater self-assurance on this score than other freshmen.[10]

Demographic and Class Variables

A number of social variables proved to have no bearing upon career salience. Among these are the education of the father and of the mother (college graduates and less than a B.A. degree); occupational status of father (high, middle, low); family income; employment of mother (full-time, part-time, no paid work); and occupational status of

---

[9] For the relationship between expected time of marriage and career salience, $\chi^2 = 25.917$; sig. = .000.

[10] $\chi^2 = 6.528$; sig. = .163.

employed mother (high, middle, low)." See appendix, pp. 335-38.

The parental families of college undergraduates do not, of course, represent a random sample of the population, being drawn disproportionately from higher educational and economic strata. Nevertheless, the demographic spread, including ethnic and religious identity, was considerable. Whatever their social origins, students who chose (and were admitted by) a secular women's college with high academic standards, affiliated with a renowned urban university, perhaps possessed shared characteristics that obliterated the impact that demographic variables might have on career salience in a nationally random sample of freshmen. Moreover, these negative results pertain only to career salience as measured by our scale, which failed to register qualitative differences. Interviews with "first-generation" college students from lower socioeconomic backgrounds strongly suggest that career motivation was linked to upward mobility. Their emphasis was upon vocational, rather than liberal arts, aspects of the college experience, and upon attaining an economically and socially secure status. Daughters of professional and economically affluent families appeared more frequently to stress commitment to work as an avenue of self-fulfillment and as an intrinsic component of a good life.

If not class, are race and ethnicity (White, Black, Latin and Asian Americans) and religion of parents (Protestant, Catholic, Jewish, and mixed) possible factors in career

---

"These social variables proved equally insignificant in findings of Simpson and Simpson (1961), Ridgeway (1978), and Tangri (1972). The latter found that class and mother's occupational and educational status have no consistent relationship to the occupationally innovative choices of female undergraduates. In a study of married women who attended college in 1968, Lipman-Blumen (1972) found that none of the usual socioeconomic and educational variables were related to sex-role ideology. Angrist and Almquist (1970) cited similar findings, except they found that career-salient students more frequently had employed mothers (see also Bose and Priest-Jones 1980).

salience? With Whites constituting 69 percent of the sample, the race-ethnic differences may not be reliable—within the limits of this sample they were not significant.[12]

Among the White students, the proportion of career-salient students did not vary by religion.[13] Here again, the finding contradicts an earlier study that reports career-oriented women were more often Jewish and less often Catholic than Protestant (Angrist and Almquist 1975). In the present sample, the proportion of Jewish career-salient women was lower than that of the Protestants, though the religious differences were not statistically significant.[14]

When the total sample, including the racial and ethnic groups (Black and Latin and Asian Americans), was divided by religion, a significant relationship emerged.[15] Catholic freshmen showed the highest rate of career salience, and this in turn is explained by the high rate among Latin-American Catholics. The fathers of the Latin-American students had on the average fewer years of schooling than the fathers of the two other minority groups. If the desire for upward mobility is taken to be the clue to career salience among the Latin Americans, we have no explanation of the fact that Black and Asian-American students, who also came from lower educational backgrounds, exhibited rates of career salience similar to that of the White majority. In this college, the Latin-American Catholic students were the most recent arrivals in comparison with other ethnic groups; as "pioneers," they may have represented an especially upwardly mobile group.

As reported earlier, maternal employment was not related to career salience. The interviews, as analyzed in chapter 5, show some of the complexities of this issue. Explanation

[12] $\chi^2 = 3.317$; sig. = .345. Our figures do not confirm the higher career expectations of Black students reported elsewhere (Cherlin 1980).

[13] $\chi^2 = 2.557$; sig. = .465.

[14] See chapter 6, page 196, for further discussion of religion.

[15] $\chi^2 = 10.409$; sig. = .034.

of the daughter's career salience should include the mother's reaction to whatever role she is engaged in, the message her experience conveys to the daughter, together with her explicit aspirations for the latter. Above all, the nature of the mother-daughter relationship affects the daughter's tendency to aspire to imitate her mother's role or to rebel against it, or, as in some cases, to experience a conflict-ridden ambivalence. Recent studies of this problem point up some of these complexities (Baruch 1972; Haber 1980; Lipman-Blumen 1972; Lipman-Blumen and Thompson 1976).

One family background factor proved to be significantly associated with the degree of career salience in the present sample. Thirty-three percent of career students, but only 18 percent of noncareer ones, described the marital relationship of their parents as "very tense" or "somewhat tense."[16] Conversely, noncareer students were more positive in their assessment of their parents' relationship, describing it, for example, as "close and intimate." At least one motivational nexus was supplied by several daughters of unhappy parents. In the words of one: "I am going to make sure that I shall never have to depend upon a man for my livelihood. I will never want to face my mother's predicament."

Psychological Variables

We know much less about the distinctive psychological characteristics of achievement-oriented young women than we thought we knew in the 1940s and 1950s—decades dominated by Freudian theory. Helene Deutsch (1945) described with assurance the pathology of the intellectual and achieving woman, rooted in rejection of the allegedly basic and healthy feminine nature. Criticizing Freudian

[16] $\chi^2 = 11.572$; sig. = .000.

theory, this writer proposed the hypothesis that the psychodynamic characteristics of an "achieving" woman are not constant, but vary with the social context (Komarovsky 1953: 31–44). At a time when society penalizes achievement in "masculine" spheres, the emergence of such a "deviant" drive and the readiness to pay the high costs of pioneering may be linked to psychodynamic processes quite different from similar achievement at a later period. As the social climate becomes more favorable to women's achievement, it is conceivable that those who are "the last to take up the new" (that is, the achieving roles) may be women deficient in intellectual strength, creativity, self-confidence, and enriching experiences. Moreover, the distinction must be made between some psychic maladjustment as the motive power for compensatory achievement on the one hand and as the psychological consequence of following a pattern defined as deviant in a given milieu on the other. Finally, it is likely that future research will reveal not one but a variety of psychodynamic profiles of achievement-oriented women. Data in the current study have some limited bearing upon these large and complex issues.

As already mentioned, the freshmen filled out the Gough Adjective Check List for "My Real Self." The career and noncareer students were compared on eleven dimensions from the list. Additional data that have psychological implications consist of the students' own assessment of their high-school social relationships.

The scores of career and noncareer students were compared on each trait, using the percentile distribution of scores in our total sample, with the figure closest to the fiftieth percentile as the dividing point. These data tell us what proportions of the scores of career, as against noncareer, students fall in the upper and lower half of the total distribution.

Heterosexuality (as defined in the 1965 Gough and

Heilbrun ACL manual of instructions for the users of the text: "to seek the company of and derive emotional satisfaction from interaction with opposite-sexed peers") did not distinguish career and noncareer students.[17] Nor was affiliation ("to seek and sustain numerous personal friendships") related to the degree of career salience.[18]

Support for these findings is provided by the students' own assessment of the frequency and quality of their high-school social life with female and male peers. There were no statistically significant differences in the frequency of "dating" or the students' estimate of the quality of friendships. The latter was based on the question "Do you feel that, compared with other girls in your high school, your social life with female friends and male friends in the last two years of high school was: 'More satisfactory,' 'As satisfactory,' 'Less satisfactory'?"

So far the evidence is contrary to the hypothesis that career-salient young women are less involved with social life in general and with male peers in particular.

To return to the ACL for "My Real Self," the scores for dominance and achievement were in the expected direction, but were not statistically significant.[19] The career and noncareer freshmen differed significantly on seven out of the eleven dimensions of the ACL selected for comparison: The career students scored higher on Self-Confidence, Autonomy, Aggression, and Unfavorable Adjectives (that is, the relative proportion of defects the student checked in describing herself).[20]

[17] $\chi^2 = .049$; sig. $= .824$.
[18] $\chi^2 = 1.630$; sig. $= .202$.
[19] It is significant to note that psychologists (California Personality Inventory) distinguished two kinds of "achievement" potential: "via conformity" and "via independence." Using only the ACL we may have minimized the "achievement via independence" of our career students.
[20] Self-Confidence ($\chi^2 = 4.480$; sig. $= .002$); Autonomy ($\chi^2 = 9.781$; sig. $= .002$); Aggression ($\chi^2 = 8.894$; sig. $= .003$); and Unfavorable Adjectives ($\chi^2 = 5.520$; sig. $= .019$).

The career students scored lower on Favorable Adjectives, Personal Adjustment, and Nurturance.[21] The ACL manual defines a low scorer on Nurturance as "skeptical, clever . . . but too self-centered and too little attentive to the feelings and wishes of others." Conversely, the subject high on this scale is "of a helpful, nurturant disposition, but sometimes too bland . . . his dependability and benevolence are worthy qualities, but he may nonetheless be too conventional" (p. 12).

The relatively higher scores of career students on Unfavorable Adjectives and on Personal Adjustment are intriguing. The ACL manual describes the high and low scorer on Unfavorable Adjectives as follows:

> From individual work with subjects who have scored high on this scale it appears that checking of unfavorable adjectives does not spring from a sense of humility and self-effacement, but more from a kind of impulsive lack of control over the hostile and unattractive aspects of one's personality. The high-scoring subject strikes others as rebellious, arrogant, careless, conceited, and cynical. He tends to be a disbeliever, a skeptic, and a threat to the complacent beliefs and attitudes of his fellows. The low-scorer is more placid, more obliging, more mannerly, more tactful, and probably less intelligent. (P. 6.)

A clinical psychologist attempted to present composite profiles of career and noncareer students solely on the basis of the ACL scores:[22]

> The emerging personality picture of a career-salient student is one of an independent, nonconforming, self-motivated individual, who has a need to assert herself,

to get things done, and to make an impression. Her intelligence is characterized by sharpness, originality, and skepticism. There may be an element of impulsivity and rebelliousness in her behavior.

Although the career-salient freshman is a vital, out-going person—interested in relationships with men and women—there is a self-centered quality to her relation-ships. Inattentive to feelings of others, perhaps somewhat abrasive, such a person is prone to experience anxiety and may be moody and dissatisfied.

In contrast, the non-career student is conventional and conforming. She gets along well with others and because of her readiness to adjust she is willing to take the others' lead. Although she may work diligently towards her own goals, she does not seek to be the center of attention. Her intelligence is likely to be more practical than original. Her conventionality may result in her being viewed by others as friendly and loyal but bland.

These profiles were sketched on the basis of polar dimensions of the ACL with no examination of the degree to which the actual scores of the two groups of freshmen overlapped and with no collaborative evidence from other personality tests or clinical interviews. Tentative as the findings are, the career-salient freshmen emerge as similar to the noncareer ones in heterosexuality and dating in high school, superior in autonomy and self-confidence, and lower in self-satisfaction.

In summary, those career-salient freshmen entering the women's college in the fall of 1979 expected to combine careers with marriage, since all but 2 percent hoped to be married. The overwhelming majority—all but 14 percent—also looked forward to motherhood. A radical change in professed aspirations has taken place among the students of this college since a similar survey was made in 1943, when only 12 percent, as against the current 48 percent, could be defined as career salient by our criteria.

The career-oriented students exhibited considerable ideological consistency in their attitudes toward gender. In contrast to their noncareer classmates, they endorsed more egalitarian sex roles, did not stereotype as negatively the feminine psyche, and were more sympathetic toward the women's liberation movement. This ideological consistency, however, was lower than might have been expected; an attempt was made to offer some hypotheses for discrepancies among life-style preferences, beliefs, normative attitudes, and ideal values. Thus, for example, the somewhat muted enthusiasm for the women's movement on the part of the careerists may be attributed to their manifest lack of realism about the problems of combining careers and family life. Serenely confident about the feasibility of their ambitious goals, they saw no need for major social reforms. Possibly the phrase "Women's Liberation Movement" carried some negative connotation. Other surprising results remain to be investigated. It is not clear why the ideals of femininity and, especially, of masculinity bear so little relation to other components of gender orientations. The results dictate caution in using interchangeably the degree of stereotyping of psychological differences, attitudes toward sex roles, ideals of femininity and masculinity, and life-style preferences.

As noted previously, socioeconomic, religious, and racial-ethnic background variables were unrelated to career salience. These negative results call for further research. The selective character of the students may have obliterated the impact of these demographic variables. However, as indicated earlier, studies in colleges whose student body is more representative of the general population confirm a similar lack of significance of these background factors. Possibly, the single variable correlations are inadequate.

Particular combinations of antecedent variables may prove more effective predictors. Such a complex explanatory model in relation to the mother as a factor in career salience has been proposed. This model was tested in interviews with highly suggestive results, as reported in chapter 5. Another finding of this study threw additional light on the influence of religion. Although formal religious affiliations were found to have no bearing on career salience, the degree of religious orthodoxy was a factor distinguishing traditional from career-committed students (see chapter 6, p. 196). As to family background, the striking finding is the strong relationship between marital unhappiness of parents (or divorce) as perceived by daughters and their career commitment.

Finally, the data on psychological correlates of career salience, based largely on the Gough Adjective Check List for "My Real Self," reveal both some psychological strengths as well as some less favorable features of the career-salient freshmen in contrast to their noncareer-oriented classmates.

5

Four Years Later: Traditionals and Converts

THE PRECEDING CHAPTER described the attitudes and aspirations of the freshmen before college could have had any impact on them. In the fall of their sophomore year and, again, in the spring of their senior year, these students filled out the same set of questionnaires. These replicated measures will reveal something about persistence and change in their attitudes. But the quantitative findings on freshmen–senior comparisons will serve merely as an introduction to the major task of this and the following chapters: to discern the processes by which different students reacted in different ways to their college experience. The analysis of the interviews of freshmen, sophomores, and seniors will illuminate these processes.

The responses on the Life-Style Index will be presented first. They bear on the centrality or salience of careers in the students' aspirations for the future, which will be the basis of the typology of college impacts. The questionnaire findings also revealed changes in the desire for children, the preferred age of marriage, plans for graduate study, and attitudes toward the women's movement.

TRENDS IN ATTITUDES BASED ON QUESTIONNAIRES

Were we to depend on one question of the Life-Style Index (see IV, p. 331) filled out by entering freshmen, sophomores, and students at the end of their senior year, the overriding impression would be the stability of responses. (A few changes are noted in the following text.)

Students were asked: Fifteen years from now, would you like to be:

		1979 (%)	1980 (%)	1983 (%)
1.	A housewife with no children	0	0	0
2.	A housewife with one or more children	7	4	5
3.	An unmarried career woman	2	3	1
4.	A married career woman without children	14	10	7
5.	A married career woman with children	76	80	85
6.	Other: what?	1	3	2
		100	100	100
			(n = 154)	

The response "Other" included, among miscellaneous items, "an unmarried career woman with children." The major change in the answers to this question was an increased desire for children. At entrance to college, 14 percent of the freshmen checked "a married career woman without children." This percentage declined to 10 percent of the sophomores and to 7 percent of the seniors. The major gain was in the vote for "a married career woman with children," making this the preferred choice of over four-fifths of the seniors.

The vast majority of the seniors who hoped to combine family life with a career, did not, however, constitute a homogeneous group. They varied greatly in the centrality they attached to work.

The crucial variable in the forthcoming analysis is career salience, as defined in chapter 4. The sample was divided into two groups. The first, "career" students, were women who hoped to have a lifelong occupation. They would interrupt their careers, if at all, only to take care of their preschool children. The second, "noncareer," was a more miscellaneous category. It was distinguished from the first by a more moderate commitment to work, the intention to withdraw from work for longer periods (until children finished elementary or high school), or to work only part-time, even when their children were grown.

The distinction between career and noncareer students, especially within the seemingly homogeneous group of those who checked "a married career woman with children," brought to light a trend hitherto obscured. Using the same criteria, only 48 percent of the total sample of the entering freshmen could be classified as career salient. This proportion increased to 62 percent by the end of the senior year. Of the remaining seniors, 35 percent were noncareer and 3 percent ambiguous. The unmistakable conclusion is that the four years of college coincided with a significant increase in the expectation to carry on a lifelong occupation, generally in combination with family life.[1]

When during the college experience did these shifts in attitudes take place? Some increase in the desire for children was already manifested in the sophomore year and continued into the senior year. The results differ for career salience. By the beginning of the sophomore year, the proportion of career-salient women had hardly changed from 1979. The striking rise in career commitment took place in the last three years of college.

Preferred age of marriage was also tested in 1979, 1980, and 1983. Students were asked: What is your best guess as to the chance that you will get married within 5 years after college? The four response options were "no chance," "very little chance," "some chance," and "very good chance." There were two married students in 1979 and 1980, and three in 1983. Though for the sample as a whole, the attitudes remain quite stable, for some students there was a tendency to delay marriage. This is seen in the rise of combined responses of "no chance" and "very little chance" from 14 percent in 1979 to 17 percent in 1980 to 21 percent in 1983. At the other pole, "very good chance" was checked by 40 percent in 1979 and 39 percent in 1983. A radical change in the age at first marriage has taken place at this college, as in the country at large. As recently as 1967, nearly one-third of the graduating seniors were already married less than one year after graduation.

As to plans for postcollege education, the entering freshmen and the seniors were asked: As far as you can tell now, do you plan to continue your education after receiving a bachelor's degree?

[1] Angrist and Almquist (1975) also found some increase in career aspirations from freshman to senior years, although the relative percentage of career-salient seniors was lower than in our sample. Some differences in the use of the Life-Style Index we adapted from that study, if anything, sets more stringent requirements for the career-salient designation (see p. 90).

		1979 (%) (n = 232)	1983 (%) (n = 154)
1.	Yes, graduate school	62	48
2.	Yes, professional school	27	36
3.	Yes, other training	4	2
4.	No, I do not plan to continue	7	14
		100	100

The decline in plans to work for an M.A. or a Ph.D. may be attributable to the perception of scarcity of academic jobs, as well as to the increase in professional aspirations requiring a specialized professional education. The last category, students with no plans to continue, constituting 14 percent of the seniors, is mixed. It consists of students who wrote "intend to take some time off, may return to school" and others who found a line of work in which advancement depended on experience rather than on a graduate degree. Still other seniors, generally noncareer ones, felt that after four years of college they wanted a temporary or a permanent leave from the regimentation of any school.

We have traced the students' intentions and hopes for their personal lives. An attempt was also made to ascertain their attitudes toward the women's movement for equality. The questionnaire dealing with this issue is reproduced as table 5.1, together with the students' responses in fall 1979, fall 1980, and spring 1983.

Fuller understanding of these statistics emerges from the analysis of the interviews that follow. Suffice it to say here that the entering freshmen were by and large indifferent to the movement because they felt that the so-called women's problem either was solved for their generation or required individual rather than collective action.

By the end of the senior year, however, endorsement of the women's liberation movement significantly increased.

TABLE 5.1

Changing Attitudes Toward the Women's Liberation Movement

		1979 (%)	1980 (%)	1983 (%)
1.	Please indicate your feelings about the "Women's Liberation Movement" in general by circling one of the choices below:			
	(a) sympathize greatly, think it is certainly justified	35	42	52
	(b) sympathize somewhat, think it is somewhat justified	54	53	40
	(c) neither for it nor against it	9		
	(d) somewhat against it, think it has little, if any, justification	2	4	7
	(e) very much against it, think it has no justification		1	1
		(100)	100	(100)
2.	Have you ever been active in the movement in any way?			
	yes	13	18	26
	no	87	82	74
		(n = 151)	(n = 146)	(n = 150)

One-half of the seniors, as compared with only slightly over one-third of the freshmen, checked the most favorable response, "sympathize greatly, think it is certainly justified." Greater realism about problems of combining family life and career, heightened awareness as a result of work experience, and influence of feminist classmates or teachers were cited in the interviews as grounds for increased sympathy. Still, given the ethos of the college, it is somewhat puzzling that 40 percent of the seniors still gave the movement only the qualified support of "sympathize somewhat, think it is somewhat justified." The remaining 8 percent were even more indifferent. As in the past, an individualism that denies the need for a social movement and, among a minority, an active hostility toward radical feminism with which the phrase "Women's Liberation

Movement" was identified appear to account for this result.

Regarding their own active participation (in a consciousness-raising group, abortion reform, day-care facilities, conferences, demonstrations, and the like), 26 percent of the seniors showed an increase over the earlier years but they constituted only one-half of the "strong" supporters of the movement and one-fourth of the total sample.

CAREER SALIENCE: FIVE PATTERNS

The global comparison of freshmen and seniors concerning career salience conceals the diverse patterns of change and persistence resulting in this final outcome. Five such patterns have been uncovered, and these illuminate the processes affecting the degree of career salience.[2]

The first group, "Noncareer Steadfast," or traditionals, consists of students who entered and finished college as noncareer (24 percent of the senior sample). To avoid the awkwardness of "noncareer," this group will also be referred to as "traditional." But a caveat is in order. The true traditionals are the minority of 5 percent who look forward to being full-time homemakers "fifteen years from now." The group of noncareer steadfast also included students who expected to work for major periods of their lives. But, in contrast to the career-salient students, they preferred to interrupt their work for longer periods of child rearing or to work only part-time, even when their children were grown.

The second pattern embraces the "Shifters to Careers,"

[2] This typology was essentially the one developed by Angrist and Almquist (1975).

or the converts. These entered college as noncareer in 1979 but were career salient in 1983. They represent 25 percent of the seniors. The third group, "Career Steadfast," were career salient at entrance to college and remained so in 1983—33 percent of the seniors. The other two types represent smaller groups. They are the "Shifters to Noncareer," students who entered as career salient, but lost their career commitment by the end of the senior year (9 percent of the total). Finally, "Waverers" fluctuated from year to year without the consistent direction exhibited by the first four types (7 percent of the seniors). (Responses by 2 percent were too ambiguous for classification.)

As we compare the five types, the analysis will attempt to locate both the characteristics of the entering student and the decisive features of the college that together accounted for the different outcomes.

All of these contrasting types spent four years at a college that has a distinctive ethos in regard to women's roles. The interviews sought to tap students' perception of a variety of institutional values. None evoked nearly so unanimous a response as the college ideology on women's roles.

College Ethos Concerning Women's Roles

The message of the college as seen by the students is conveyed in the following excerpts from the interviews:

> The ideal student of this college is a self-confident, independent, ambitious woman—in a word, an achiever.

> I don't think this college discourages femininity in general, but it surely does play down the full-time housewife role.

> This college attempts to give women the sense of their own worth, not just as helpmates to the opposite

sex. You can tell that some professors and advisers are really pushing you to make something of your own life.

We are constantly reminded that the college ranks first in the proportion of its graduates who get Ph.D.'s and are accomplishing things in the professional world.

This college aims to groom intelligent and talented women as future leaders and innovators in all fields. It attempts to equip women with tools to do their best in academics and to make it in the outside world.

As evidence, the students cited the president's and the dean's formal and informal speeches; the literature published by the college; the releases of the Public Relations office; the outside authorities invited as speakers; and the explicit statements of the faculty, combined with the cues conveyed in faculty-student interaction. (One student reported: "Professor X lost interest in me when I told him that I decided not to go on to graduate school.")

In view of the perceived ethos of the college, a methodological issue may be raised regarding the validity of student responses. Might they not be merely an expression of conformity with prevailing values? Confidence in responses is heightened by the probing questions of the interviews, which served as a strong safeguard against perfunctory conformity. The proportion of career-salient students was as high among the interviewed 65 seniors as among the 154 seniors who returned the questionnaires. Only a longitudinal study of postcollege years could confirm the students' degree of lifetime career commitment.

The student consensus about institutional values must be distinguished from the social structure of the student body, its alignments, factions, and values. Those present a much wider diversity. The following analysis of patterns of change and stability in life-style preferences will reveal the countervailing factors and cross-pressures that led some to withstand, withdraw, and, occasionally, rebel against the values espoused by the college even as others were inspired to strive for these goals.

The logic underlying this exploration assumes that the choice between career and noncareer preferences involves a form of cost-benefit balance. To begin with, the traditional role may vary in its appeal from positive anticipation to an attitude of disdain or repulsion. The role of a career woman, independently, may appear alluring or not, attainable or out of reach. The search for determinants of the disposition of women to choose one or the other role has been the subject of a large body of writing. Psychologists and sociologists have sought answers in the culture of the family; the interaction of the daughter with her mother, father, or siblings; and a great variety of personality traits. I shall cite some data on these antecedent variables as they interact with the college experience, but it is the impact of the college that remains the primary concern.

The following analysis of the patterns of change and persistence is based largely on the seventy interviews with the sophomores and sixty-five follow-up interviews with the same students in their senior year. Some of the hypotheses suggested by the interviews will be tested with the total sample of 154 seniors.

THE TRADITIONALS

These traditional students were the 24 percent of the sample who entered and finished college as noncareer in their preferences for the future. These students were not alike in all respects. (The same is true of the other types sharing the common feature of the classification. Each type contained various subgroups that arrived at the same outcome by different routes.)

Among the traditional students, some had few misgivings about the sequential pattern of work, withdrawal for child rearing, and return to work, within a fairly conventional form of family life. Others, also relatively at peace with such a prospect, nevertheless were tempted to explore alternative plans. They were deterred by vulnerability to setbacks or by some uncongenial feature of an early occupational choice or of any demanding career. This combination led them, as we shall see, to fall back, with varying degrees of conflict, on the life-style preference expressed when they entered college.

The theoretical problem posed by all the traditional students is to discover the processes that shielded them from what they themselves perceived as the nontraditional institutional values, especially from the influences that transformed others who were also traditional as entering freshmen but shifted to career plans in 1983.

The following analyses are based largely upon the interviewed subsample of sixty-five students.

Familial Values

The considerable ethnic and religious diversity of the students meant that their precollege years were spent in a variety of familial subcultures, some deeply religious with strong emphasis on female-male differences and segregated gender roles and others relatively egalitarian. The first finding characterizing traditionals is that more of them than of the other types received a strong message from their families, a message situated within a traditional ethnic and religious background, that the proper role of women was to be homemakers and mothers.

A case in point has already been cited in the introduction, of a student from a tight ethnic community who, after an initial rebellion against her familial background, "returned to the fold" in her senior year. This involved strong family expectations to live at home after graduation, enter the family business (thus putting her college education to a practical end), and marry soon thereafter. From feeling hostility toward her mother's role as a full-time homemaker, the student eventually came to realize that many aspects of that role appealed to her:

> I would really like to be like one of my sisters-in-law. She got married when she was twenty-one, she had a baby at twenty-six. She's very happy. She's not the domestic type—she's not the bridge-playing, tennis-playing type at all. She's very down-to-earth. And she's such a great mother. She does very well what is now the most important part of her life.

However, while certain traditional rights and responsibilities of marriage and motherhood appealed to this student, she differentiated herself from her own mother, who was the "bridge- and tennis-playing type," and realized that she still needs some work, both for personal fulfillment when children are somewhat older and in the event that her marriage should not work out.

Another illustrative case is that of a Chinese student who upheld parental values in the face of several more assimilated Asian friends who often questioned her strict adherence to "old-style" values.

> This Chinese student described her father as extremely traditional and he objected to her coming to this college, causing her to rebel against his wishes. Both parents were indifferent to any future career for her. She spent

a great deal of time with them at home and in church, respected their prohibition against dating non-Asian men (her comment: "It must be the same for every ethnic group, isn't it? Parents like their children to marry inside the group."), and agreed with their desire that she marry and be primarily a child rearer. Interestingly, her independent and feisty younger sister developed an interest in science, and now "my parents want her to be a doctor. For them, being a doctor is the only profession that counts and this is part of their Chinese background."

This case also illustrates the conflict of Chinese-American parents between their desire for prestige and family honor on the one hand and the old values about women on the other.

Based on the interviews, the two ethnic groups with strongest resistance to career orientation and the modern roles for women were Orthodox Jews and Chinese Americans. In the total sample of 154 seniors, the proportions of traditional or noncareer students were nearly identical for all Jews (Orthodox, Reformed, or assimilated), Protestants, Asians, and non-Latin Catholics. The Latins had a lower proportion of traditional and, conversely, a higher percentage of career-salient women. The small group of Black students was more traditional than the Latins (see chapter 4 for the relationship between religion and career salience of entering freshmen).

Not all traditional students came from ethnic minorities. Some nonethnic daughters came from warm, closely knit families, and they admired and wished to emulate their traditional mothers. A Catholic daughter of native-born parents, a talented music major who hoped to continue composing and performing, nevertheless planned to go home to live after graduation and to marry her high-school boyfriend in the near future. To quote from our notes from the interview: "This student hopes to re-create her parental family: four children, each spaced two years apart; possible freelance work in music when children are young; community and volunteer work (like her mother), and return to full-time work when the youngest child is in high school."

Several noncareer students looked forward to this sequential pattern, which, in many cases, repeated the work patterns of their mothers. In sharp contrast to the career and the "converts to career" students, the traditionals expressed no concern about the adverse effects upon career opportunities so prolonged a withdrawal from work might have. Their naiveté about the realities of the job market may have been the product of their inexperience and their only moderate career drive.

Peer Groups

For most of the traditional students, friendships tended to be with equally traditional friends. This was certainly one mechanism that shielded them from the influence of the prevailing college ethos. Chinese and Asian students, through membership in the Asian Students' Club, tended to associate with others who provided affirmation of their values. The Orthodox Jewish students, by eating together on the Kosher meal plan, received similar reinforcement. This is in sharp contrast to other religious and ethnically identified women who, by interacting with members of different groups and exposing themselves to different values, underwent changes in life-style preferences. Friendship homogeneity was often accompanied by a lack of identification with the mainstream of college thought, a feeling of not being one of "them."

Members of ethnic and religious minorities were not the only ones to express a "them/us" mentality—other traditional students also voiced it. In some cases, this view was accompanied by self-doubt and conflict. D., a white Protestant daughter of native-born parents, a French major, was living off campus with her boyfriend. She saw college as a place to explore intellectual and personal growth and did not envision a full-time career for herself. Her circle of friends did not approve of what they saw as excessive ambition typical of women in the college. She both shared their attitude and was somewhat uneasy with it:

> Most of my friends are not directed. They are unsure of what they want to do and they may end up in jobs that they hate—it's depressing. We make fun of all those premeds and prelaws, who have a passion for something and go after it. A lot of people at this college have real self-confidence, are organized and independent. Maybe we make fun of them because they have something we don't have.

Although she would like to work, probably to teach in elementary school, she would prefer to work part-time and devote most of her time to child rearing. Perhaps because these attitudes are not deeply rooted in religion and ethnicity, she experiences more conflict than the traditional students just cited. D. reflected: "I can imagine myself in a few years with kids and teaching school. It is old-fashioned. . . . I'd be in a position so many women have been fighting to escape. Yet it is a position I really wouldn't mind being in." If she experienced some misgivings, they were allayed by the fact that her values were shared by her boyfriend, her sister, and a small group of close friends.

Academic Performance

A plausible hypothesis is that the noncareer students performed less well academically than the career students. Contrary to this expectation, the grade-point averages of the noncareer and career group for four years of college were similar.[3] In fact, 54 percent of the traditional and 51 percent of the career students averaged 3.3 (B+) or above. What appears to be more significant is the reaction to the initial disappointment in grades experienced, as pointed out in chapter 2, by about half of the freshmen. The noncareer students appeared, whatever their grades, to be more easily discouraged and convinced that they lacked some essential quality necessary for a career, be it motivation, competitiveness, talent, or other traits. For D., her initial poor performance in her chosen field of design was so crushing a blow that it drastically changed her orientation to college:

> I hated that I wasn't good at design, so I just threw it all away. I had thought that I have a talent for it, but then I realized that I had probably liked the idea more than the job. It was at that point that I decided to have no ambition and to just enjoy school until I graduated.

Another student, originally thinking of going to graduate school and perhaps becoming a stockbroker, did not do well in her first two years, and became less and less oriented toward a defined career: "The whole struggle made me feel very frustrated. Now I'm not worried about it at all, in terms of my future. I know now that I can only do so much."

---

[3] Contrary to our findings, Davis (1966) cites some evidence that career-oriented women had received higher grades.

To repeat, the traditional students performed, on the average, as well as the career-oriented ones in terms of grades. The hypothesis suggested by the interviews is that those traditionals who did not come up to their initial expectations were more easily discouraged. Attracted as they were to the traditional life style, they may have more readily assumed that they lacked the capacity, the drive, and the competitiveness required by a demanding career. By contrast, the career-steadfast students, discussed in the following chapter, coped with initial disappointment in various ways, including changes in majors, without relinquishing career aspirations. Moreover, a distinction must be made between the motivation for high academic performance and the career drive. The traditional group included students with high academic averages but no interest in a lifelong career.

The traditional group stood in contrast to both career-steadfast students and shifters to career in two other respects. These were their lack of interaction with the faculty and their unsatisfying job experiences during college years.

Relationships with Faculty

In comparison with career-steadfast students, a smaller proportion of traditional students had contacts with their teachers outside the classroom and fewer instances of on-campus internships with professors or of recommendations by the latter for outside jobs during the college years. While the traditional women often found their teachers intellectually stimulating, they were reluctant to initiate contacts with them. In the words of one such student: "I don't care to interact with my professors. I don't seek them out the way some students do, who are on a first-name basis. I feel the distance and I don't feel like breaking it."

There were exceptions, even among the traditional. D., the English major, changed her mind about the inaccessibility of the faculty. She explained: "Mostly through my own probing and pushing, I broke the barrier. Before I thought that they were unconcerned, but if you really know what you want to ask and are specific, they respond to you." For her, the presence of an intellectually stimulating female teacher was more important than that of a male teacher, because it "gives you a sense of your own possibilities." This sentiment was echoed by only one other student in this group, who admired highly a female teacher because "she was working on her doctorate, was working full time, and had two children." With these few exceptions, the traditionals either expressed no preference for a teacher's gender or else favored male faculty.

The interviews with traditional seniors illustrated anew the familiar generalization about selective responses to the social environment. The very feature of the institution that stimulated the ambition of one student might discourage another. Female faculty members who served as role models for one student evoked this reaction in a traditional senior: "Two of my professors had kids and within two weeks they were back and it seemed like such a difficult thing to do. They were superwomen. I admired them, but I realized how difficult it really is to successfully combine work and family."

Another illustration of contradictory responses to an identical stimulus is drawn from the students' reactions to a visiting lecturer who described a five-year litigation under Title VII involving a professional woman versus a giant corporation. The woman eventually won the case, but the economic and psychic costs of this battle aroused such deep indignation in one student that, on her own testimony, she became "radicalized." But another member of the audience recorded in her diary:

After hearing the guest lecturer speak today, I was much more informed of the degree to which women are discriminated against in our present society. My reaction to her statement that each of us graduating and entering the job market would be discriminated against upset me a great deal. I jokingly said to a friend, "I think I'll drop out and marry rich." This was a joke, but it's not that funny. This lecture made me wonder why I'm going through all this trouble, when I'll probably never get what I deserve, or what I'm worth. It's very sad that we are striving for equality and getting so little accomplished. The knowledge of this inequality reduces my incentive to strive.

Working During College Years

In their interviews, career-steadfast students and shifters to career repeatedly described the crucial role internships or work experience played in clarifying their choice of occupation.[4] By contrast, the traditional students reported more negative experiences with work. They found themselves oppressed by the nine-to-five routine of full-time employment or they became convinced that they lacked some quality necessary to "make it" in the world of work.

One student who had thought of going into international finance or becoming a stockbroker had already developed strong misgivings by her sophomore year: "I was working categorizing jobs and their skills at the placement office. I saw for the first time what a stockbroker really does, and I'm not sure I have what it takes. I don't have that competitive instinct, that drive." And a similar remark by another student: "I would like to succeed in a business job, with all the money and prestige that it brings, but I don't

[4] An internship, unlike a job, generally carries no stipend and places a responsibility upon the supervisor (or the so-called sponsor) to serve as a mentor in providing a broader interpretation of the work of the establishment, occasionally rotating job assignments.

want to sit in an office from nine to five and type reports. I don't want to be some minor official in the business hierarchy, yet I would hate even more being the top corporate manager who is always insecure in his job."

Two other students who originally intended to be stockbrokers or financial analysts gave up their plans after work experience. The "number crunching" was not what they had imagined business to be. Moreover, both began to feel that the competition and pressure would be excessive. Another student, a psychology major, loved children and enjoyed her work at the campus toddler center. Yet she decided that work with children would be too draining.

The negative image of the nine-to-five work week was contrasted with a countervision of a job with flexible hours and time to pursue other interests. A noncareer student states this view:

> I have a friend who graduated from Stanford and became a broker for a major company. He's a big success. But all he's interested in is money. He's all work, no time out. He has no time for love, no girlfriend. And that's my view of the women here who want full-time business careers. They're just like that.

Among the various elements that dampened the lure of a lifetime career, this last excerpt echoes the students' revolt in the 1960s against the "rat race," the single-minded dedication to "make it" in an imperfect society at the cost of humane values.

Conflicts of the Traditional Students

In the 1940s and 1950s the majority of students at this college had looked forward with serenity to life as a homemaker. In contrast, the noncareer seniors of 1983 intended to work for major periods of their lives. But their ambivalent attitudes toward work generated considerable anxiety. Their choice of occupations was hindered by their perception that they did not quite fit into the world of work. The anticipated familial obligations were one factor restricting the range of suitable jobs. Another was the resistance toward the demands and pressures of the occupational world. It is not surprising that a higher proportion of the traditional students, as compared with career-steadfast ones and shifters to career, reached the end of their senior year unsure of occupational choices. Some perceptive students recognized the circular process that stymied them. As one such senior noted:

> I realized that one can't work full time and raise children. Maybe I feel this way because I'm not sure of my occupational and career objectives. If I knew what I wanted to do careerwise, the responsibility for children might not assume such a major importance and such an obstacle to work.

Others blamed themselves for lack of persistence in exploring job opportunities, and hoped to find interesting jobs effortlessly, even as they recognized their dreams for the fantasies that they were.

By graduation time a Chinese-American student who had originally thought of becoming a writer had abandoned that plan and had tentatively considered becoming an elementary school teacher. Her indecision seemed to stem partly from lack of self-confidence and partly because a career was not seen as central to her future.

> I'm in a quandary. That's why I'm not doing much of anything next year. I'm not going on to graduate school because my head's not in what I'm doing. . . . I think I'll try to get a job after I graduate, but I haven't even

written up my résumé, so you can see how disorganized I am. All I know is that graduate school is definitely out. Maybe I'll get two part-time jobs, one related to education and the other totally unrelated, just to explore.

An English major who thought she would teach in a private school talked about all her "quirky" friends who had found a multitude of interesting jobs after graduating from college: one travels as a wine expert; another, Phi Beta Kappa, ended up as a drummer in a band. She concluded:

> Maybe I'll just go out there, explore, and find something wonderful I want to do. I'm undecided now, but if I only could decide, I could do it—that has a lot to do with people here telling you you can do anything you decide on doing. . . . Maybe I'll just take a job after graduation to earn money and use my time to figure out what I want to do. Maybe I shouldn't be so lazy and shouldn't just expect things to happen. I guess I really should be thinking about these issues. I want to enjoy my last semester. I could take my GREs [Graduate Record Examinations] and apply to grad school, but I don't know what I'd be going into. There are people at this college who have it all planned and are interviewing for jobs. I don't want to do that.

The indecision about the choice of an occupation was not the only conflict typical of this group. The students could not insulate themselves so completely from the mainstream values as not to worry about wasting a good mind and a good education. One Chinese-American student expressed her concern this way: "Sometimes I do have ambivalent feelings about wasting my education. I think it will be totally wasted if not put to good use. And I feel that I have something to offer the world—but I just don't have the ambition."

Qualms about her real motives for choosing a traditional life style worried another student, a daughter of native-born Jewish parents. She looked forward to homemaking and was "crazy" about children, but she wondered:

"Why do I like cooking and cleaning? Do I want to spread sunshine? Do I want people to depend on me?" This student has a long-term relationship with a man whom she might marry. She now cooks and does the laundry for her boyfriend. She enjoys it, but misgivings arise when her roommate asks in disgust: "Are you really doing his laundry?" "My problem is," this student sums up, "to make sure that I am enjoying the traditional role authentically and not out of some deficient self-esteem and an excessive need for endless encouragement."

Doubts about her priorities concerning family and work were expressed by another noncareer student:

It would be nice to try writing, but I'm lazy by nature. But it would be nice to have the option to do whatever you want, and not to feel that when you have kids you always have to think if you're making the right choice. I think bringing up children is a very important thing and has to be taken seriously. And my career would not come before raising children. But I also don't think it's right for a mother to be home full time all the time. You get spoiled. I see a lot of kids of my generation who can't do anything for themselves. My mother was home full time when I was thirteen to sixteen. I don't think it's healthy. If a mother is unhappy and sacrificing her life for you, it's not good.

The majority of the noncareer students, however, did

not share these misgivings about their life-style preferences. The values that supported them are seen in their lukewarm attitudes toward the women's liberation movement in comparison with career-steadfast students. For one thing, they tended to minimize the problem of women's oppressed status. For another, they criticized the tactics of dealing with such problems as did exist.

The following quotation from a student on the Dean's List for every semester of her college career typifies this traditional women's denial of the women's problem: "I am not now and have never been subject to any discrimination. I have never been deprived because I am a woman, either in my family or elsewhere." And, again, one religious Jewish student took a stand against women rabbis in a course on Judaism, arguing that the Orthodox position did not imply female inferiority: "If women can't get up early to go to the synagogue, it is because of their *superior* obligations of taking care of the children and the family. It reflects the mistaken devaluation of family roles to view these sex differences as female disabilities."

Among the traditional students who did recognize the existence of unsolved problems, some objected to the movement's militant tactics. A student who entered college as a convinced feminist had become, in her own words, "more moderate" over the four years. She is more loathe, she said, "to ram feminism down people's throats."

All in all, those traditional students who did acknowledge the existence of women's problems saw them as best addressed on an individual level. The few most hostile to feminism felt that the college did not adequately esteem their own life-style choices.

SHIFTERS TO CAREER (OR CONVERTS)

As freshmen, the shifters to career held life-style preferences similar to those of traditional students. Yet by the end of the senior year they expressed a determination to pursue an uninterrupted career. The comparison of these two groups appears especially promising for an understanding of processes of change and persistence of attitudes toward careers. More specifically, the theoretical task is to ascertain which particular background factors, on the one hand, and which features of the college experience, on the other, far from reinforcing the traditional attitudes held at entrance, aroused career aspirations in the converts. It is clear from the outcome that, compared to the traditional students, the shield that protected the converts from change was not as impenetrable. Quite the contrary. Some factors made them open to whatever in the college experience awakened, rewarded, and stimulated an interest in a career. The converts constituted 25 percent of the senior sample.

Ethnic and Religious Backgrounds

A smaller proportion of interviewed converts had strong ethnic or religious identification upon entrance to college than was true of the traditionals.[5] Moreover, by the end of their senior year, the converts changed their beliefs in some respects or testified to an even more radical secularization.

One of the major factors in these changes was the greater openness of the converts than of the traditional students to interaction with classmates of different religious and ethnic groups and different values. For some, an

---

[5] Nine out of twelve traditional, seven out of twelve converts, and only eight out of twenty-seven career-steadfast students came from ethnic or religious groups that prescribed strongly traditional roles for women.

increased interest in women's rights (in response to teachers and courses, college administrators and classmates) created a clash with what they began to perceive as the restrictive norms embedded in religion.

The tendency of the traditional students to limit friendships to homogeneous cliques stands in contrast with the positive interest expressed by the converts in people with different value systems, particularly in the area of sexuality and gender roles. Interviews threw light on the interplay between the exposure to different values and personal changes.

For example, a religious Catholic student from the South had entered college thinking that "I couldn't function with a man who wasn't my equal in religious devotion," but by 1980 her attitudes were already changing. Although she maintained close phone contact with her parents and felt that her values were still similar to theirs, she became more tolerant of and more interested in other religious, ethnic, and racial groups.

> I changed the most in my religious intensity. When I lived [at home], I was very religious. I belonged to religious groups, taught Sunday school, and went to church every week. Here I don't go to church that often, but I still feel very strongly about my religion. ... There are other things that impinge upon my life now. At home religion was an important part of daily life. Here it's not. Here my work is more important to me, as well as having new experiences with friends. Other people here are not very religious. They go to services once in a while. When I was [home], all of my friends were Catholic and we did things around the church.

By 1983 her attitudes had changed even more radically,

and she described her involvement with the church as "near zero." When asked to explain the change, she replied: "I was really very religious for a long time, but now I'm trying to eschew organizations that are blatantly sexist, namely the Catholic Church. I stopped going with my family to church this past summer."

Another religious Catholic student maintained her strong religious sentiments while at college, even though they were not shared by her friends on campus. In 1980 she said that it would be absolutely essential for her to marry a Catholic, since her children would have to be raised Catholic; in 1982 she was involved in a serious relationship with a Jew and was thinking of marrying him.

> My conflict comes from the church's attitude that women's natural calling, or part of God's plan, is to be wives and mothers. There's nothing wrong with being a wife or mother—some women should devote their lives to being wives and mothers if that's what makes them happy. But the church should also recognize that women are desirous of having careers and that must be part of God's plan as well. I can see how the church adds to women's oppression by taking away options from them and making them feel guilty, but faith is a matter of personal conscience and individual decision, and I feel it's right for me to be a career woman.

This student's mother supported her daughter's right to make her own decisions, so that the changing attitudes did not cause family conflicts. In fact, the student attributed her changing views to discussions with her parents and friends at college and to a course in religion.

A Jewish student entered college with no interest in a career. Although not particularly religious, she had a strong sense of Jewish identity, buttressed by her mother and an all-Jewish circle of friends in high school. In the course of her sophomore year at college, she began to develop friendships with non-Jews, which her mother began to criticize, particularly her growing friendship with a Black student. Here is testimony of her growing emancipation:

> My mother feels that I should associate with my own kind. When I asked her what that meant, she said that she wanted me to have Jewish friends. She was afraid that people who weren't Jewish would put me down or destroy me or do something to me. I told her that I was not going to segregate myself from the rest of the world, that there are good people who are Jewish and there are good people who aren't Jewish, and that I could gain a good deal from having relationships with people other than those of "my own kind." When I was in high school, all of my friends were Jewish; I suppose it was because of my mother's influence that I didn't seek out friends who weren't Jewish. Now that I'm at college in a big city, I feel that I can gain a lot through exposure to different religious and ethnic points of view.

The major finding with regard to friendships of the converts became apparent as we compared the 1980 and 1983 interviews. The senior interviews included references to changes in friendships over the college years from those with traditional values to classmates committed to careers. Sometimes the students saw the new friendships as an important cause of their own changes; others saw them as merely reflecting changes already underway. But, by the end of college, it was rare for a career-salient convert to be surrounded by traditional friends. Whereas the traditional students gravitated toward peers supportive of their values, the converts were increasingly attracted to like-minded friends, although several maintained other friends as well.

Early in college a student planning to be a lawyer, whose mother was a staunch feminist, turned to a circle of more traditional friends because she was tired of hearing about feminist issues from her mother.

My friends here are all old-fashioned, traditional women who want families and who want to get married, not because I want that but because I don't have to deal with feminist issues. They don't talk about women's issues, they talk about family and home and such subjects. . . . I like to play up the feminine, I like to be a woman, I want to use my feminine characteristics to get what I want. It's an individual struggle and I can use my femininity to gain some ground. If I have to do it that way, that's okay with me. I'd rather be a traditional woman in that sense than a staunch feminist.

Yet, in her senior year, she was attracted to friends who were pursuing careers.

The friends I'm making now all seem to be as career motivated as I am, which is different from the friends I had earlier. The thing I found most attractive in the two friends I'm now closest to is that they're both traditional and progressive. But they do have this image of themselves as superwomen: "I'm going to have a career, have children, and I'm still going to make dinner." I don't think it's possible.

One southern student, even in high school, had experienced a sense of difference from her classmates and had left her hometown partly for this reason.

Most of the friends I grew up with were concerned with finding good husbands and settling down. They were also very soft-spoken; they wouldn't argue with men and they would defer to men's opinions. I never felt right there because I didn't think this was the correct way to interact with men. But I couldn't assert myself because I was alone and afraid of being a freak. Part of the reason I came [here] was because I was hoping to find other women who felt as I did.

In contrast to her earlier friends, her new circle of friends at college supported her growing commitment to a career.

My friends here have been a very strong support network for my ideas and opinions; they're all very career oriented. They want to make it in the world and they also believe in women's rights. I feel more at home with my friends at college than with my friends back home. I argue when I am home and try to point out to them how they are degrading themselves, but they just laugh and say that when I fall in love it will be very different.

To sum up these findings, the converts, in contrast to the traditional students, came to college with different ethnic and religious values. Theirs was a weaker identification with traditional dogmas about women's roles rooted in certain subcultures. This in turn made them more open to interaction with classmates of diverse groups. The impact of these encounters took the familiar form of cumulative, circular processes. With respect to women's roles, these encounters exposed the converts to feminist values and this, in turn, was followed by reassessment of prior assumptions. Changes in their attitudes over the college years led to increased selectivity in friendships. Their closest friends became classmates who shared career aspirations. Finally, interaction in these homogeneous groups reinforced these common values.

But peer groups are only one of several decisive factors in changing aspirations of the converts. Another background factor, family attitudes and family relationships, proved to have a dynamic of its own in its interplay with the college experience.

In contrast with the traditional seniors, as noted earlier, the converts identified less strongly with traditional dogmas about women's roles characteristic of some ethnic and religious groups. Related to this background were differences in parental values and aspirations for their daughters.

Family Values and Relationships

Most parents of converts were supportive of careers for their daughters, much more so than the parents of traditional students. To be sure, these supportive parents sometimes expressed ambivalent views, stressing the importance of marriage and motherhood, but this was outweighed by their encouragement.

The explicit parental stand on the preferred life style for their daughters is not the only form of parental influence. The indirect message conveyed by the total configuration of marital and parent-child relationships is equally significant. The converts brought to college certain predispositions to seek alternatives to parental models. They were, so to speak, in the market for alternatives. The college experience made latent dissatisfactions with parental models manifest, led to reassessment of previously taken-for-granted features of parental marriages, and, at the same time, pointed to new and more congenial goals.

Important in this process is the relationship between the mother's role and parental marriage on the one hand and the daughter's life style on the other. The negative findings reported in chapter 4 are not conclusive; they call for a more complex explanatory model. The interviews with converts begin to reveal the complex sets of variables that must enter into an adequate explanation.

The proportion of mothers who were primarily home-makers was nearly identical for the traditional students and converts. The critical difference lay in the degree of the mother's satisfaction with her own role. More of the mothers of the converts were dissatisfied homemakers. In some cases the daughters surmised, without explicit mater-nal confidences, that their mothers regretted the decision to stop working when they had children. In other cases the homemaker-mother (and, indeed, both parents) strongly encouraged their daughters to reach out for career oppor-tunities they themselves missed.

A student who entered college as noncareer became increasingly career oriented and applied to several law schools in her senior year. Her mother, having given up her artistic career, strongly urged her daughter to have a career, not merely a job. All through college her father, as well, wanted his daughter to enter a profession he never had. He was instrumental in getting his daughter summer jobs in the legal field.

The perception of maternal dissatisfaction with her role was not the only ground for the daughter's rejection of the maternal model. A few converts felt that full-time mothering had had a negative effect on their own upbring-ing. One student planning a career in banking or financial management expressed no qualms about sending her own children to babysitters or nursery school and working full time. Her own mother had not worked outside the home, but she did not want to repeat her mother's concentrated domesticity.

I often wished that my mother did work. There was a point in my life, around junior high school, when I didn't want her around. I wanted her to do something herself and, as I got older, my brother and sister would say the same thing: "Why don't you go out and get a job?" It was not that she seemed particularly bored or dissatisfied, it's just that she was always underfoot. All my friends' parents were working, and I wanted my mother to be like them.

She complained that her mother had been overprotective and "stifling."

By the end of the senior year converts adopted an ideal of marriage that differed markedly from the traditional mode. One of them, who planned to go on to graduate school in English literature, spelled out this difference:

> My parents have a good marriage, but it's rather traditional. My mother cooks my father a separate dinner— she makes chicken for the kids, but my father hates chicken and won't eat it, so she cooks him a steak separately.... My mother doesn't think twice about it, but when I see it I think about it for myself. I wouldn't want my husband to act that way. My father is spoiled and somewhat of a big baby.... I would expect equality in the domestic tasks.... My father never cooks and insists that my mother cook special meals for him. I would want my husband to share in the cooking and cleaning up afterward.

A senior planning a career as a mathematics professor observed in her own family a transition from a traditional (mother a full-time homemaker) to a relatively egalitarian marriage when her mother started her own business, working from their home. The student approved of this change and felt that her mother had been dissatisfied being just a housewife. As for herself, she never got to know her father when she was young: "It was a very traditional household when we were young. My father was always out of the house working late and my mother was home taking care of the kids. For a long time, the only thing I knew about my dad was what my mother told me." Now the household is run more democratically and the authoritarian structure has given way to a family council that makes decisions for the family.

A Latin-American student who entered college with no career aspirations increasingly realized how unsatisfactory her mother's role in marriage was and how important it would be for her to avoid repeating her mother's mistakes. She reported in her senior interview:

> My mother is totally dependent on my father. It's only recently that she got some freelance translating jobs. . . . For her, it's liberation time. She's got twenty dollars a week to call her own. My father dishes money out to her like he owns it. He will put her down and demand his dinner. He makes her feel worthless. I think she's gotten a little bit of self-esteem partly from me.

So much for daughters of full-time homemakers who, for a variety of reasons, departed from their mothers' path. Converts with working mothers present a different pattern. Some felt that they missed close contacts with their busy mothers and entered college with strong doubts about following their mothers' example. The change in their attitudes requires an explanation.

> In one such case the student felt that her mother did not present her with the model of a woman who had successfully combined career and family. People were hired to take care of the student and her siblings and she never had a close emotional relationship with her mother. The latter had always urged her to have a career.

This student, noncareer at entrance, attributed the change in her plans to two circumstances. One was a series of positive experiences with children in her part-time jobs, which increased her desire to have a family. Even more important was her contact with a strong and warm professor who so successfully combined career and motherhood as to dispel her doubts.

In another case, the parents were divorced when the daughter was a child, forcing her mother to work full time. The mother embarked on a successful career in corporate business and became a staunch feminist in the face of the discrimination she met with. The daughter was influenced by her mother's predicament after divorce, her success in business, and her constant feminist indoctrination. The latter generated some resistance.

> I know that discrimination exists, but I don't want my mother to constantly point it out to me. I don't want to be confronted by the fact that this is a prejudiced world. My mother sees prejudice everywhere she turns, and I just don't want to have to look at it that way. I want to see things that are going on for women that are positive.

Nevertheless, when it came to her own plans, the daughter became increasingly committed to a career in law and applied to law schools. She was sufficiently influenced by her mother's negative attitudes toward women's place in the corporate world to decide on a different course. At the time of her final interview, she planned to open her own law firm in order to maximize her control over both her workplace and her work schedule so as to allow for child rearing.

So far the discussion has considered the predispositions

that students brought to college. But what of the influence of the college years?

Of the college experiences, the influence of peer group, already discussed, is the major catalyst of change. Other influences of the college experience include positive relationships with faculty in out-of-class interaction, female role models among teachers, successful work and internship experiences while at college, and the college ethos supportive of occupational achievement for women. The new values acquired due to these experiences led some converts to reassess and reject previously taken-for-granted traditional parental marriages.

In contrast to the traditional students, the converts had the capacity to take advantage of the resources provided by the college. They manifested a greater sturdiness in the face of initial disappointment in academic performance, greater initiative in seeking contacts with professors, and a more purposeful search for internships and jobs. Each of these tendencies produced a cumulative, reinforcing cycle of experiences that moved them further toward career salience, as shall be demonstrated.

Academic Performance

As noted earlier, there was no difference in the grade-point averages of traditional students as opposed to career-steadfast ones. Nor did they differ for the converts, of whom 51 percent had a grade-point average of 3.3 or over. (These figures are based on total samples of each type, not merely on the smaller groups of interviewed students.)

The level of academic performance, as measured by grades, apparently bears a complex relation to career salience. Poor grades discourage the latter, but high grades do not necessarily guarantee it. Students repeatedly cited low grades as the discouraging factor in choice of a major or of a particular occupation. A low grade average in general might have had a negative effect on the students' career intentions. But this effect was obscured in the comparison of various groups because some traditional students had very high grades. High value placed on academic performance, good methods of study, and competitiveness were quite compatible with the traditional orientations. Being on the Dean's List for each year in college did not necessarily kindle an ambition to pursue a career.

The interviews do suggest a different reaction to initial disappointment in grades on the part of traditional and convert students. The former tended to become more easily discouraged and to assume that they lacked some quality essential for achievement in postcollege years. The lure of the traditional life style may have made such inferences more plausible. The converts, on the other hand, sought ways to improve their study methods or to redefine grade expectations without changing their goals. A case in point was a straight-A student in high school who was very depressed by her B average in her freshman year. In her interview in 1980, she stated: "I'm going to work very hard and to give it more than 100 percent, but if B's are all I am capable of, there's nothing I can do about it. I am interested in my courses and I shall just have to accept the fact that I shall not have a phenomenally high average at college."

In addition to the effort to improve one's study habits or to redefine academic expectations, the converts found another method of recouping their self-esteem or another source of reassurance. They initiated, and succeeded in establishing, more frequent contacts with the faculty outside of the classroom than was the case with traditional students.

Relationships with Faculty

Four of the converts resembled the traditional students insofar as they did not initiate contacts with teachers, giving as reasons fear of authority or a sense of impropriety of using the professor's office hours unless one had something very specific to ask. But eleven of the fifteen interviewed converts did establish contacts with faculty, which they believed to be an important element of their college experience, ranging from intellectual encouragement to relationships in which more personal issues were discussed. In seven of these cases, the teacher mentioned as most important was a female professor who served as a role model for the students. In one case, a student who had an uneven grade average and initially a low commitment to a career developed an interest in psychology and sought an internship in the field. The professor she worked with for a year became a role model, solidifying her intellectual interests and convincing her that perhaps career and family were not incompatible. In describing this mentor, the student remarked:

> She had a balance in her life that I had always wondered if someone could achieve. She has her career and her husband—they have two children. She has a handle on things—she loves her work and what she's doing, yet she also has a family which is very important to her.

Another student hoping to become a college mathematics professor initiated contact with several teachers in the subject seeking a teaching assistantship, stressing confidence in her abilities:

> Even though I'm only a sophomore, I know I can speak with confidence about the subject. I developed a friendly relationship with the woman who chaired the Mathe-

matics Department, and we discussed issues that involved women and mathematics—math anxiety, sexism in the discipline, etc.

Still another student, planning a career in psychobiology, responded in the same manner each time she suffered a setback in a course or in her grades or became indecisive about her future career: she initiated an internship with a professor or sought out an outside laboratory job. Through the internships and the job, she clarified her career direction and gained invaluable work experience.

Working During College Years

Just as contacts with the faculty were higher in this group than among the traditionals, converts had more rewarding jobs. Thirteen of the fifteen converts viewed their work or internships as important influences on their career commitment.

This college, situated in a great metropolis, provided the students with exceptional opportunities to participate in professional settings of great variety. Economic research on state legislation, stage managing a dance repertoire, cancer research, developing demographic profiles for marketing research, editing in a publisher's office, clerking for a lawyer, interviewing for a project to locate and reinvolve the isolated elderly—these are a small sample of volunteer and sometimes paid work of students during intersessions and summers. During the 1981–82 academic year, 700 students in the college participated in the internship program.

According to the interviewed converts, such participation in professional settings was a major influence on their career goals. In some cases it increased the student's confidence that she could meet the challenge of an occupation she had aspired to; in other cases the internship pointed to a career direction for a previously uncertain student and thereby solidified career aspirations. Again, students sure of a general field narrowed down their interest to a specific occupation. The attraction of work and financial independence, observation of how successful professional women handle themselves in work situations, the obstacles yet to be overcome for women in a given field—these and other firsthand experiences were cited as by-products of internships and jobs that made the world of work appear more familiar. Finally, these sometimes reinforced commitment to a career by lowering the appeal of full-time homemaking. As one student put it: "I can't any longer see myself staying home full time with the children." The excerpts from interviews will both illustrate these generalizations and add some telling details about the operative processes.

A senior enrolled in the education program described to an interviewer an episode that helped to convince her that she could meet the challenge of teaching. "One day, she faced her fourth-grade class in panic—the teacher was ill and she was left alone to teach. Although success in coping with the class was not immediate, she learned that she could, in fact, deal with this stressful and challenging situation."

The student referred to earlier, who intended to become a psychobiologist, heard of a summer scholarship, applied, and spent three months working for one of the college professors doing biological research at a well-known laboratory.

It was an ideal experience. The people there were great. There were graduate students and scientists, and two of them were recent Nobel Prize winners. Working with people like that was just what I wanted. . . . Then some days all I did was lab work. It was so satisfying because you can connect all these little events in the lab with a larger theory. And it was great to have an idea at dinner and then be able to go do an experiment that same night. Sometimes I'd be in the lab until midnight.

For a student majoring in psychology but unsure of her precise future occupation, a part-time job was crucial in determining her career.

When a guest lecturer for a survey research company spoke in one of her classes, she asked the professor to set up an interview with the company. She got a part-time job, and continued for one year doing survey research and political polling. She gained self-confidence and on-the-job training and she replaced her previous fear of competitive situations with a belief that "I'm going to meet competition everywhere and I hope to meet it head on and do well."

A student hoping for a career in computer science had a summer job working in an office, reviewing records.

In the process, she learned two things: that women can work and have babies successfully, and that large wage differentials between men and women still exist. She saw coworkers who had recently given birth back at work within weeks, and this convinced her that a mother's working doesn't necessarily do harm to a child's development. Observing the wage differentials made her more determined to be a successful career woman, especially when the experience was repeated in a second job in her future field.

Compared with the traditionals, converts were more decided about occupational choices. Eight of the fifteen students were very sure of their future career by graduation, four were fairly sure (for example, sure of a career in business, unsure whether in banking or financial management), three were unsure. The increased probability of a full-time, lifetime career for the converts was accompanied by increased certainty about the choice of career as well.

College Ethos on Feminism

The converts included among the influences that increased their career commitment the ethos of the college with its strong support of women's achievement. A student planning a career in journalism had attended a Catholic girls' school and compared it with the college:

> In high school the attitude of the nuns was that you have a career but completely abandon it when you marry and have children. Here the administration projects the image of their graduates as tough, independent career women who, oddly enough, combine this with marriage and family. But they really don't emphasize the family part. . . . There are great role models here. . . . What was new to me was the notion of a women's network, that women would help other women up the corporate ladder.

Some students were radicalized by a combination of an experience of sexism and of the shared condemnation of sexism in group discussions at college. This consciousness-raising is illustrated by a student planning to enter graduate school in English literature. She had once planned to be a professional athlete, and continued to keep in shape by daily running. The following incident sensitized her to sexist attitudes.

> I noticed there were two men who ran at the same time every morning. I was running with a girlfriend and we

were faster than the men and we kept passing them. Finally one turned to the other and said, "Look at those two pieces of ass move." I was extremely offended at this and went back to my dorm and discussed it with my friends. I was surprised to find that other friends had had all kinds of similar experiences where they were put down by men because they were better than men in certain areas. . . . My group of friends are not anti-men, we don't want to reject relationships with men, but we're very aware that we have to assert equality in our relationships or else we'll fall back into traditional or stereotypic patterns.

Coming to this college was very important for her. Although she had been sympathetic to the women's movement in earlier years, she became more assertive and vocal in defending her beliefs, no longer remaining silent when she heard demeaning comments about women.

A minority of the converts, although they approved of the college ethos, criticized the lack of attention paid to motherhood and the future family roles. As one student put it, "Families are treated as out-of-date, something that happened in the bad old days." In a similar vein, these critics felt that insufficient attention and advice were given to the problems of balancing career and family.

The Conflicts of the Converts

This criticism of the college on the grounds that it neglected the contemporary difficulties in combining family life with a career reflects the anxieties some converts continued to feel about the future. If the college, in extolling achievement and careers, stressed one horn of the dilemma, parents, as has been noted, sometimes were ambivalent, oscillating between conflicting positions, especially if they felt that their daughters were moving to either extreme: "Will my daughter find a satisfying personal life if she becomes a career woman?" A case in point is a student whose father had died when she was young and whose mother had been very supportive of a legal career for her daughter. As graduation approached, however, the mother became worried about her daughter's dedication to her future profession. The student, who was not concerned about marriage, felt confused by this sudden switch:

> I have this quest to prove myself to my family. I've gone to prep school all my life. I'm here now. I think to get married would be a letdown. I think I'd hate myself more than anything else. All my life I've heard push, push, push. Make us proud. And now my mother is sort of turning the tables on me: "Yeah, you can get married if you want. I want grandchildren." But it's sort of falling on deaf ears with me. She's concerned about it because I've never shown any interest in it. We don't talk about it because we just end up fighting. She thinks my perspective is really askew. The funny thing is that none of my friends are really involved with anybody.

Another senior complained about the constant pressure she received from her mother not to delay marriage. Her mother was afraid her daughter would be cut off from friends and lonely her entire life if she followed her present course. The daughter described her position in this way:

> I have always been too dependent. It's in this way that I've accepted the traditional role of a dependent woman. I cannot rise above that without being on my own for a while. In a marriage you develop mutual dependencies. I don't want to go from being a dependent daughter to a dependent wife. My mother thinks my views are much

too extreme. She can't understand why I'm so violently opposed to marriage right after I finish my education. She was opposed to my going to this college because it is a women's college. She thinks I have been isolated from men for too long. I am female centered. I grew up in a house of all women and I went to a private girls' school for the first seven years of my life. I told her I have no trouble interacting with men, but I relate better to women and have a greater affinity to women. I'm sorry if she can't accept that, but that's me.

Of fifteen interviewed converts, eleven had had long-term relationships with men by the end of their senior year; four had no such experience. The change to high career salience was often accompanied by a changing idea of the kind of relationship the students wanted to have. Eight converts ended previous liaisons because the men with whom they were involved remained traditional while they themselves had changed. (Additional information on relationships with men is presented in chapter 8.)

In conclusion, it should be noted that the explanation of noncareer orientation of converts at entrance to college is problematic. On the basis of the interviews conducted in 1979, it would appear that they were troubled by the difficulties of balancing a desire to raise a family and the demands of a career, as well as by a lack of confidence in their own abilities to cope with the latter.

What during the four years of college had increased career aspirations by the time they were seniors? This central theoretical question can be answered more confidently. Clearly the latent misgivings about traditional life styles became manifest, and interest in careers mounted as had the students' confidence in their ability to attain new goals. Among the features of the college experience that operated to produce these outcomes were the ethos of the college and the influence of peers. These led to a reevaluation of traditional family patterns and their replacement with a more egalitarian model. Relationships with professors and a positive experience in an internship or a job were also decisive in changing aspirations for the future.

6

Four Years Later: Career-Steadfast Students, Defectors, and Waverers

THE CONTRAST between the traditionals and the converts, presented in chapter 5, contributed to our understanding of the processes involved in their respective reactions to the college experience. The analysis of still another type of student, the career steadfast, indirectly confirms the findings about the converts.

CAREER-STEADFAST STUDENTS

Career-steadfast students were those who entered as career salient and remained so by the end of college; they constituted one-third of the total sample of seniors. The background factors that proved influential in predisposing the converts to become career-salient students and the features of the college experience activating, as it were, these predispositions also proved to be significant determinants of career salience for career-steadfast students.

The differences between the two groups were of degree. For example, a lower proportion of career-steadfast students than of converts came from ethnic and religious families embracing traditional dogmas regarding gender roles, and a higher proportion testified to strained marital relations between their parents. A higher proportion of career-steadfast students initiated close interaction with the faculty. The similarities and the differences among career-steadfast students and the other groups will be presented in the following pages.

Ethnic and Religious Background and Peer Groups

While some of the career-steadfast students were strongly identified with ethnic and religious groups that prescribed traditional roles for women, there were fewer such cases than among either the traditionals or the converts. What impact did the confrontation between these traditional beliefs and the new approaches acquired in college have?

Several of the religious students did not reject their religious beliefs but modified them, and all experienced conflict. This conflict in itself testified to the students' openness to elements of the college experience in general and to interaction with classmates of diverse backgrounds in particular. One religious student described her conflict in this way:

I've had serious conversations with some friends, also

religious. We talk about Adam and Eve and I know that man has evolved from the apes. The more I get involved in academia, the more conflicts I have with religion. I have conversations with my boyfriend and he asks me how can I believe in the Immaculate Conception. It's a matter of faith, but it's weird because everyone is saying to me, "I can't believe you're saying that [even though] you're so involved in science."

Another student, a religious Catholic planning to go to medical school, echoed these sentiments and described her changed attitude to religion:

I consider myself confused. I'm almost at the point where I can say I don't believe in God, but when I say that I feel like a real shit. And I feel so guilty. I can't make up my mind. Because all the science courses I've taken have explained to me how life begins and how molecules first came together to form life, and in genetics I've learned all these mysteries that the church was supposed to explain. I'm beginning to think of religion more and more as a very personal thing and it's nothing like church or Catholicism.

The college experience has also made this student increasingly question the church's teachings about women. This added to her feeling of alienation from the church, although she thought the role of women in the church was improving.

An Orthodox Jewish student found her increasing interest in feminism a source of conflict with her religion. Although, in contrast to traditional students, the career-steadfast did not close off friendships with diverse groups, this particular student had only superficial contacts outside her religious group. (According to her, "I don't have anything in common with those who aren't Orthodox Jews and don't see the possibility of forming friendships with people who don't share my interests.") In her case, the operative influence was not an out-group friendship, but new ideas in the classroom and the ethos of the institution at large.

Another Jewish student, Jewish-identified but not Orthodox, described her growing alienation from more traditional Jewish women:

> These women are really looking for nice Jewish premed boys who would buy them a house in the suburbs. They have their whole lives planned out, what they'll do during the day, how they'll furnish their homes, etc. ... I wanted to meet other people, not only of other religions, but of different life styles.

As to racial and ethnic origins, the women steadfast in their goal of a career also differed from the traditional students. The Asian career students came from already fairly assimilated families. One, whose father was a professional man, did not like to associate exclusively with other Asian students. Another was from a mixed marriage, and her parents did not have any particular expectation that she should associate with, date, or marry an Asian. She too had an ethnically diverse set of friends. One student, who was half Japanese, was the only to identify strongly on campus with other Asian students, although she expressed her sense of identification as deriving from her working-class background and a feeling of similarity to other minority students.

Two Black students, however, both from the Caribbean, associated almost exclusively with other Blacks, and experienced what they described as racism at college, which increased their sense of detachment from the rest of the student body. They were both active in Black student organizations. Very little of their college experience took place in close contact with White students.

In summary, fewer career-oriented students, in comparison with the traditional ones or the converts, entered college as strongly identified with ethnic and religious dogmas linked to traditional definitions of gender roles. Even the deeply religious students reacted to the college experience in a distinctive manner. Unlike the traditionals (but similar to the converts), they were more open to interaction with diverse classmates who challenged and modified their attitudes. Having entered college with greater interest in women's issues, they responded to the institution's feminist ethos. This, in turn, led to further questioning of the traditional dogmas embedded in religion regarding women's roles.

The part that peers played in socialization for nontraditional roles was inferred from both 1980 and 1983 interviews. The drift away from high-school friends in the freshman year was described in chapter 3. This drift was accentuated in career-salient students who belonged to the more traditional high-school cliques. One student, a fairly religious Catholic from a traditional Irish working-class background, continued to maintain ties to her small town and to her Irish club at home. Yet, increasingly, her circle of career-salient Catholic friends at college became more important, and finally she reluctantly gave up older friendships.

> I remained friends with my best friend from high school until the end of my sophomore year, but then we started to drift apart. We were going in such different directions, I couldn't relate to her any more. When she was in

school she wanted to be a lawyer, but then she quit
college after a year and if she goes back to school I'll
be surprised. A lot of it is family problems, but now
she's just waitressing, and a lot of it is lack of motivation.

One student, planning to go to graduate school in the
sociology of science, similarly began to "sift out" from
among her high-school friends those with whom she had
less and less in common, eventually turning more to her
career-salient peers at college.

The weakening of ties to high-school friends (a change
that was not limited, of course, to the career-steadfast
group) was striking in the extent to which, in the senior
year, the career-steadfast students confined their friendships
so exclusively to classmates who shared their values as to
claim that there were no traditional women at this college.
This was the only one of the five student types to
misperceive the diversity of student attitudes.

For the converts, peer support was occasionally one of
the determining factors in a change in orientation, whereas
for the career-steadfast students peer support served to
anchor or reinforce career intentions as well as feminist
values. Several career-salient students who at college entrance had very little interest in feminism credited college
friends with introducing them to feminist ideas. These
ideas, they testified, affected their behavior and reinforced
their desire to succeed in careers. It also made them more
sensitive to sexism in all of its manifestations in people's
behavior and in themselves.

A student who had planned to go to graduate school to
study English had been sympathetic to feminist ideas but
had not been involved in any activities when she entered
college. By her sophomore year, she had become actively
involved in conferences, demonstrations, consciousness-
raising groups, and rape counseling, and she saw her close

friends as being responsible for exposing her to these ideas and activities. This is how she traced the change in her own development:

> In my freshman year, I wanted a family and career, and family was a bit higher. This year I can sense a dramatic change, that I'm more concerned with career and I want to pursue a career and then have my family, and if my family caused problems with my career, they would have to be worked out. . . . I had a friend from high school who's at this college. She was living with someone and they'll probably marry. I just see her as someone who's very dependent on this person. Career-wise, she couldn't make it on her own without this other person, and I resent it.

By contrast, this student admires another classmate who had been living with a boyfriend ten years her senior. The boyfriend wanted to get married.

> My friend moved out and they are now just seeing each other. She said to him: "Look, I don't know where my life is going. I'm not sure what I'm going to be doing. I'm not working yet. I don't think I want marriage." I was standing in the background and I was applauding her for this.

"Consciousness-raising" by classmates is illustrated in another case. One student recounted how, in her sophomore year, several of her friends introduced her to feminist ideas, but she had problems with them.

> My friend urged me to be more vocal about my feelings toward feminism, not to try to smooth over the situation when men were making disgusting or sexist remarks. I said that I wasn't secure enough to argue when men

made sexist remarks. When I was in high school I didn't have a normal social life. . . . This is the first year I've gone out with guys, and I don't feel secure enough to assert myself.

Yet, by her senior year, when she was interviewed for financial analyst jobs, this student was very aware of sexism in the interviewing process and very capable of standing up for herself. These experiences made her even more determined to get the job. As a woman, she now felt that to make it in a man's field was a "mission."

Family Relationships

Notwithstanding ambivalence and, in a few cases, outright opposition, the parents—and particularly the mothers—supported the career goals of this career-steadfast group of students. Only seven out of twenty-seven career-steadfast students who were interviewed reported serious parental disapproval or ambivalence. Among this minority, the strongest opposition came from fathers who had traditional views about women's roles.

Two or three mothers in this group expressed ambivalence toward a daughter's career goal. One student, who planned to be a set designer, claimed that her mother, a full-time housewife, was both supportive and troubled:

My mother has not been a career woman. Sometimes she takes pride in my achievements and sometimes she feels threatened. She feels that my being a career woman may reflect badly on her own choices. I feel that a lot of the anxiety she's been expressing to me about my future is more an expression of anxiety about her own life.

In a couple of other cases, mothers expressed some

general uneasiness about the price their daughters will have to pay for becoming "career women."

In contrast to these exceptional cases, the career-oriented daughters generally received positive encouragement of their aspirations from their parents, directly and indirectly. A Caribbean student from a working-class family who planned to become a doctor described her family's support: "My father is always telling me that I'm intelligent and to keep working because he is sure I can make it. My mother makes comments like: 'I can't wait till the day you're a doctor.' I can't let them down and I can't let myself down. This makes me work harder."

With the popular diffusion of psychology, some students were ready to attribute unconscious motives to their mothers when the pressures were felt to be excessive.

> I call my mother maybe once a month, but she calls every week to check up on me. She was very proud of my grades last year, but I told her at the beginning of the year that I wasn't doing as well. This was a mistake, because now she calls all the time to ask what I get on my tests and am I studying hard enough. My mother wants me to be on top of everything. She pushes me to be an overachiever. I wonder whether she wants me to fulfill her own frustrated ambitions.

Another career student complained about the excessive pressure from her mother to pursue a career. The ironic twist here was that this pressure was of a recent origin and came as a consequence of her parents' divorce. Prior to it, the student said her mother "pushed me to be a domestic homebody."

So much for the direct expressions of parental attitudes toward careers. With respect to indirect influences, two quite different patterns emerge. First, career goals were strengthened when mothers were dissatisfied full-time homemakers, and especially when parental marriages ended in divorce, leaving mothers without resources. Second, the career orientation was also present in daughters of mothers who worked full time, provided the daughters felt that their mothers' occupation did not impinge negatively upon their childhood and that relationships with mothers were positive.

A Hispanic student with divorced parents dropped out of school and then returned, aiming toward a future career in business. One of her major motivations was her mother's position in marriage: "I wouldn't want to be as unhappy as my mother was. With so many children, she was dependent on my father. She couldn't write a check or make a move without him. He didn't want her to work. It was a terrible marriage which she couldn't escape."

Homemaker-mothers' experience served as a negative role model even short of such a dire outcome as in the above case. One student, who planned to go to medical school, had urged her mother to go to work. The latter's brief foray into the work world ended after only a few months, because of her husband's opposition.

> It made me very upset because I knew she liked it. Not so much the job, but getting out and doing something on her own, something constructive. That's the one thing we really strongly disagree on. Not that she doesn't want me to do things like that, but she just doesn't think she could ever go out on her own and do anything, support herself, or even hold a part-time job. She just doesn't think that she could because of my father.

Another student saw the toll that a traditional marriage had taken on her mother—anxiety, nervousness, frustration.

I remember a week ago she was having an anxiety attack on the telephone. She was talking real fast and was really upset. Her main problem was financial and the day-in, day-out routine. She was comparing herself to my boyfriend's mother who is semiretired and travels. My mother's only twenty years older than me. She doesn't exercise. She can hardly move. I just look at her and say, I've got to have my own interests. I don't think it's good to live for others and expect them to achieve to make you look good.

The final case of rejection of a mother's full-time homemaker role is described below:

My mother never worked and I think she would have been much better off if she had. She would have been happier, and that's also true of my grandmother. My grandmother was a real rebel. Then she got married and was left at home with the kids. She didn't drive, so she couldn't go anywhere.

She ended up smoking like a fiend, nervous, and an alcoholic. She and my mother both needed a career as an outlet. My mother's reason for not working was just that she thought she ought to be at home because she was needed there. My father never would have objected; he would have welcomed the extra income.

Some career-steadfast students were critical of their parents' traditional life style, even when the students considered the marriage to be satisfactory and, occasionally, even when the mother held a job. An art history major, although approving of her parents' solid marriage, wanted something different for herself:

Ideally, I'd like a marriage in which both husband and wife share equally the task of raising children and keeping house. I think men miss out on children because it's assumed that women will handle the job. . . . My parents had a traditional marriage—my father took the leadership role. I think husband and wife should have equal decision-making powers in the family. My father always insisted that he was the leader. I find it very annoying. My father insists that my mother and I serve the food or clear the table.

Others were more indignant about the traditional model of marriage. A student majoring in psychology hoped that she would never experience her mother's financial uncertainty. Her mother worked full time for minimum wages. One of this student's major goals in her career is financial security, which she saw as linked to her parents' type of marriage.

Despite the fact that both my parents work full time, my father expects my mother to prepare all the meals and have them ready when he gets home. He doesn't even get up to get himself a glass of water. My mother gets up early, because my father leaves early. She feeds him breakfast. Then she feeds my brother. Then she goes off to work. But she has the opinion that that's the way it is and it isn't going to get better, so why complain.

Because of the mothers' dissatisfaction with life, or because of the daughters' own disapproval of parental marriages, a higher proportion of career-salient than of traditional students considered their full-time homemaker-mothers as negative role models.

Turning to the daughters of employed mothers, we find that career-steadfast students had a higher percentage of working mothers than all the other types of interviewed students.[1] Some grew up with working mothers; in other cases mothers resumed careers more recently. But the interviews with these students brought to light another factor: these daughters did not feel that their mothers' work had adversely affected their own childhood. They enjoyed close relationships with their mothers. This appears to be a precondition of their wish to emulate their mothers' life style. In a few low-income families, in which the mothers' work was a necessity and rarely a pleasure, these mothers of career-steadfast students were proud of their daughters' professional goals and upward mobility.

The interviews revealed that dissatisfied homemaker-mother and satisfied working mothers, provided the relationships with working mothers were satisfactory, were important factors for the career-steadfast young women.

Academic Performance

The grade-point average of career-steadfast students was not any higher than that of traditional students or converts. Nor were they spared disappointment with their freshman grades. Yet only six students out of this entire group expressed continued and deep concern about their inability to match academic expectations and actual performance. The great majority displayed coping mechanisms that helped them either to weather or to overcome the early failures.

Disappointing freshman-year grades were for this group a sign that study habits had to be changed. A physics major looked back on her first year when she received two C's

[1] The career-salient freshmen, as pointed out in chapter 4, did not have a higher proportion of employed mothers. Apparently it is the steadfastness of career salience through the four years of college that related to working mothers. However, one study has found that it was the father's disparagement of the housewife role, not the mother's dissatisfaction with it, that was most strongly related to daughter's work aspirations (Ridgeway 1978).

in her physics courses and stated: "Freshman year was a year of great readjustment. It threw me back on my own resources—how to budget time, not only among courses, but within a course, when to start research for a paper, when to start writing."

But improving methods of study was not the only coping mechanism. In several cases, resilience in the face of disappointment had its origin in a stubborn refusal to be conquered by a bad grade. A premed student felt at a distinct disadvantage entering this college with the inferior preparation of a small-town high school. Though she found she could not compete adequately in her first introductory course, she did not get discouraged:

> I just don't give up. I didn't like the idea that other people were determining my life, that my chemistry professor, by giving me a bad grade, will determine whether or not I get into a medical school. I learned how to calm down, psych myself up, and realize that I'm in a 'battle zone.'

Another student, planning a career as a writer, entered with a strong sense of class inferiority. She felt that everyone came from a wealthier, more refined, and more educated background than she did. She considered transferring to a municipal college, but decided to stick it out. She acknowledged that it was largely her stubbornness that saw her through her first year, when she finally became convinced that she belonged at the college. She plunged into her work, got involved in campus organizations, and began to feel increased self-confidence.

An art history major was also extremely insecure when she first got to college, and worried about her ability to compete. Yet she overcame those feelings:

Given a challenging situation, I'll always face it if I really think that I can do it. In the case of sports, or something I think I am genuinely incapable of, I'll walk away from it. But a challenge like school, I'll work hard and confront it. For example, if I found a course I wanted to take and people warned me the professor was hard, I'd probably take it anyway. Competitive situations make me work harder.

Other strategies for countering the discouraging effects of a bad grade, whatever their ultimate success, helped students maintain self-confidence in college. One student was dead set on a medical career. She avoided the discouraging effect of mediocre grades in the sciences by taking other courses in which she did better:

I just kept to the grind and learned how to study and be self-disciplined. The first semester of my sophomore year, I got an A in art history, and it was a real boost to my self-confidence. I got a bad grade in chemistry. I hadn't taken the prerequisite, so I knew why. And then I got a couple of A's in other courses and this gave my self-confidence another big boost.

The career-steadfast students were not immune to the feedback they had received from their grades and competitive performance vis-à-vis classmates. However, when unfavorable, this feedback did not undermine their apparently more sturdy sense of identity but, on the contrary, stimulated their potential for coping.

Improved study habits, resilience, and persistence were not the only factors anchoring or increasing career salience. As in the case of the converts, two other reinforcing factors were at work: interaction with the faculty and work experience.

Interaction with Professors

Eighteen out of twenty-seven students in this group reported high to moderate degree of interaction with their professors—ranging from receiving crucial advice about a major or career, to personal encouragement, to receiving internships or research experience. These students referred to this interaction as a significant element of their college experience. Those who did not initiate contacts attributed their reluctance to two factors: large lecture classes in their majors and their own shyness. Said one student: "I put them on a pedestal; I haven't gotten to know them."

The reinforcement and support for the student's career goals received from out-of-class contacts with a professor were illustrated by a Puerto Rican student. The influential person was a female English professor with whom the student studied as a freshman. This student described the process in this way:

> During the course, I had conferences with her and she showed a personal interest in me and devoted time and extra effort to helping me with my writing. I think she gave me extra attention because she knew that I speak Spanish at home and that was why I was having problems writing in English. After the course we kept in touch. . . . She knows of my career interest and often sends me information and pamphlets. I'll never forget her. She always told me how much I had in me and how much I can accomplish.

Similarly, other students reported strong support and advice from professors, both male and female, about majors, career options, and personal issues.

A significant finding of the section of the interview concerning the faculty was the frequency with which career-steadfast students mentioned a female professor as their role model (fifteen out of twenty-seven); this generally occurred when the professor exemplified the career woman who balanced her personal and work life. Career-steadfast students look for encouraging examples that this was not an impossible dream. One student, having decided on a law career in her junior year, was in some conflict. Sometimes she thought she would not have any children, at other times the combination of a law career and child rearing seemed feasible:

> I'm encouraged by one of my professors who has a fourteen-month-old baby. She hires someone to care for her baby. I feel some ambivalence about working [when I have] preschool children, but if I found someone I could trust, I would. I see more and more women doing it. I don't think it's a real deprivation for the child. In my professor's case, her husband is also involved in bringing up the child. That's encouraging.

Internship and Work

Just as interaction with the faculty was high in this group, so was work or internships. All but one student in this group had such experience. All testified that it either served to reinforce their early occupational choice or was instrumental in their changing to another occupation. Specifically, twenty students had jobs or internships in their intended future occupations that reinforced their original choices.

Career-steadfast students initiated such work experiences more frequently than students in all other groups. Having entered college with the expectation to follow a career, they may have been more strongly motivated to "test" occupations.

The work experiences reinforced career salience in several

ways. For some, it was the first heady introduction to the exciting world of their future career. For others, undecided about future occupation, a successful internship led to an occupational choice; for still others, the experience increased self-confidence in their ability to attain a previously tentative occupational goal.

A computer science major initiated job searches every summer through the college placement office. The summer before her senior year was especially rewarding: she received an internship in a computer firm across the country, which, impressed with her performance, eventually offered her a choice job after graduation.

> I was thrilled with everything about the firm: the work, the people, the company, and the weather [of the region]. I was very proud of what I accomplished. They gave me a project to do on my own. There was a problem that I had to solve, working entirely on my own. Of course, I could go to others for help, which I did, because I never would have gotten anywhere just reading those thick manuals. But it was my project and I completed it and I learned a lot. My program was actually going to be put to use after I left. In fact, they're using it now.

Another student, who was undecided about her future career, thought she might be interested in law after taking a sociology of law course. She subsequently obtained an internship with the American Civil Liberties Union, working on a children's rights project. The experience convinced her both of her interest in law and of her competence to make it through law school.

> As soon as I started working here, I felt that I had found a niche, I felt I was in the right place. I'm impressed with the professionalism and dedication of

the lawyers working here and the extent to which they are able to improve people's lives. The lawyers are receptive and encouraging. I've asked them about law schools and they've offered to help me. They've offered to write recommendations for me.

A student who had temporarily dropped out of school because of indecisiveness about her career direction looked for and found a job in a new field, geology, when she reentered college. She walked into a geochemistry lab, introduced herself, and asked if they needed help for the summer. As a result of this experience, she discovered that she wanted to pursue a career in geology. Here, again, we note a circular process in college impacts. A greater proportion of career-steadfast students entered college with definite occupational plans. The rest of this group, by virtue of their career drive, were also eager to test out occupations. This accounts no doubt for the active pursuit of internships and job opportunities through the use of the college placement office or contacts with professors. When the actual job experiences turned out to be satisfactory, they, in turn, reinforced career salience.

College Ethos and the Feminist Movement

The majority of career-steadfast students perceived the college ethos as championing careers and achievement for its graduates, and increasingly so as their college years progressed.

A premed student, for example, who in her sophomore year had said that she preferred coed classes and saw no practical reasons for a women's college, by graduation had noted discrimination against women in some of her coed classes and in her future profession. She became, as a result, more sympathetic both to a women's college and to feminism. Another student put it this way: "This college is really special because it is supportive of women. Students can really grow here and experience themselves as bright women. The female faculty encourages women and helps them develop."

But there were some opposing views concerning benefits to be derived from attending a women's college. One student who planned a career in computer science did not see any particular reason for an all-women's school and, on the contrary, thought it might ill-equip one for the realities of the work world:

If you come to a women's college with the impression that you are going to get away from that intimidation, then I think that's the wrong attitude. If you go to classes that have all females, when you leave the college, you're not prepared. Because you're only used to being around women and then, when you come into a business and find males, you're not going to do a good job because you're not used to speaking up when there are males around. So if you come to school with that attitude, then I think there's a lot to be learned. If you're just coming to hide from everything, and to be with women only, then I think you should have gone to a coed college.

The students' attitudes toward the desirability of maintaining a women's college were distinct from their support for the goals of the women's movement. The majority (twenty-two out of twenty-seven interviewed career-steadfast students) felt progressively more supportive of the movement while in college, although they had various interpretations of both the priorities of needed reforms and appropriate strategies of change.

The unambivalent endorsement of the impact of college upon feminist ideals is illustrated by a premed student who had a history of unimpeded academic success at college and claimed that the college had changed her philosophy:

> I've become more sympathetic to the women's movement while here. Although I have always had ideas which you could call feminist, my self-conscious identification as a feminist has increased. I've come across instances of discrimination and, once I left the sheltered environment of the college, I ran across things that have just made me stronger in my beliefs, like discrimination in the sciences.

Another senior also attributed to the college her support for women:

> I consider myself a feminist, not a textbook feminist, but a feminist nonetheless. I know nothing about what happens on campus in terms of women's organizations, but there was a popular rock group composed of five women who took the country by storm last year. I hated their music, but I'd support them because they're women. . . . If I make it in my career, I'll always hire a woman before a man. I attribute this to this college. They gave me a lot of financial aid and help and I just feel that women are more loyal, dependable, brighter. There's a real support network here and my feminism is a very gut thing.

Qualified support for the women's movement, ambivalence, and opposition were also expressed, but by a minority of five in this category of twenty-seven students.

Some students made the distinction between "liberal" feminism (women's right to education and to high-level jobs) on the one hand and "radical" feminism, which they opposed. The term radical was used by several of the steadfast students to refer to some groups and organizations of the women's movement on campus and in the public sphere. Often it was equated with lesbianism and "screaming, strident women." Those who were sympathetic to feminism, but had some trouble identifying with the movement, usually used these two characterizations.

A student planning to have a writing career voiced some of this ambivalence when she described her own sympathies and problems with feminism and feminists:

> I've become sensitized to the women's movement because of the experience I've had with college men [in the affiliated college]. When I came, I felt I had a healthier attitude. I tried to give men the benefit of the doubt and I would judge people according to their personality, rather than sex, but men treat women here abominably. . . . There are some aspects of the women's movement with which I can't agree. I hate watching screaming women on TV yell about women's issues and women's rights. Those people are just angry, and their anger doesn't come out of self-respect, but out of their inability to do anything about the situation.

A very few students in the steadfast group felt negatively about the women's movement altogether, usually because of what they felt was its irrelevance to their lives. A premed student explained her attitude:

> I'm fed up with the women's movement. You don't need to go to a feminist school to know you can be a doctor. I knew I wanted to be a doctor before coming here and this college just brings that issue into everything. The fact that the college president had to rationalize inviting a man to speak at our graduation is just ridiculous.

Finally, a few strongly identified feminists, who were

active in feminist groups on and off campus, voiced criticism of the college ethos and of their classmates for not being feminist *enough*. One student, an activist feminist when she entered college, planning a career in journalism, described critically her classmates and the college ethos:

> A lot of women have found out that you can make $40,000 a year and have a child and do all that without calling yourself a feminist. Women's liberation to them means going out and being able to be an executive. Women here want careers, but they're so afraid to make the connection between what women did for us thirty years ago. They dissociate themselves from the struggles that went on before. The two images at college are one, that you can have it all—executive and mother—every woman should want to be both; and two, the feminist image, those women who remain marginalized from most of the school because they're seen as too radical or lesbian. Even if you're an executive *and* a mother, have you really solved the problems of women in our society?

In summary, the career-steadfast students were the most sympathetic toward the women's movement of all the five types studied. Some entered college career salient and feminist, but many became more identified with women's causes while in college. They attributed their greater involvement to strong classmates who increased, by example and through discussions, the students' awareness of the sexism still prevailing in our society. The students' own experience of sexist and discriminatory practices in relationships with men in the affiliated college, or in work, contributed to their interest in the women's movement. A few students observed perceptively that, were it not for the influence of feminist classmates, as well as the general college ethos, they might have taken the sexist experiences for granted. Thus, consciousness-raising both preceded and was strengthened by individual experiences of sexism. A small minority of career-salient seniors were hostile to what they termed "radical" feminism.

Conflicts of Career-Steadfast Students

The career-steadfast seniors were not oblivious to the problems they will encounter in trying to combine career, marriage, and motherhood, as most of them hoped to do. Their anxieties will be illustrated presently. They appeared, however, to be somewhat more confident than the converts that some accommodation can be worked out by temporarily lowering career goals or providing child care while continuing full-time careers. The following case illustrates stages in the development of one still-anxious student:

> This student planned to be a lawyer. When she entered college, she felt certain that she wanted neither marriage nor children, because these would interfere with her career. In the course of the four years of college, she changed her attitudes, and she attributed the change to three influences: a long and satisfactory relationship with a man, a positive experience working in a day-care center, and her favorite aunt as a role model. She is more desirous of having a family, but she still describes herself as "confused": "Children would be a conflict with my career. I enjoy them and I think I always knew I enjoyed little kids, but I knew that if I was going to make it—in capital letters—in this society, I was going to have to reject family life, at least at the start, so that I wouldn't be classified as "the marrying kind." Perhaps I can stay home for a couple of years if I have children, but I am still quite worried that both marriage and children would detract from my chances to fulfill my career goals."

The prospects for accommodation took several forms.

Some students echoed the hope for the transformation of work schedules by the time they have children, however unlikely they felt that this reform might come about. For many, part of the attraction of a particular career was its compatibility with child care. A premed student, as her medical career approached and her thoughts about children became clearer, thought it less possible to take a block of time off from work. Instead, she looked around for alternate models of child care.

> I would like to nurse my children, so I couldn't send them away to day care while they're still infants. I've thought of hypothetical situations and wondered how I could do it. Maybe I could have a bassinet in a back room in my office. I would cut down on my medical practice, but not stop altogether. I've heard of women having babies while they're still doing their residencies.

For the student going on to a computer science career, part of the future conflict has already been resolved. She chose her future employer partly based on the firm's policy of flexible time:

> They've offered me a lot. The company has a flexible time system. You can come in early or late, as long as you work eight hours a day. You can even work at home if you want. There was a woman there who had just had a baby, and she was telling me how wonderful flexible time was for her. This is great for when you have a family and need time. They give males time off for children too, like maternity leave for women.

Again, a senior planning to become a geologist was encouraged by the fact that the man she lives with would be willing, she was sure, to share in child care.

In comparison with the studies of women at the same

campus in the late 1940s and the 1950s, the author was
struck by the ease with which some students admitted the
priority of careers. A premed student expected both help
from her future husband and paid child care. She had no
qualms about adding: "If I didn't think both things could
be done well, I'd sacrifice the children, because I've already
made a commitment to my work."

A married student, planning to attend graduate school
in sociology, tried to describe her own changes as she
became more committed to her career:

> I went schizo at some point. I'm not a feminist and I
> can't identify with the feminists on campus—they're too
> militant. I don't know how to explain the change. I
> came from a sheltered background and I only knew one
> way to be. The people I was with freshman year talked
> about careers, but somewhere along the line they became
> more traditional. Maybe I just got so interested in my
> career I got selfish. I decided that I was going to do
> something and if I found someone to live with, fine.
> I've learned that if I want something, it doesn't mean
> that I'm a bad wife or a bad mother. If I want something,
> I need it, and it's good for me.

A few of the career-steadfast students were prepared to
make concessions and lower career goals. A student planning
to go to law school saw the potential conflict between
work and family in this way:

> A woman can't totally isolate her career from her family.
> She can't totally close out the child to go to work every
> day, and if the job demands total concentration and if
> the woman can't provide it, I don't think she should
> feel intimidated or bad because she can't provide that
> total attention.... She should put it up front, on the
> line, when applying for a job. If she had a child, she

should tell her employer that she had a child and that the child might call her at work occasionally, and so on.

Finally, the next senior was one of the very few who seemed untroubled by the problem of juggling career and family:

I know many women who are educated and bright, had careers at one point, got married, had a kid, and that's it. I just feel they're not happy with themselves now. I feel like if they were more established before they had kids, then it would be much better. As for myself, I know that if I was married and had children and I was not working at what I wanted to do, it would adversely influence my family life.... As a child, I was very independent because my mother was working at two jobs and I grew up with a key around my neck, fixing dinner for myself and so on. Kids are capable of taking care of themselves for the most part, like I did.

So far, in this and the last chapter, three career projectories over the four years of college have been analyzed: the noncareer steadfast (or traditional); the shifters to career (or converts); and the career steadfast. Next are the students who changed their orientation from career to noncareer, either as early as in their sophomore year or by the time of the senior interview.

FROM CAREER TO NONCAREER
(DEFECTORS)

The number of students in this category is too small to
warrant the systematic analysis of the interviews presented
for the first three categories, which together constituted
82 percent of the senior sample. Instead, three cases will
be presented representing different patterns of "defection"
from careers.

Since the defectors entered college as career salient, it is
not surprising that they shared some characteristics of the
career-steadfast students. The first case illustrates a career-
oriented freshman who became, at the end of college, a
somewhat conflict-ridden and reluctant "defector."

V. indicated in 1979 her intention to major in economics,
a decision she followed. She came from a traditional
Protestant Eastern European family, with both parents
working full time and her mother performing, in addition, all the traditional domestic functions. Her parents
had high expectations of her, with her mother more
supportive of career goals than was her father, who
laughingly predicted that she would be married in a few
years and "at home raising kids."

The issue of children was a source of conflict as early
as 1979. At that time, V. thought she might not have
children at all, to enable her to pursue a career. Or else
she would start a family in her thirties, having established
herself solidly in some occupation. She explained—
reflecting, perhaps, both the culture and the reality of
her parental home—"Traditionally speaking, children
are always in a woman's picture. But, if I was deeply
involved in what I was doing, I wouldn't want to have
that conflict." As for the women's movement, in 1979
she objected to the militancy of its adherents.

By 1980, after one year of college, the interview revealed developments generally associated with career salience. V. said that she felt more self-confidence and security in her work and had done well in her major. She was much more sympathetic to the women's movement as a result of classroom discussions about discrimination against women and through close friends who introduced her to feminist ideas. She expected more from female professors and found them more inspiring. She appreciated feeling part of a community of women scholars. All in all, college had increased her awareness of women's strengths and of her own potential for accomplishment. Yet, by her senior year, several developments tilted the scale against an uninterrupted career. What were these developments?

She became surer that she would want to have children. Her temporary jobs not only failed to anchor her interest in a specific occupation, but raised doubts whether her soft-spoken, mild personality would fit her for a business career. In her own words:

> I'm having doubts about whether I can swing it all. I've been hearing too many horror stories about trying to balance work, kids, and marriage—the exhaustion and running around trying to get everything done. I don't know whether I can do it all. Maybe I am not really suited for a superwoman career role.

She was late in starting to date. In her senior year, she established a serious relationship with a man. While she was not against shared parenting, her current boyfriend was fairly traditional and would probably expect her to take care of their children.

This student was described as a conflict-ridden defector because, even as she expressed her fear of trying to be a "superwoman," she dreamed "that for me the solution may be in finding a job with the least possible pressure, perhaps part-time, and in persuading my husband to help me with the children."

The next case presents a different pattern. For B., a senior, the decision to moderate career goals was less of a compromise than an acknowledgment of her real desires and interests, temporarily obscured by early fantasies of a career. For all the setbacks that were involved in arriving at her final decision, there is in the end less conflict and a more wholehearted conviction that she found her right path. B., a religious Catholic freshman, entered unsure of her major and future occupation, but hoping to work, even when she had young children. Her mother had never worked and B. felt that she would have had a more fulfilled life had she had some occupation. The college influenced B. by making her more aware of women's problems. In 1980 she felt more sympathetic to the women's movement. This she attributed to the actual experience of discrimination in a job and, more important, to the friendship with two classmates who "raised [her] consciousness." At times, she found it difficult to reconcile her Catholic beliefs with feminism, especially on the issue of abortion. She continued to be career salient in the fall of 1980.

By 1983, however, her aspirations for the future changed. Unlike the more prevalent tendency toward some weakening of religious sentiments, B. became, if anything, more devout. All her close friends were church-going Catholics, even if they were equally troubled by the discrimination against women in the church.

Between 1980 and 1983, B. had undergone a change in her philosophy of life. By 1983 she began to view her future work as an expression of a religious commitment to improve society rather than an ambition for personal success. She criticized the success drive of many classmates. How much this shift to "meaningful service" was affected by disappointing college grades cannot be determined. But when, in the summer of her junior year, her father urged her to try out a summer job in advertising (one of the possible occupations she had considered at one time), she refused: "I'd probably feel like I'm doing something to pollute the world, rather than reform it."

Her outlook was affected by serious involvement with her Jewish boyfriend. Her parents were not opposed to this relationship, they were only insistent that the children be raised Catholic. As for her, her boyfriend's agnosticism bothered her more than their different religions. His career would involve a change in residence and she was prepared to follow him. Perhaps her desire for a large family was equally important in the new vision of her future.

> I want four or five children, and I see the possibility of taking time off from work for each one. The space of time might be ten years. I wouldn't be able to have an adequate career and raise a family at the same time. I'm more willing to sacrifice my work than children.

To sum up, by her senior year B. felt that her flicker of interest in a full-time career was more of a response to other people's expectations of her. She has recognized that she really wants to raise children. Her sympathy for the women's movement has declined: "They want all women to go out and get jobs, but they neglect the other alternative."

This student developed a very satisfying relationship with her boyfriend, and her major concern was living her life in a way consistent with her religious beliefs. At her last interview she felt she could do this best by raising children and being involved in social issues.

The next and final case is the story of S., who remained career salient until the beginning of her senior year. Several themes emerge in the series of interviews with S. over the four years. The first is the salience of other interests outweighing occupational goals. During the first year, it was the membership on an athletic team, with strong competition with another female athlete; and during the first two years, S. was preoccupied with her popularity with men. This preoccupation was all the more absorbing because she was slow to begin dating and combined some romantic naiveté with a longing to "make it" in a sophisticated, "liberated" clique.

Her academic performance was satisfactory, but she changed both major and prospective occupational choice several times. Her final enthusiasm turned out to be disappointing: "I went into [the field] in a very naive way. Father always said it was 'a noble profession.'" But the more she learned about the realities of it, the less appealing it became. "Even if I made it through graduate school, I'd have to start with some minimal job."

The strongest factor against a profession turned out to be the dread of the commitment, the dedication that it would require: "What about the family? What about all the other things I may want to do—say, learn to ski?" She confessed the fact that she was only a B− student had depleted her drive.

S. came to the conclusion that she did not, after all, want a time-consuming "set career." She felt there were many more attractive possibilities, such as working at home or opening her own store. She was turned off by those all-absorbed, preoccupied professionals whom she met: "All they think about is their work." She thought she would end up in some retailing job that would leave enough time for her other interests.

It would appear that, at this stage of her development (S. was only twenty), there were too many social pulls and problems to balance and resolve to allow the concentration required by a professional choice. The short-lived enthusiasms for a number of majors and careers were, perhaps, expressions of familial pressures and the very ethos of the college, which she deplored but could not disregard.

The introduction to this chapter referred to the cost-benefit schema in the choice of life styles. The defectors relinquished career goals when they moved from fantasy to the more realistic view of the persistence and dedication a career demanded. Occasionally, as in the case of B., the major factor that led her to become a defector was the strong appeal of the more traditional large family and a philosophy of volunteerism.

THE WAVERERS

The few waverers oscillated between career and noncareer orientations without the consistent direction observed in the foregoing types. They were subject to more cross-pressures and greater conflicts than the other types, but the nature of the conflicts was no different: "It's a waste to go through four years of this college and then be a housewife"; but "The goals are set too high for me here. I have a constant dread of failing"; "If I could find some occupation that would fulfill my interests, I could work hard, but here I am, a senior, with not the slightest idea of what I'd want or could do"; "I want a family and I doubt that I have the stamina to balance family and a career"; "I have a serious relationship with a man who has quite traditional views of marriage"; and the like.

If the waverers did not reveal new determinants of life-style preferences, their case histories illustrate the complexities and intensity of their conflicts.

SUMMARY

College impacts must be studied in relation to the characteristics of entering students. It was this postulate that directed the classification of career orientations on the basis of attitudes toward careers expressed both at entrance to college and in the senior year. This classification proved sound, since the types were, in fact, found to differ in a number of respects.

Among the background social factors, we found ethnicity and degree of religious orthodoxy to affect the impact that the college would have on career salience four years later. The intervening variable was the family ethic as to women's roles. The traditional definition of women's roles differentiated Orthodox Jews from other Jews, unassimilated Asian families from others more assimilated, and the like. This finding explained the generally negative results reported earlier on the relationship between the major religious affiliations and the degree of career salience at entrance to college. The formal classification of religious affiliations obscured the differences within each religious group. The decisive feature was the degree of traditionalism as to women's roles, rooted in ethnicity and religion, but varying within the major ethnic and religious groups.

The relationship of the mother's role to the daughter's degree of career commitment proved complex. For example, the homemaker-mother served as a negative role model when the mother was dissatisfied with her role or when the unhappy parental marriage or divorce demonstrated to the daughter the high costs of such a life of dependence. The homemaker-mother served as a positive role model when the mother was satisfied with her role, provided the mother-daughter relationship was warm and close and the mother's aspirations for the daughter were traditional. The interviews provided an outline of the complex explanatory model underlying the relationship between the mother and the degree of the student's career salience.

Career-steadfast students had a higher proportion of working mothers than did the other types. But a working mother was not an invariable determinant of career salience in daughters. Some daughters felt deprived of sufficient nurturance in childhood and had, therefore, some misgivings about following their mothers' example. The father's influence on his daughter's career orientations was not studied as systematically, though some references to it were cited.

The impact of college was considered in respect to several features of the college experience that were found to distinguish the traditional, the converts to career, career-steadfast students, and the other types. These distinguishing factors included: patterns of interaction with peers, more specifically the degree of homogeneity (with respect to ethnicity, religion, class, life-style preferences) of social cliques and friendships at various stages of college; the extent of interaction with female and male professors; the degree of satisfaction with work experience and internships; and the ethos of the college.

Contrary to expectations, the various types did not differ in grade-point averages for the four years of college. If some students were discouraged by poor academic performance from a wish to pursue a career, others, if disappointed in grades, changed majors, remaining committed to careers.

Moreover, high academic success did not necessarily ignite career motivations.

We found no differences between the traditionals and careerists in the proportions of students who did not date at all or dated infrequently, and students who dated often or had steady relationships. The assumption that career salience is a characteristic sublimation of frustrated personal relationships with men is not supported by the interviewed sample. In fact, each of the major types—that is, traditional, convert, and career-steadfast students—had about the same proportion of nondaters, occasional daters, and past or current "steady" relationships.

7

Occupational
Decision Making

MUCH of the recent research on occupational choices
of women undergraduates has dealt with specific occupations—those that women intended to enter and those they
have ruled out. An important issue has been the extent of
innovative, as against traditional, occupational goals and
accomplishments, as ascertained in longitudinal studies of
college graduates.

This chapter focuses on the *process* of occupational
decision making. The problem is not primarily to account
for the choice of business, science, social work, medicine,
journalism, or some other occupation. It is to trace the
various influences, and the conflicts involved, either in
coming to a definite choice or in remaining uncertain by
the end of the senior year.

The data on which this chapter is based consists of

TABLE 7.1

Degree of Certainty of Occupational Plans

	1979 (%)	1980 (%)	1983 (%)
Completely undecided	25	28	14
Considering 2 or 3 specified occupations	52	42	34
Feels quite certain to enter a specified occupation	23	30	52
	100	100	100
	(n = 232)	(n = 196)	(n = 154)

questionnaires filled out by total samples in 1979, 1980, and 1983. The questionnaires elicited occupational plans as well as the degree of their certainty and provided a typology of occupational choices in college. To interpret the processes of occupational choices among the contrasting types, we shall turn to the interviews.

As far as certainty of choice is concerned, table 7.1 demonstrates a general trend toward crystallization of plans.

As seen in the table, only 23 percent of the freshman sample specified an occupation they "felt quite certain" to enter. The proportion of "certain" choices increased to 52 percent of the senior sample. This leaves a substantial number, however—nearly one-half—of students who reached the end of their senior year vacillating among two or three fields of work or completely uncertain.[1]

It is tempting, but unrealistic, to attach value judgment to these categories. Those certain of their postcollege field of work have not always arrived at their decision rationally, sure of the nature of the occupation and its compatibility with their basic interests and abilities. The "shifters" may,

[1] Contrary to our results, the percentage of students able to be specific about career or job choices declined across the college years in a study by Titley, Titley, and Wolff (1976:107), but Angrist and Almquist report findings similar to ours (1975:52).

occasionally, prove more open to unanticipated, but promising, options. Whatever these objective assessments, there is no mistaking the students' own subjective reactions. The uncertainty about future plans at the end of their senior year was, for most, a source of anxiety. The author has already referred to the significance that students, even those classified as "noncareer," attached to work. Nor was the significance limited to the question of economic survival. Fulfilling work, even if interrupted for child rearing, was viewed by the great majority as a component of a good life.

More significant for our purposes than the degree of certainty is the understanding of factors involved in exploring, discarding, deciding, or remaining uncertain about postcollege fields of work. As an introduction to this analysis, six major patterns of occupational choices have been identified among the 154 students who were members of the sample throughout the four years of college. This classification is based on their responses to the questionnaires on occupations filled out in 1979 and in 1983. In the subsequent analysis based on interviews, the 1980 responses will also frequently be included.

PATTERNS OF OCCUPATIONAL DECISION MAKING: 1979 AND 1983

The six major patterns are classified on the basis of two dimensions: the degrees of certainty of choice and the similarity or differences in specific occupations listed on the freshman and the senior occupational questionnaires. The patterns include:

		Percent (n = 154)
1.	*Constancy*—a certain choice, identical in 1979 and 1983	19
2.	*Shifting*—ending in complete uncertainty or three unrelated choices in 1983	29
3.	*Crystallization*—from several options in 1979 to a certain choice in 1983, related to the earlier options	14
4.	*Radical Change*—from a certain choice in 1979 to a radically different certain choice in 1983	4
5.	*Discovery*—from complete uncertainty or a number of options in 1979 to a certain choice in 1983, unrelated to earlier options	14
6.	*Change to Relative Certainty*—from uncertainty or a number of options in 1979, ending in two possible *new* choices in 1983	15
7.	*Miscellaneous*	5
		100

Constants

The single most conspicuous characteristic of the twenty-nine cases in this category is the predominance of two career choices: twenty-five students were planning careers in either law or medicine when they entered college, and their career objectives remained unchanged during college.

All of the interviewed constants made their choice long before arriving at college; some traced it back to junior high school. For many, high-school courses had already solidified a particular interest that continued through college. For several of the students, good grades in biology encouraged them to pursue a medical career. Others had part-time work experiences that channeled their career direction.

Parental Encouragement. Students in other groups often testified to parental encouragement of career aspirations. What distinguishes the constants is the strong family support for the particular occupation, a support that often preceded college and continued through the college years.

A number had a close relative (parent, sibling, aunt) in the chosen occupation.

An apparent exception to parental encouragement turned out to confirm the broader generalization that the encouragement of significant adults was a factor in constancy. One student, planning to go to medical school, had a tense relationship with a critical mother and an aloof father. Her boyfriend's mother, however, a doctor and a professor of medicine, gave her strong encouragement and practical advice about her future career during her college years.

Once they arrived at college, the constant students encountered many of the same problems, setbacks, and disappointments that the other students faced. What, then, were some of the factors fostering persistence?

Coping with Setbacks. Many of the students, particularly the premed ones, experienced anxiety about grades, even though most in this group perceived themselves as doing well academically. When grades were not high enough, the students showed strong determination to overcome the problem. Adaptation took several forms. Some worked harder; several went to advisers or professors and discussed concretely how to improve grades or whether to be alarmed about them; several gathered about them a group of friends in the same program (particularly premed) and worked collectively to improve grades. Several students in this category, although quite worried about grades and performance, claimed to like the pressure since it made them work even harder. What seems probable is that, because the career goal was initially so well defined, students in this category mobilized their own and the school's resources more quickly and efficiently when they saw their goals threatened.

A case in point was a psychology student who loved most of the courses in her major, then took one in which she did poorly. Apprehensive about approaching the professor, she repeatedly sought out the teaching assistant and received both encouragement and concrete assistance in course work.

Jobs and Internships. Apart from seeking and receiving assistance from the faculty in overcoming academic problems, the constants reported positive experiences in jobs and internships. To begin with, *all* the constants had some work experience in their future occupations while in college. In comparison with the other groups, they may have chosen jobs more purposefully and carefully. It is conceivable that those whose exposure to work in the chosen field proved unsatisfactory did not remain in the constant category. In any case, the constants reported that work strengthened their conviction that they could succeed in the chosen occupation. For several, the work experience not only reinforced the original choice but also served to specify the area within the occupation that attracted them most. The processes involved in these outcomes were exemplified in the interviews.

One Hispanic premed student was determined, despite occasional difficulties, to be a doctor. Her adviser and teachers encouraged her when her grades were down, and she worked hard to improve them. She got an internship in medical research and this helped resolve the dilemma of her shyness. She decided that she could do medical research, since she could avoid being in constant contact with many people. The internship also strengthened her self-confidence in her ability to succeed in research.

A student planning a career in television production had worked for a TV station before college and continued her work during college. She gained specific knowledge of different jobs in the field and decided exactly what she wanted to do when entering the field.

Finally, a premed student revealed in the interview some

moral misgivings she felt about the medical field both in contacts with premed classmates and in her observations in an internship. She was repelled by the mercenary values that, as it seemed to her, permeated the field. She was more interested in scientific research and respected researchers more than she did clinicians. Yet she worried about her financial future were she to confine her work solely to research. Long talks with her major adviser reassured her that she could combine research and medical practice without compromising her values.

Support of Peer Groups. Paradoxically, despite the widely held view about the competitiveness of the premed and, to a lesser extent, prelaw students, peer groups emerged as one of the major sources of support in overcoming setbacks. In explaining this seeming paradox, some factors seem to offset the alleged rivalry of these preprofessionals. The academic program requires these students to take many courses together, leading to formation of friendships. A greater proportion of constants had a close friend pursuing the same career goal than was true of the other types. It was not surprising, therefore, that the constants frequently referred to being helped by friends to remain "on track." Having friends who were experiencing the same difficulties demonstrated that one's problems were not unique. Shared enthusiasms also reinforced constancy of goals.

In summary, the described experiences of the constants illustrate the circular, mutually reinforcing processes. They entered surer of future occupations;[2] they read possible setbacks less negatively and forged ahead; they obtained more help from professors and more encouragement from family; they chose more work and internship projects related to future occupations, which reinforced their original decision. For premed students particularly, the presence of

[2] Contrary to this finding, Angrist and Almquist (1975:72) found no association between career commitment and the certainty of occupational choice.

a friend or a circle of friends pursuing similar occupational goals often meant the difference between an alienating, frightening, competitive environment and a supportive, shared academic experience.

As to conflicts typical of this occupational pattern, given the constancy of choice, it is understandable that the stress experienced was about performance. "Will I get into medical school?"; "What will I possibly do as an alternative if I don't?"—these questions often punctuated the interviews. Self-doubt was expressed, but underlying stress and doubt was a very strong motivation to succeed.

Shifters

This pattern represents students who, at the end of their senior year, were either completely uncertain about occupational goals or listed three unrelated possible choices on their 1983 questionnaires. This group represents the highest degree of uncertainty of all occupational patterns of our typology. The theoretical problem is to attempt to account for this indecision.

Some of the shifting students entered college uncertain about occupational goals, much more so than, of course, the constants. Only six of the forty-four shifters indicated a certain occupational intention in 1979. But this initial attitude does not distinguish them from the other occupational patterns, which also contained many who were uncertain upon entering college.

One major clue to what distinguishes them was provided by the fact that the proportion of traditional students was higher among the shifters than among any of the other occupational patterns. Of forty-four shifting students, 39 percent were traditional and an additional 11 percent were defectors from career salience. By contrast, among the constants, only 10 percent were traditional, and there were no defectors.

Given this lack of career orientation, a number of the attributes of the traditional student, as described in chapter 5, were found to produce uncertainty as to occupational direction. As repeatedly stated, the traditional students were not free of anxiety about future occupation, but they were hindered in arriving at a decision by several factors. Some of these were the consequences of their traditional orientations. Others may have been at the root of traditional preferences, that is, the common origin of both.

Given the primacy of familial responsibilities, the shifters tended to eliminate from consideration demanding careers that would entail an excessive sacrifice of competing concerns. Moreover, their weaker career drive cut short the persistent exploration and testing of occupational goals, as well as the stubborn coping with setbacks characteristic of many career-salient students.

The shifters who experienced disillusionment in initial occupational choice, as well as those who entered without any goals, were more easily discouraged and more passive. They did not mobilize the resources of the institution to arrive at an occupational choice. Their disillusionment with an occupational option they had considered initially was generally brought about both by poor grades in relevant courses and by loss of interest, as the reality of the field replaced fantasies. Four interviewed students abandoned medicine as an initial choice after having received poor grades in sciences. Five dropped other fields because of poor grades. A student who had intended to become an architect (she had been fascinated watching her uncle sit at his drafting desk "working at those incredibly beautiful designs") soon discovered that she "hated the mechanical work and hated that I wasn't good at it."

Among the shifting students, a few experienced an added conflict that stymied still further the process of occupational choice. This was the case when parental aspirations for a high-status profession exceeded the daughter's interest or abilities. A premed student who did poorly in required courses and abandoned medicine as her future profession waited almost a year before telling her father, anticipating his disappointment at her defection.

A Chinese-American student vacillated among different occupational choices because of a clash between high parental expectations and her own temperament. She confessed:

> It is hard to have to live up to standards that are set for you by your parents. I am the only one of my brothers and sisters to attend college, and they have dreams about my future. Sometimes I wonder what would happen if I decided to drop everything and goof off, and then I think that I would be such a disappointment to them.

If excessive or uncongenial parental pressures immobilized these students, paradoxically, the relative indifference of some other parents had a similar effect on a few shifting students. This inference is drawn from the comparison of several occupational types. Among the constants and the radical changers, close and supportive parental involvement in occupational decisions (rather than an uncongenial pressure or indifference) served to sustain the student's own motivation.

The majority of the interviewed shifting students had no significant interaction with professors in general or discussions with faculty about occupational choices in particular. One such student explained: "I don't like to talk to professors. If I have a problem, I'll solve it in other ways, say, by talking to my friends."

More striking is the fact that over one-half of the shifters either had no work or internship in the four years of college or, more likely, chose such work randomly, unrelated to a possible occupational goal. As indicated earlier, for the constants such work constituted a strong factor in reinforcing or specifying an occupational direction. Students in the shifting category tended to seek out work or internships less frequently, not only than the constants, but also than the crystallizers or the discoverers. Moreover, of the minority who did select work as a test of occupational plan, one-half found the experience unsatisfactory. Its value, if any, was to eliminate a possible option. One student, an urban studies major, worked for the City Planning Commission and also for a private research firm and became convinced that the field was too technical and too dry for her. Another student decided to do some elementary school tutoring, but remained uncertain about teaching: "Would I like it? Would I be good at it?"

The passivity of the shifters in relation to faculty, internships, and other college resources led to a sense of alienation from the academic program and a loss of self-confidence vis-à-vis work. The grades of the shifters were no lower than those in other occupational categories (48 percent of the constants and 46 percent of the shifters had a four-year grade-point average of 3.3 or above). Whence, then, comes the sense of inadequacy experienced by the shifters? The interviews suggested a set of interlocking processes.

In comparison with the other patterns, the shifting students appeared less well integrated into the academic program. They did not approach teachers as readily to check their own perception of their academic performance. Consequently, they had fewer reality checks when they were dissatisfied and less encouragement from professors that might have counterbalanced feelings of self-doubt.

In an institution that values achievement and with many classmates who were clear about future work, the uncertain seniors felt inadequate. This may explain their worries about lacking the "right personality" for the occupational world, or about lacking "motivation" and "academic involvement." The majority were uneasy about reaching the time of graduation uncertain of their future work. In the words of one student: "I am afraid for my future. Of course, if we don't feel like going any more for those job interviews, we always have the little option of getting married, having some kids, and just diddling around for a while. But then I'll be in my thirties and still not know what to do with my life. This scares me."

The shifting group included also some career-salient students whose occupational uncertainty did not derive from traditional life-style preferences. Some of these career-salient, but shifting, students also encountered failure in their occupational plans and were profoundly discouraged by this. That is, not all career-salient students had the resilience, tenacity, and purposeful search for alternatives that helped others to overcome the initial disappointment. But an initial blow to self-esteem does not exhaust the explanation of the career-committed shifters.

Two other conflicts impeded occupational decision making by some career-salient shifters. One was a compelling academic interest or an artistic skill that had poor prospects for employment. A student whose wish was to become a writer came under strong pressure from her family to settle on a more practical major and vocation. "Writing is fine," argued her brother, "but you can do it on the side." Succumbing to this pressure, she set up some interviews with corporate recruiters late in her senior year, remaining uncertain of her future. The difficulty of translating a passionate interest in writing, history, or other of the humanities into a marketable skill in the present employment situation stymied these students.

Another conflict involved deeper moral values that can best be conveyed by an illustration. A student whose academic performance and motivation were high expressed great contempt for any competitive work. Whatever the deeper psychic reasons for this attitude, she declared that she was not going to devote her life to the "scramble up the academic or the corporate ladder." This ideological rebellion against the competitive "rat race" devoid of humane values blocked some students from active exploration of career opportunities. Similarly, a few students dedicated to religious and humanitarian concerns felt at a loss to find a suitable occupational niche.

In contrast to the majority, the postponement of a career choice was somewhat less stressful for the students who entered college with the strong conviction that its function was that of a liberal education. This was especially true when the family supported this philosophy. Students from a lower socioeconomic class had, on the other hand, to face the insistent question of their families: "But how are you going to make a living with this major?"

The few for whom the issue was not fraught with anxiety were occasionally deeply integrated into the academic program with strong intellectual and, sometimes, political interests. There was no lack of personal development and no flagging of their career drive, but these students had a feeling that they were bound to come to an occupational choice in time. We might speculate that these students, sustained by their intellectual interests, did not feel as purposeless or afloat as did other shifters who remained relatively uninvolved in the academic work. Another hypothesis is that parents for whom the primary function of college is intellectual growth are likely to be more economically secure and more able to support a daughter's extended search for her true vocation. This is in contrast with the more practical orientation of lower-income families whose daughters had to be self-supporting.

If the shifters illustrate the forces impeding the choice

of a congenial occupational goal, the next three groups offer a close view of how the college experience leads to a discovery of an occupational direction by the end of the senior year.

Crystallizers

The students in this category entered college listing two or three career options they might pursue. By the time they graduated, they had picked one occupation that was related to one or more of their original choices. For this reason, their occupational decision making was characterized as a narrowing-down process, since what was generally involved was the increasing appeal of one of the options, with elimination of the others.

Crystallizers tend to be career salient. Of all the patterns of occupational decision making, the constants and the crystallizers had the highest and nearly identical proportions of students who were career steadfast. Only 10 percent of each group were traditional, that is, noncareer, in 1979 and 1983.

For this group parental influence tended to be less critical than college experience in arriving at a decision. The original uncertainty among two or three occupational interests occasionally reflected a conflict between personal interests and family pressures. More frequently, it stemmed from a plurality of interests on the part of the student herself. One freshman entered college interested in law, journalism, and music. All three reflected different interests and talents on her part, and she looked to the college experience to help her decide among them. Another student listed three possible occupations when she arrived in 1979: medical doctor, social worker, or work in the Foreign Service. She definitely wanted to enter a helping profession: "to be of service to the poor." Although medicine interested her, she was uncertain whether she would be competent as a doctor and looked to the college experience to test her abilities in various areas.

Parental influence appeared to be less important than it was for the other occupational groups in the sense that it did not withstand opposing forces exerted by courses, professors, and work. For these students, it was the college experience that served to crystallize the occupational choice. The majority of interviewed crystallizers testified that college courses played a very important part in their final career decision. Given several interests at entrance, they tested, through a sampling of courses, both the appeal of these competing interests and their own abilities. Grades in various courses became one way to gauge future competence in a profession. We did not find among these students the kind of dramatic disappointments and self-doubt that characterized the shifters—perhaps because these students did not have their heart set at entrance on a particular career. A student who listed her occupational options as musician and chemist when a freshman had decided by her second year that she was not a good enough musician to make a living as a performer. Although she rejected one of her options, she also had some difficulties with her chemistry courses. Given her interest in science, she had received disappointingly low grades in chemistry. At the same time, she took physics courses, was excited by them, and performed well. This indicated to her that she should shift her interest to another branch of the sciences—physics. Likewise, a student who intended to be a college professor of either mathematics, physics, or chemistry had such a positive experience in her math courses and did so well academically that she felt this helped her decide to become a math professor.

The crystallizers had closer and more positive contacts with their professors than did the shifters. Most of the interviewed students in this group had initiated contact with their teachers. For several, the relationship was central in their decision to reject a certain career choice and to embrace another. Such a mentor relationship is illustrated in the following excerpt:

> The parents of a student strongly urged her to enter medicine. She herself was interested in medicine, as well as journalism and computer science. Eventually, however, it was the student's own academic experiences (including a negative reaction to some aspects of medicine) that were more influential than parental pressure. This student took a premed program, but had many doubts as to her interest and competence in medicine. She was fascinated by sociology courses and realized that what she really wanted to do was academic research in the sociology of science. It was primarily her relationship with a sociology professor, who introduced her to the sociology of science and then encouraged her in her growing interest, that helped her see a way to combine her interests in medicine and sociology.
>
> For the student who chose to become a math professor, it was her "inspirational" mathematics professor who first encouraged her, helped her make some academic contacts, and suggested that she serve as a teaching assistant in the department.

In addition to college courses and mentor relationships with professors, internships and jobs played a major part in helping these crystallizers arrive at a decision. An Asian student vacillated between medicine and physical therapy. Her science grades were very good and she felt encouraged to consider medicine. Her job in a health clinic gave her added confidence that medicine would be the right choice for her.

A shy and somewhat insecure freshman wanted to work

with children, either as a child psychologist or as a
sociologist. Two teachers helped steer her toward the
program in elementary education. But it was not until this
student taught at a public school that she realized how
appealing teaching was to her and became confident that
she had what it took to become a good teacher.

The richest insight into the impact of a job on occupational decision making is provided by the case of a Black
student torn between journalism and law. Having been
involved in high-school journalism and public affairs, she
received added encouragement in her writing ability from
her college teachers. Law attracted her too, but she was
apprehensive that it was a cutthroat and competitive career
and one discriminating against women and Blacks. However, a part-time job in the legal department of a city
agency caused her to decide in favor of law. The decision
was made because she discovered that her previous negative
perception of some aspects of law was unfounded. Additional factors were the attractions of this field and an
increased confidence in her abilities to meet its challenges.
An excerpt from her senior interview will highlight the
processes at work:

> The young lawyers at the agency have been really
> interested in me and my plans for law school. They go
> out of their way to encourage me. The very fact that
> there are so many Blacks and women working here is
> in itself reassuring. I am no longer worried about law
> being too competitive for me. In the first place, it isn't
> that competitive. Over the summer, the law office
> seemed relaxed; the lawyers were just confiding in each
> other—they weren't out to cut each other's necks. It
> surprised me how laid back it was. Besides, I figured I
> can learn to deal with what competition there is and
> maybe be more competitive myself.
>
> The best part of the job is that I am doing things

lawyers actually do, writing up files. It's sort of fun doing that instead of sitting around Xeroxing. I'm getting the feel of a law office, and I'm not wasting my time. I see what they do all day. I work in the law library and when I'm not busy I read cases. And the lawyers talk to me a lot about what they're doing.

Changing personal values were also a factor in final occupational decisions. The case just described included another factor, not previously mentioned, in explaining the shift from journalism as an option to the choice of law. The student explained the changes in her values over the college years. Having been involved in high-school journalism and public affairs, she was attracted to the glamour and the moral mission of uncovering government corruption. By the time she reached her senior year, her priorities had changed, and control and autonomy in the workplace became her major consideration. Having her own law practice, she felt, would give her power over the conditions of her work.

The student referred to previously who decided on medicine over social work and Foreign Service had also changed her moral outlook. By her senior year she had become so critical of American foreign policy that working for the government would, she felt, go against her values. Moreover, she became convinced that as a physician she would be more effective than a social worker in helping the disadvantaged.

Still another student changed her evaluation of an occupation, this time less as a result of a new perception of its nature than of a new recognition of her own needs. This engineering student, despite her high grades in engineering courses, realized that working with people would be more satisfying to her. By her senior year she hoped to combine her interest in urban planning and management.

In summary, the process of narrowing down occupational choices could be described as a trying on of different occupational hats during the college years. Courses, professors, and jobs were all involved in this effort to achieve the best fit of occupation and the student's personality. These features of the college experience contributed to the final choice by providing a more realistic picture of the occupation in question, as well as a clearer self-definition in terms of level of confidence in one's ability to achieve in a given field, one's interests, and values.

Radical Changers

Radical changers constituted only 4 percent of the total sample of seniors. These were the students who entered college certain of an occupational goal and ended having made a radically different, but equally certain, choice.

Much like the constants, the radical changers traced this interest in the occupation at entrance back to high school or even earlier. One student had known since the age of ten that she wanted to be a doctor, following in the footsteps of her physician father. Strong familial support for a high-status professional career was combined in this group with close contact and discussions with family members over occupational decisions, but no pressure for a particular occupation.

The college experience led the radical changers to reevaluate the intrinsic appeal of the early occupational goal or of their capacity to attain it. The student who embarked on a premed program, an A student in high school, failed dismally in science and math courses. But she got an A in history "without batting an eye." History had been her passion in high school. She realized that she had chosen medicine largely to emulate her father and win his approval. She switched to history as an academic career.

In contrast to the shifters the radical changers, whatever their disappointment with the initial failure, became strongly attracted and eventually committed to a second career choice. Small as the number of the radical changers is for conclusive results, two factors appear decisive. They expressed a strong motivation to find their future occupation during college years. Second, they were more influenced than either the constants or the shifters by college courses and by professors. Each of the interviewed students referred to a course or courses considered crucial in determining her newly chosen occupational goal. Moreover, in their major fields, these students felt strongly influenced and inspired by their teachers. They expressed positive attitudes about courses and professors.

After poor academic performance in their first-year courses, they improved their grades and, consequently, their self-confidence in courses related to their new occupational goals.

Work experience proved important for a couple of students in identifying the new career interest, but was less of a factor than the academic program.

The radical changers resembled the constants in the high level of motivation and in the ability to utilize the college resources. They differed from the constants in that their course work and contacts with the faculty were central in their discovery of the new occupational choice, replacing the one initially held but abandoned.

Discoverers

These students entered college uncertain of future occupations and ended committed to a certain goal. By contrast, the crystallizers differed in making the final choice out of the options listed at entrance to college. The discoverers entered college without any pull toward any occupation. Students in this category were exposed to strong parental pressure to find a "practical" career. Unsure of the specific occupations insistently advocated by their parents, they nevertheless shared the parental view of college education: its purpose was not to introduce students to the liberal arts and sciences, but to prepare them for an occupation. "You have to learn for a practical reason," commented a student. Despite the fact that she enjoyed her courses, she was "going crazy" because she did not arrive at a practical occupational choice. All in all, the combination of strong parental pressure with their own indecision created a high level of anxiety in the discoverers.

These discoverers, though they sampled courses with a view to arriving at some decision, remained uncommitted for the first couple of years of college. Most of the interviewed students in this category felt disappointed with their grades. Pressed as they were to find an occupation, they described themselves as not highly motivated academically, not working to their potential, not having disciplined study habits, lacking in academic focus. In view of this self-description, it is not surprising that all of the interviewed discoverers made their occupational decision after an internship or work experience. Very few had close ties to professors.

In sum, the discoverers combined both a strong external or internal pressure to find a career during college with a somewhat low motivation to become integrated into course work and relationships with professors. The anxiety about a decision was resolved for them more by a practical work experience that introduced them to their future occupation than by academic or intellectual interests.

Changers to Relative Certainty

Five patterns of occupational decision making have been reviewed: constancy, shifting, crystallization, radical change, and discovery. This leaves the changer to relative certainty, students who moved from uncertainty or a number of options in 1979 to two possible choices in 1983. Two features distinguish these students from categories already described. Unlike the shifters, they ended with two possible occupational goals, rather than with virtual uncertainty. Unlike the crystallizers, their senior goals were not related to any considered in previous years.

In summary, 19 percent of the seniors stayed with the same occupational goals they expressed as freshmen. At the other extreme, 25 percent of the seniors listed three unrelated choices or acknowledged complete uncertainty. The majority followed the patterns of choice just described.

Overall, in interviews the freshmen exhibited ignorance of the world of work, the range of possible occupations, and the nature of each. In view of this ignorance, it is not surprising that their intended occupational goals were so often based on fantasy. The trend toward increased certainty involved three processes: a more realistic recognition of both negative and positive features of an early occupational plan; a changed perception of their own abilities, interests, and values; and, finally, a discovery of an appealing occupation they had not been aware of prior to college.

Much of the literature on occupational decision making, as pointed out by Angrist and Almquist (1975), dealt with male undergraduates. The orderly progression of narrowing down of choices from a general field to a specific occupation described by Ginsburg and associates (1951) was true of only a minority of our students. On this score, Angrist and Almquist (1975) were correct in stressing indecision and dramatic shifts in women's occupational decision making. The women in our sample were more highly motivated to seek occupations with high status and high earnings.

In conclusion, the identification in this chapter of six distinct patterns of occupational decision making suggests that any of the current emphases on a single theory is likely to give way to a more complex interpretation as future investigations continue.[3]

[3] See R. W. Titley, B. Titley, and W. M. Wolff (1976) for a review of several theories of occupational choice.

PART III

Women and Men:
Roles in Flux

8

Emotional, Intellectual, and Power Relationships with Men

I N this and the next chapter, relationships with men are analyzed for the light they throw on role strains (difficulties in fulfilling social roles); specifically, on those strains linked to current social changes in gender perspectives. Hence a caveat is in order. If relationships with men appear too problem-ridden, an unrelieved portrayal of pain and friction, it is because the aim was precisely to uncover the disturbed aspects of these encounters. Some balance is provided by the attempt to discern conditions that exacerbated and, conversely, alleviated particular types of strain.

Since role strains are difficulties in fulfilling roles, the study attempted to discover the normative scripts underlying the intersexual interaction of this particular sample of college youth. The analysis sought to distinguish ideal, as contrasted with "operative," values and norms. This is the background against which the interpretations of strains are presented.

Female and male undergraduates interact in various statuses, as classmates, club members, in musical and dramatic societies, on athletic teams. Their purely social relationships are further subdivided into various categories. Dating and romantic partners, for example, differ from "just friends." The latter appear to adhere to more egalitarian norms than those governing the *early stages* of a romantic involvement. Among "just friends," women are more likely to pay their share of expenses for joint activities, feel freer to take the initiative in calling their male friends and perhaps also in asserting themselves and in self-disclosure. This all contrasts with the early stages of dating behavior. These normative differences, in fact, created problems for some egalitarian women on first dates: "If I offer to pay, would this convey a misleading signal that I have no romantic interest in the guy?"

The great majority of interviewed students felt that the campus did not provide sufficient opportunities for meeting the male undergraduates of the affiliate college. Since the women's and the men's colleges are adjacent, some dormitories are coed, and cross-registration makes many classes virtually coeducational, the refrain about the difficulty of meeting men appears, at first glance, puzzling. Granted that by the middle of the sophomore year many women in fact participated in social relationships with men of varying degrees of intimacy, adjustment, and duration, all the same, dissatisfaction with social life was prevalent. Even the satisfied minority admitted, in the words of one student:

You really have to make an active effort to meet men

here. There aren't many opportunities for men and women to come together. In classes you don't talk to the men very much, and after class you just leave and they leave. You have to make a real effort to talk to people, to stop them after class, and you can't be shy. You have to put yourself on the line and you have to take risks. If you're shy or somewhat backward, you're not going to meet men here. There's a lot of pressure here to be popular with men, or at least to have dates for the weekend. I was more successful than my suite-mates because I had been taught to smile, to be friendly and outgoing.

What students described as the dearth of opportunities to *meet* men had in reality other causes. As the interviews progressed, the students themselves bore witness to another interpretation. The problem was less one of literally meeting men than of establishing mutually satisfactory relationships in this period of changing gender roles.

Before presenting various modes of role strain, some clarification is in order. To begin with, the phrase "feminine (or masculine) role" is not a single prescription but a cluster of subroles pertaining to different aspects of inter-action, such as the initiation of contacts, patterns of communication, rules of chivalry, economic obligations, presumptive balance of authority in case of conflicting interests, and the like. Second, while the traditional gender roles have long been deeply etched in social consciousness, perceptions of egalitarian roles are fraught with confusion. The rhetoric of "independence" sometimes equates it with a state of unrelatedness to others. "If I want this reassurance from my boyfriend, am I getting too dependent?," worried a student.

Apart from the confusion as to the ideal of egalitarianism, the remaining social obstacles to its realization create additional problems. A concrete situation requires the couple to improvise roles. Given, then, the blurred concept of the ideal and the remaining social constraints, each is plagued by self-doubt: "Is this demand excessive, is this stance a betrayal of my ideals?"

The discussion will begin with early stages of dating, which illustrate a particular mode of role strain, that is, an uncertainty about norms regulating behavior in a given context. The first section will amply demonstrate ambiguity and the need to "play it by ear."

The ambiguities in the early stages of dating are more easily resolved by trial and error than the deeper conflicts, resulting from current social changes, in more lasting relationships.

The next mode of role strain to be illustrated is a clash between a traditional male and a girlfriend who expects a more egalitarian intellectual, emotional, or power relationship. As might have been expected, the reverse conflict was less prevalent, but sometimes it was the male who attempted to develop greater independence in his traditional girlfriend.

Turning from interpersonal to intrapsychic conflicts, some that stem from a clash between some idiosyncratic psychic wish on the one hand and an internalized value on the other will be illustrated. A militant feminist who is sexually aroused by male sadism would exemplify this type. Simultaneous allegiance to two irreconcilable values would be another variety of intrapsychic stress.

The interviews pointed to other aspects of role strains. With traditional and egalitarian gender roles coexisting in the public consciousness, each sex may reach out for the double dose of privileges—those of each role—laying the burden of all obligations upon their partners. Occasionally, under the guise of egalitarian ideology, the man may conceal even from himself some self-indulgent motive or a wish to avoid responsibility. More rarely, a "liberated" woman who insists on all the obligations of independence has so internalized the traditional female role that she absolves her male partner of all domestic duties. In such a case the woman takes on, at her own expense, the double burden of obligations.

Another mode of role strain has more exclusively social, rather than psychological, roots. We termed it "socially structured scarcity of resources for role fulfillment." It will continue as long as society does not remove social obstacles now blocking the newly emerging goals of an increasing proportion of women.

These are analytical distinctions. Some cases do approximate one or another of these "ideal types," and we shall begin with them. But, given the complex clusters of norms implied in a "gender role" and the varieties of idiosyncratic personality traits, many combinations causing conflicts are likely to be fused in any given relationship.

DATING RITUALS IN FLUX

The First Move

Even the feminist freshmen and sophomores who condemned the male prerogative of initiating a dating relationship as still another symbol of patriarchy hesitated to violate this norm—that is, to literally make the first move. In subsequent interaction, and certainly in established relationships, women and men appeared equally free to contact the other, modified in either direction by the struggle for power or degree of individual involvement.

A self-assured and gregarious sophomore felt that, unlike most of the women she met at college, she did not think it was wrong to call up a man and was rewarded by positive reactions of the men. Significantly, she added: "But, of course, I would never call up anyone I had just met."

The strongest sanction against violating the male prerogative of the first move was the male interpretation of such initiative as a sexual come-on. Men described such aggressive women as "sluts." Indignant as the women were at this inference, they hesitated to expose themselves to the risks, unless they were among the very few who did so with full knowledge of the implications. Some women learned their lesson through trial and error. A freshman who eagerly anticipated intellectual exchanges with male, as well as female, classmates sadly came to the conclusion that the men she went out with were interested solely in her body. She recounted her first experience:

There was this one guy in my philosophy class who was really bright. He used to make brilliant comments in class and I wanted to get to know him so I could talk to him about philosophy. So I approached him and asked him whether he would like to go out for a cup of coffee. My intention was to talk about the lecture, but when we sat down, all he wanted to talk about was how I felt about sex, and when we could go out on a date. I kept telling him that sex wasn't the reason I asked him out. I was trying to be honest and straightforward with him, but he just wouldn't believe it. He thought that the reason I asked him out for a cup of coffee was a sexual come-on. I never asked another guy out on a date.

Deprived of the right of initiative, a woman attracted to a man might resort to active but indirect tactics of frequenting places where she would be likely to meet him or persuading a disinterested suitemate, who had also met the man, to invite him to a party.

Some strong feminists berated themselves for their timidity and the failure to live up to their egalitarian ideals. Wrote one student in her journal:

> There is this guy whom I find incredibly attractive but I cannot speak to him. I don't know if it's fear of rejection, or fear of being perceived as too forward, or, most likely, a combination of the two. In any case, I feel incredibly stupid. I know that one day I will look back on this and hate myself for it, but something inside keeps stopping me.

Who Pays?

There were many well-established relationships in which expenses were shared or otherwise regulated without causing any conflict whatsoever. On the other hand, the payment for joint activities was mentioned in the interviews as a source of embarrassment often enough to warrant its inclusion as another example of anomie, or an absence of shared norms.

Some women, intent on pleasing a new male acquaintance, confessed their puzzlement: "Will he be put off if I offer to pay my share or does he expect it?" Others had strong feelings, either traditional or egalitarian, only to be confronted by the indignation or mockery of a male companion.

Defraying the expenses of a date conferred power upon the male but, with changing customs, many undergraduates apparently found compensating advantages in the emerging custom of sharing the costs. This was all the more understandable when a man embraced those egalitarian innovations that served his self-interest while still clinging to traditional male advantages. A woman describes just such ethical inconsistencies:

> I expect a man to pay for me the first several times we go out, but this one guy would make fun of me. "What kind of an independent woman are you? You don't even offer to share the expense?" But she had other grievances against him. He never asked her what she wanted to do. He would come over and tell her that they were going to a poetry reading or to a museum, whether she was interested in his plan or not. She went along with him, but she acted sullen and he would get angry and ask her what was the matter. She would tell him and then *he* would get sullen and stop talking. Finally she got so fed up with his treatment of her that she ended the relationship.

Another student felt that her former boyfriend was both cheap and a hypocrite. He was not above taking advantage of her by always expecting her to share expenses. At the same time, he wouldn't allow her to call the waiter for a bill or to give her share of the money openly.

Another aspect of restaurant behavior was also ambiguous. A student who was working part-time as a waitress made fun of some traditional couples:

> It really annoys me when the guy gives the order for both of them and the girl just sits there. This happened last week. He knew what she wanted, but he kept messing up the order. He was going, "Scrambled eggs, right?" and she'd answer (almost in a whisper), "Yes, with bacon" and he would turn to me and say, "And

with bacon." She was telling him instead of telling me
and I was thinking, "Oh, come on, what are you, some
little wimp?"

The Symbolic Significance of Money

Adding to the uncertainty or conflict about sharing
expenses was the symbolic significance of money in defining
new relationships as "just friendship" or dating. "It's
somewhat ambiguous," declared one sophomore: "If you
go out with a guy and you pay for your own dinner, you
don't really know whether you're on a date with him or
whether you're just going out as friends. I prefer the guy
to pay on the first or second date because that sets up a
dating relationship." She gave the following example of
what, she hoped, might be the start of a dating relationship:
"Some guys, friends of mine, were going out to the
movies. There was one guy in the group that I was
interested in. I stayed with him all evening and when we
got to the movie theater I stood right next to him. He
looked at me and I looked at him and he said, 'My treat.'
I said, 'Don't be ridiculous, I'll pay for myself.' And he
said, 'No, if you're with me tonight then I'll pay for
you.' "

The Familiar Cues Are Misleading

There are other illustrations of problems that stem from
diversity of norms. A freshman who came from a provincial
high school that combined more permissive sexual norms
with more traditional gender roles describes her confusion:
"I was really shocked by this guy's liberated attitudes
[toward women], it posed real worries for me. I thought
'If he's offering me a joint, why isn't he kissing me?
Doesn't he like me, if he doesn't kiss me, if he doesn't

attack me?' In high school offering a joint was a pick-up line." This student concluded perceptively: "It was a question of getting readjusted to new cues."

CONFLICT WITH TRADITIONAL BOYFRIENDS

A student complained: "My boyfriend is always asking me: 'So what are you going to do with your life after you graduate?' I am telling him that I don't exactly know. I may want to go into the field of psychology. He is constantly pressuring me about this and it annoys me."

Another student credited her boyfriend with striving to make her more independent. He insisted on her clarifying *her* own views instead of placating him with facile agreement. He demanded that she read newspapers, become politically active, and go to antidraft meetings. All this was congruent with her personal agenda of development. Yet, welcome as it was, his influence conflicted with her natural fear of disapproval and her reluctance to "make waves."

It is not surprising that cases in which the boyfriend was the feminist of the couple were rare. Much more prevalent were clashes between more traditional males and their girlfriends' new egalitarianism.

In a number of cases the role conflicts between traditional men and egalitarian women contributed to the termination of the relationship; at other times they were chronic stresses of couples held together by other ties.

In some cases, the clash of role expectations was virtually all-embracing, with the boyfriend wishing to play the stereotypically masculine role in all of its aspects and an increasingly rebellious girlfriend. Other couples illustrate some more limited lack of complementarity in their expectations.

In the first two of the following cases, the relationship began early in high school and ended after the young woman's first year of college, as a result of changes in her attitudes. The stages and the processes of her development are illuminated in the interviews.

"I Refuse to Be an Appendage to a Man"

A college sophomore described several stages in a relationship that began in high school and broke up three and a half years later after the young woman's first year of college. According to her, nearly all through high school, she had had a very sexy and handsome boyfriend, one year her senior. During the first year of college, she began to see him and herself in a new light and to recognize how irreconcilable their mutual expectations had become.

The case illustrates a young woman's increasing striving for equality. Specifically this entailed her growing refusal to subordinate, as a matter of course, her occupational plans to those of her boyfriend; a heightened importance attached to studying and other activities to further her own goals, even when these conflicted with his convenience; and a demand to be taken more seriously in intellectual discussions.

This awakening came gradually in the course of the first year of college:

> He showed not the slightest interest in her aspirations. When she expressed her belief that men and women needed to achieve equality both in mutual commitment, as well as in commitment to careers, J. [the boyfriend] said: "Well, I'll be willing to listen to whatever positive

plan you have." But she recognized his complete indifference to her ambitions. When she tried to work it out with him, he just said, "That's the way things are."

Her frustrations weren't limited to J.'s lack of interest in her life plans. He was, she felt, always trying to get control of their relationship: "When people were asking me questions, he'd cut me off or finish the sentence for me." When she tried to tell him something that interested her in a course, he would remind her that he'd already covered those subjects. Once they went to a conference of a group to which both of them belonged. J. was chairman of a section and he explained to her that it would be inappropriate for her to speak from the floor but he would be willing to convey whatever she had in mind. "He had a very chauvinistic attitude toward women and he made me feel like an appendage to him."

As she ended this relationship, she began to wonder whether she'd ever find a man able to empathize with the woman's need for some autonomy, as well as for tenderness and understanding.

This woman ended her account perceptively. "My sharpened feminist vision led to our breakup." She found herself rebelling against the view that the ideal woman, unlike the man, finds her basic fulfillment in a personal relationship. At her final interview she felt this notion merely provided an ideological rationale for male dominance, because the woman's concessions to the man can then be rationalized as the quid pro quo in the unique rewards she derives from the association. By contrast, the man, because he is also expected to find fulfillment in other roles, expects her to make the necessary adjustments to his interests.

The next case illuminates in greater detail the process of alienation in a relationship with a high-school steady boyfriend. The couple broke up in the middle of the young woman's sophomore year at college. In the interview she traced her change from being "a little girl," who molded herself to fit the boy's traditional ideal of femininity as well as his special emotional needs. In retrospect, she recognized that "in the back of my mind I think I always wanted to do something with my life, I wanted a career." But it was desperately important for her self-esteem to have a steady boyfriend. She must have known that to tell him the truth would have angered him. He would have said: "You don't love me. Why are we going steady? I'll just find someone else who wants to marry me and be a good wife." The case describes the early phase of the relationship as well as the process of change.

> The student recalled her "little girl" role in high school. She asked her boyfriend's advice about everything—her clothes, her makeup, her hairdo. He was thrilled by her dependence: "He would plan our life for us, marriage when we graduated from college, a nice house, and two children. I used to go along and say I could hardly wait. Maybe I really felt that way in high school, but I suspect I needed the security of a steady boyfriend. I was afraid to be without a man."

In the interview this woman traced her change from the "little girl" into a more independent and self-confident woman in the course of which she would no longer tolerate her concealed dissatisfaction and she would see more clearly her boyfriend's shortcomings.

> As both entered college, she an Ivy League school and he a less prestigious institution, new problems emerged. He began to feel that he wasn't as bright as she and felt intimidated and resentful of her intellectual superiority. Whenever she tried to get into an in-depth conversation with him, he would make fun of her by saying, "Well, I know you have brains and you don't have to prove it

to me all the time. Why don't you just talk like a normal human being? Why are you trying to show me how superior you are?" He was also very traditional in his attitudes toward women. When they went out, he would go through all the correct behavior, not out of consideration, but because he thought that's the way men should act. For example, when they went out to a restaurant he would order, often without consulting her about what she wanted to eat. That must have made him feel very suave and sophisticated, but it placed her in the role of the dummy. She reported the following incident: "One time I wanted to hear this concert. D. [the boyfriend] didn't want to go but he went through the motions of asking me what I wanted to do. I repeated that I wanted to go to the concert. He got out the newspaper and found the times and place for a movie he wanted to see and told me that we were going to the movie. I got very annoyed and told him that I didn't want to go out at all and he said that if I didn't want to go to the movie, then we would just stay home. I didn't want to stay home, so we wound up going to the movies. I didn't fight with him very often because he got very defensive."

Another problem with the relationship was that D. tried to interfere with [the student's] work. During finals he would call her up and try and pick a fight with her so she'd be too upset to do well in her finals. She said he called her three or four times during finals week and just found little things to pick fights about. She knew that the fights weren't significant and that it was D.'s way of making sure that she didn't do well on her finals.

The most significant effect of this student's freshman year of college was a growing self-confidence and the realization that she did not have to have a boyfriend in order to be a complete human being. She attributed this change to the independent attitudes of women she met at college. Her two best friends served as living examples that a woman can be happy and enjoy life and self-respect without a steady boyfriend. These young women were sociable but selective, and they did not fall apart if they didn't have a boyfriend for several weeks or months. They wanted to have boyfriends to share a good relationship, but they were not desperate and did not feel humiliated by a lull in their social life.

This student's boyfriend was very upset about the changes in her personality. He kept asking her, "What happened to my little girl? You're not my little girl any more. You don't need me. You don't depend on me." The young woman felt that she was able to end this unsatisfactory relationship precisely because she was not so security-minded and felt she could make it on her own.

Her newly found self-confidence was also reflected upon her return home during the Christmas holiday, when she found herself able to participate in discussions with her relatives in an adult way.

The break with her high-school boyfriend was inevitable, but the pain and anxiety were eased by a new relationship with a male classmate who had all the qualities she missed in her first love. Here are our notes on her account of the new relationship:

A. [the new boyfriend] is very interested in her studies and talks to her about them. He is completely supportive of her desire to have a career. They are able to study together. During finals they were often together studying or just being quiet with one another. A. didn't try and tear her down or make her feel bad while she was taking exams. Rather he would try to comfort her if she was having trouble in one of her classes. [The student] said that A. is very intelligent, and they have in-depth conversations and he helps her to probe into intellectual arguments. She said she's grown a lot more intellectual with A., that she can have an intelligent interchange with him and not feel that he's intimidated by her intelligence. He doesn't want her to act dumb. A. said that would bother him, if she tried to play down her intelligence; he wants her to grow intellectually and he wants them to grow together as well. Their relationship continues to grow and she's very happy with A. She hasn't told A. that she loves him because at this point she doesn't know what love is. She said because her relationship with D. was so destructive, she's very loathe to tell someone else that she loves him until she's absolutely sure that that's the person she wants to spend her life with. She said that A. doesn't pressure her at all to tell him that she loves him, that he's happy with the relationship as it is and that he allows her a certain amount of freedom. Neither of them is seeing anyone else, but she knows that A. wouldn't desert her if she wanted to see someone else. She feels a lot freer and more independent since she broke up with D.

Two relationships of shorter duration were strained and terminated due to similar conflicts with traditional men.

A college freshman set on becoming a doctor met an air force cadet who was "smart and cute and funny" and appeared to be equally attracted to her. She soon realized, however, that he was not at all supportive of her hope to combine marriage with a medical career. He would get very angry when her need to study would occasionally interfere with their social plans, trying to convince her that she was wasting her time on an unrealistic ambition. She, in turn, would be infuriated by his attitude.

She remembered an incident that finally revealed to her the abyss separating them. They were dining with an engaged couple and the girl was talking about how she couldn't wait to get married and have kids and be a mother, and her boyfriend turned and poked her and said, "You hear that?" She just groaned. Her boyfriend just couldn't understand why she didn't feel that way too. That was pretty much the end of the relationship, and soon after that she broke up with him. "That's when I had the feeling, forget it. I can't deal with this."

A conflict over "male chauvinism" broke up another relationship that lasted a year and a half. The woman found much to admire in her boyfriend, such as his honesty and openness. But, with all his understanding, he could not accept her commitment to a career. He felt it was a "slight to his pride." The break came when she discussed the opportunity to study abroad in her junior year. She argued: "Listen, I love you, but I have things in life I want to do, things like an education and a career are important to me. . . . We had a lot of arguments over it and I just got sick of it."

She concluded that men tend to have an old-fashioned picture of women. She would be willing to make some concessions, but she would never marry a man who would want her to give up her career once she had a family.

So far the cases have dealt with male friends and lovers who were so much more traditional than the women in all aspects of their gender attitudes that the relationship eventually dissolved. But similar problems sometimes plagued ongoing affairs. If the relationships endured it was because the conflicts were less extreme, more limited in scope, or offset by compensating ties, if only the fear of loneliness.

Finally, "male chauvinism" was the reason given for terminating association at an early stage of an acquaintance. One student was attracted to a man in one of her classes.

She was soon turned off, however, by his chauvinistic attitude toward women. Talking about his girlfriend, he said: "Well, she's a really cute little piece of fluff." The student "got disgusted and said that he could hardly care about a girlfriend if he thought of her as 'a piece of fluff.'" "Well," he went on, "she's very decorative and also very good in bed." "I couldn't wait until he left," she concluded. "I run into him occasionally, but I no longer feel attracted to him."

Male reactions to the women's struggle for "personhood" are known to us only through the women's testimony. Mutual accusations and defensive countercharges are rife. An interviewed sophomore reported that the suitemates of her boyfriend talk about the women's college "in a very derogatory fashion. They say we are snooty, sophisticated, motivated, driven women who really care more about ourselves than about relationships with men." Her own boyfriend was more understanding, but he too held that these women give men a hard time. Some women were soft and feminine at one time but career-driven at other times, putting down men as oppressors. In his view it was the women's confusion that was the root of the problem.

Intellectual Rivalry Between the Sexes

As discussed earlier, the women perceived the college climate to be excessively competitive. Students allegedly measured their own performance against that of classmates. When self-esteem is based on such comparative ranking, one does not always wish one's rival well. Competition for entrance to professional schools added a pragmatic ground for rivalry.

In the past, competition between the sexes was minimized by stricter differentiation of roles. Women might be superior to men in empathy or other expressive qualities and men might excel in reasoning ability without arousing defensiveness in either sex. They competed for different rewards and measured their worth by different standards. We may assume that competition within each sex was greater than that between the sexes.

No one could expect that the male and female undergraduates of the two colleges could today be free of some degree of intellectual rivalry. The only open question is twofold: First, do men or both sexes still expect that men should enjoy a clear margin of intellectual superiority, so that mere equality is a defeat for men? Second, are women more likely than men to play down their abilities in the face of intellectual differences?

I shall cite some illustrations of survivals of both phenomena, of some expectation that the male should be the one to enjoy a margin of intellectual superiority, if differences exist, and that in sensitive situations women are more likely than men to play down their abilities. These issues were not probed in every interview. Despite the lack of spontaneous references and the occasional illustrations, it seems clear that for the sample as a whole, these were not problems of great urgency.

The sophomores testify:

One student felt that she had gained enough self-confidence over the year to feel freer to argue with the men in her classes. Then she added a qualification: "I would argue less strongly if I were interested in the guy socially. You can't be adamant if you expect to be asked out."

Still another sophomore called her boyfriend feminist in his attitudes but less so in his behavior. He was raised in a traditional home and expects some traditional behavior from women. For example, he expects her not to talk too much when he's talking to his friends and, certainly, to support his views. He becomes upset if she argues against his views in the presence of his male friends.

A freshman was disappointed in lack of intellectual interchange with male undergraduates. She gave an illustration: "Visiting a male acquaintance, she saw a copy of *Ulysses* on his desk, a book she'd just read. She wanted to know what he thought of it but he cut off this conversation by changing the subject."

Whatever the stereotype of sex differences in intellectual abilities, there was, among most women, a strong admiration for those who stood their ground in discussions with men and a disdain for women who "played dumb." A sophomore recollected:

> Last year, there was this one woman on the floor who was terribly competitive with other women about her marks and her intelligence. Then I saw her with her boyfriend and she acted like a twelve-year-old. She kept looking at him in an adoring manner and saying, "Oh, you're so bright! I never would have thought of that." I was infuriated by her playing this game. I would rather see women compete as ferociously as they do at this college than act stupid.
>
> Perhaps, women are not totally at fault. A lot of the college men I met are not all that secure about their intelligence and want a woman who acts less intelligent than they are.

The educational and intellectual differences between one sophomore and the boyfriend she intended to marry presented a major problem:

> The young man went to work in his father's business after finishing high school. They "complement each

other" and are very happy except for this educational difference. She wishes he had a larger vocabulary and spoke more correctly, and they had lots of fights over it. It got to the point where he said: "Either you accept me the way I am or you don't. You'll have to make your decision."

For our purposes the significance of this case lies in the student's final statement: "I still think it would be more acceptable if the wife were not as intelligent as her husband than the other way round. That's probably why I'm so defensive about it."

The Longing for a Sensitive Man

The young women's longing for psychological intimacy with men is evidenced in their depiction of "My Ideal Man" (see chapter 4). "Warm" and "sensitive" were each included as a desired attribute by some 85 percent of the sample who filled out the Adjective Check List. The interviews corroborated this finding because some conflicts in intersexual relationships were precisely over this issue. The typical idiom of youth—for example, "He is into macho" or "He is into sensitivity"—reflects the awareness of the problem. All the same, it is the women who press for sensitivity and the men who are on the defensive.

When the boyfriend of one of the freshman respondents looked over her Adjective Check List for "My Ideal Man," he was incredulous: "But you described a woman, not a man." In the ensuing discussion, she accused him of not listening well and not revealing his own feelings. The boyfriend was indignant: "Well, what you apparently want is a sister, not a man."

Another student described a relationship dating back to the eighth grade when the boy first told her he had a crush on her. At one point throughout the vicissitudes of their long association they even talked about spending their lives together. This relationship was virtually over by the middle of the woman's sophomore year.

> In retrospect, this young woman sees her boyfriend as a good-looking, tough, athletic man, still sexually attractive to her but utterly closed up and uncomfortable communicating his own feelings or listening to her open talk.
>
> Interestingly enough, this student accepted her boyfriend's shortcomings until her freshman year at college. Her two college girlfriends taught her by example what sharing of feelings and perceptions can be like. She became more open about herself, and that was the kind of communication she now wants in relations with men. She recalled an incident that suddenly crystallized her dissatisfaction. She was telling [the boyfriend] about the changes in her personality during the freshman year, explaining how differently she was perceiving things and people, her growing maturity. This, she felt, was a big transformation. Having talked for some time, she turned to him: "Well, what do you think about all this?" And he said, "Think about what?" "He wasn't even listening to what I was saying. He was daydreaming and not making any effort to know me."

Another freshman attributed the breakup of a friendship to the man's lack of sensitivity and understanding.

> In this case the woman explained that she was more involved in the relationship but faulted her boyfriend for his failure to sense the depth of her attachment. In any event, the boyfriend would visit her often and they would have long phone talks about *his* problems.
>
> The break came when *she* called him in a very troubled state because her family was "giving her a hard time." She was telling him about her childhood and her

relation to her family. She had been talking to him for some half an hour (such lengthy exchanges were not unusual for them) when she stopped, realizing that he hadn't responded. "Oh, are you finished?" he asked. "Okay. I have to do my chemistry homework now."

"I felt extremely exposed and hurt," concluded the student. "Whatever his feelings were for me, he should have been more considerate and understanding."

We shall return to this woman in the section on problems in relationships with sensitive but dependent men. Having become wary of emotional involvement as a consequence of this disappointment, she stopped dating altogether until she met a very sensitive man who was willing to wait without pressuring her sexually or emotionally.

Whether or not men can satisfy the women's desire for deeper psychological intimacy, they have become increasingly aware of it. One woman assured us that this awareness has entered the strategy of sexual seduction used by some men:

She described an encounter with a male student during freshman orientation in the course of which he revealed much about himself, including his vulnerabilities and fears. After some four hours of talking she felt that they had a beginning of a good friendship that "might develop into something more." As he walked her to the dormitory, he began to make his pitch. He was looking for someone to sleep with "on a regular basis, not just a one-night stand." He was very persistent and it took some effort to get him to leave.

This young woman, who was sexually experienced, summed up the encounter with this observation: "I think there is a definite trend away from macho men who try to impress the woman by showing that nothing fazes them. I have noticed that now, when they want to seduce you, many men think that they'll score the most points by being open to the point of revealing very personal feelings and even fears."

INTRAPSYCHIC CONFLICTS: EMOTIONAL NEEDS CONFLICT WITH EGALITARIAN IDEALS

The feminine role strains described so far represented two types. The more numerous were interpersonal conflicts between egalitarian women and their more traditional boyfriends. Anomie might be too extreme a designation of the second type, as illustrated in the shifting dating norms. But that mode of strain did stem from the absence of shared norms and the resulting confusion of an actor who had to "play it by ear" in a relatively unstructured encounter.

We turn now to a third mode of role strain, that is, the intrapsychic conflicts in regard to gender. The idiosyncratic aspects of the woman's personality may conflict with her own internalized ideal of femininity. Another variety of intrapsychic conflicts stems from simultaneous allegiance to irreconcilable values, frequently elements both of traditional and of feminist ideologies. These are analytical distinctions that are likely to be fused in any personal experience, though some rare cases approximate one or another of these "ideal types" of intrapsychic strains.

Feminist Women Attracted to Macho Men

Several women confessed an exceptionally strong wish to be "protected" by a man. A problem arose when they were humiliated by the sense of helplessness that such dependence on a man carried. A clash between idiosyncratic emotional needs and internalized ideals was experienced by some women who were sexually and emotionally attracted to macho men "who take charge of things." But such men were not likely to support career ambitions or other egalitarian ideals that were also essential components of the woman's personality.

The following interview offers a fuller description of these strains:

> A sophomore, who broke up with a boyfriend because he wanted a traditional wife, deprecated her preoccupation with studies, and opposed her aspirations to become a physician, described her predicament. "My friends are all guys who are really with it, who understand my ambitions, and yet the guys I find myself attracted to are old-fashioned." She likes guys who "take charge of things," who can be protective and come to her defense if necessary. Once at a party, some guy, drunk, started talking dirty to her. The man she was with hit him and told him to get out: "I like it when guys do that." Her former boyfriend said that if he could find the guy who made an obscene call to her, he's break his neck. She got annoyed at this reversion to primitive macho ways that reduced her to a cave woman status. She'd like him to know that she can take care of herself. At the same time she felt warm and protected to be taken care of in this manner.

This student reported that she resembled her mother in her dependency on male protectiveness. But she certainly would not want to follow in her mother's footsteps in planning her own life. Her mother was a housewife who "was capable of so much more."

A somewhat similar problem was experienced by another student. She needed the security of a steady boyfriend because she had a terror of loneliness. At the same time, it was not easy to find men who shared her intellectual standards and supported her feminist ideals. She explained:

"My experiences with men [in the affiliate college] were extremely disappointing. They treat women abominably." One man with whom she had a serious relationship in her freshman year "allowed her to be herself" for the first few weeks but then began to put her down. Whenever she disagreed with him he'd mock her: "Well, isn't that cute? You have such original ideas." The irony of it was that they were attracted to each other by their ability to analyze ideas. But he began to feel threatened by her and wished she were somewhat less intelligent and a bit softer.

She fell very much in love with another man who gave the impression of being spontaneous and charming. Theirs was a painful affair. It was mostly sexual. He was afraid of emotional commitment. Besides, she eventually realized that he did not respect women. He in effect admitted he thought that women were merely appendages to enhance his image. He said to her that he would have nothing to do with a woman who wasn't good-looking, that women had to enhance his image. The student said that he was very competitive with other men. She told the following story: "I hadn't seen L. [this boyfriend] for about a month. He called on a night when I had a date with someone else. I was still in love with L. so I broke my date to go out with him. I told L. about it. I said, 'I broke a date with somebody else just to go out with you.' L. was very proud about that. I later found out that he told the whole story to the guy I had a date with. I thought that was really disgusting behavior."

In these and other interviews, women confessed to emotional dispositions that ran counter to their ideals either of themselves or of masculinity. As a result, they were humiliated by their own wishes in relation to men or they despised in men the very traits they found attractive. As a rule, the intrapsychic conflicts arose because of an emotional attachment to traditional gender roles in women with liberal or egalitarian ideology.

But intrapsychic conflict did not always involve such a clash between the desired (traditionalism) and the desirable (egalitarianism). Another type is illustrated by the student who internalized a combination of traditional and feminist values that made future problems inevitable. For example, one feminist student's ego ideal contained many elements of traditional masculinity such as professional ambition and a strong drive for achievement and economic affluence. "It's extremely important to me to have done something with my life. When I'm dead I don't want to be forgotten. I wouldn't mind being one of the few women in history books. I'd love it actually." She admired this drive for success and achievement in both men and women. Her boyfriend had it and, she thought, was brighter than she.

Having modified traditional gender roles to the extent of demanding achievement of women, this student remained traditional in exempting men from domestic duties and responsibilities for child rearing. Although she wanted children and fully realized the importance of nurturance for young children, she explained that she could not have any respect for a man who would not also, as she did, want to try to make his mark in the world. She was opposed to the idea of a man staying home to take care of the children: "I think it's a cop-out, I would see him as a failure, as someone who just gave up." This combination of values generated a great number of problems as to the timing of marriage and childbearing in relation to her career and ways of balancing career and child rearing. She and her boyfriend saw these problems intellectually and though the student felt "panicky" sometimes, they "handle the strain by not really facing up to their future problems and sometimes joking about them."

In a period of changing gender roles, it is understandable that both sexes would be inclined to claim the privileges of the traditional and the egalitarian roles, even if this imposes upon their partners a double dose of obligations. The case just described differs in that the young woman's values (rather than practical exigencies) imposed upon her a double dose of obligations. She was "modern" in her drive for personal achievement and "traditional" in her definition of the husband's role.

Problems with a Sensitive but Dependent Man

The student mentioned earlier whose unhappy love for an insensitive man made her wary of any emotional involvement met a man to whom she explained at the outset that he could expect nothing but friendship.

He was considerate, patient, a wonderful listener, and quite open about himself. They began to see each other frequently and he let her take her time without pressuring her sexually or emotionally.

One day she told him that she felt their friendship might develop into something more. In her sophomore year they began an exclusive and steady relationship.

When asked, she expressed some dissatisfaction with this affair. She felt K. [the boyfriend] was way too dependent on her, too focused on the relationship to the exclusion of other possible relationships with male friends. He had no close friends at school. He is very sweet and shy and has a hard time reaching out to some of the more jocklike men at the college. Whenever K. was lonely or wanted to talk, he relied on her for support and for understanding. She felt guilty if she didn't really want to listen to him, to be his confidante when at times she might want to be alone or be with her friends. She felt that K. resented her other friends. He wasn't warm or open or friendly when they were around. He would withdraw and wait until they left and then be very warm and affectionate with her. She wasn't sure whether he was jealous of her other friends or just wanted to spend the time alone with her.

This case illustrates the dissatisfaction of the woman with the price she found she had to pay for the sensitivity and expressiveness of her boyfriend. He was, she felt, something of a deviant among the college men and dependent on her to the exclusion of other ties. His lack of self-sufficiency put great demands on her time and required her to be isolated from her own friends. She felt guilty when she could not be available to him. She began to wonder whether she would ever meet a man who combined sensitivity with a degree of self-sufficiency.

SOCIALLY STRUCTURED SCARCITY OF RESOURCES FOR ROLE FULFILLMENT

The final mode of role strain is pervasive and will be emphasized in the final chapter of the book. It involves anticipated problems in combining career and family life.

This apprehension increased over the four years of college and was particularly acute for career-salient seniors. The timing of marriage, the realization that success in a career requires maximum dedication precisely at the stage of the life cycle that is optimum for childbearing, the absence of good childcare centers, the assumption that industrial time clocks are not to be tampered with—these and other obstacles to the preferred life style were, by the senior year, all too obvious.

It is possible that the title of this secton reflects the author's value judgments. It assumes that the obstacles to fulfilling the role of a career-mother are not intrinsic but are remediable by various social inventions. As it stands now, much in the ethos of the college extols such a goal in the absence of social supports that would facilitate its realization.

One student's anxiety about the future will serve as a prototype of this mode of role strain:

I have a very serious relationship, and it frightens me. Every two months or so I have a crisis and want to break up with him. He just sits back and waits, and within a week I'm back knocking at his door. He just laughs and makes fun of me. We kid around about getting married, but whenever the talk gets too serious, I back off and he shuts up. . . . It's so scary because I want some time on my own. I don't want to give up my career to get married and raise a family right away. But I don't want to lose this man because I love him and would eventually like to get married to him. Five or six years is a long time to wait. I'm not ready to commit myself to him and then wait five years before we get married. That's too much of a strain. . . . I've thought about this a lot. When I do settle down and get married, I'll want kids. And I want to stay home with my kids when they are young, until they are five or six. But most career advances are made between the ages of thirty-five and forty-five. I certainly can't wait until I'm forty-five to have kids. It upsets me to think that I will either have to sacrifice my career or having kids. It's not a fair choice to have to make. It upsets me already. I can't work part-time when I'm thirty-six or thirty-seven, because I'll never get anywhere in my career if I do. I want a family, not just a career. I don't want to grow old without a family around me.

So far this chapter has described various modes of strain in intellectual, emotional, and power relationships with men. Female and male undergraduates interact in various statuses. In the next section, two female athletes analyze a status-set conflict[1] on the athletic field and in their social life.

ATHLETES: A STATUS-SET CONFLICT

The female athletes were swimmers and divers who trained together with men in the same pool and gym.

Long daily training sessions generate a sense of mutual respect. Male athletes are generally superior to women. They can afford, therefore, to watch sympathetically the women's interaction with the coach and applaud their progress and dedication. The intercollegiate meets enhance the sense of solidarity, and each team feels a genuine satisfaction in the success of the others in competition with other colleges.

[1] "Status-set" is the cluster of positions that a person occupies. Thus a female undergraduate is a daughter to her parents, a student to her teachers, a teammate to her athletic team, a female to males, and so on (Merton 1968: 434–438).

Both males and females, not incidentally, train in situations where they can observe and admire each other's bodies.

This account would appear to describe a setting in which cross-sex friendships and romances would develop. This expectation, these students assured us, is belied by some countervailing factors.

The "jocks" are generally traditional males expected to play "macho" roles vis-à-vis women in social contacts. They know exactly how to act in partying with "groupies" (young women, some from other city colleges, who adulate athletes). The men flirt with the "chicks," strut, tease, and try (often successfully) to "make" the female companion of the evening. These familiar partying strategies do not play well in relationships with female athletes from the affiliate college. "Hi, chick" would be too contemptuous and impersonal an approach. The easy male superiority established in athletic activities does not necessarily extend to intellectual abilities, cultivated tastes, and sophistication, which come into play in social relationships away from the gym and the pool. Female athletes, unlike male athletes, may, if anything, be less stereotypically traditional and more competitive than the average female student. The women themselves are confused, being attracted by the physical attributes of the men and, at the same time, repulsed by the macho attitudes they evidenced on social occasions.

This was the explanation, offered by some interviewed female athletes, of the difficulty of establishing social relationships with men whom they see daily in long training sessions. Men and women can be classmates, coworkers, club members, and also form mutual romantic relationships, provided they can play roles appropriate to each social context. But this flexible shifting of roles was excluded in the athletes' case because the roles linked to the different statuses were not only distinctive but contradictory. The colleagueship on the team contrasted so sharply with the somewhat contemptuous and exploitative attitudes toward the partying "chicks" that a strict separation between the two sets of role partners offered the easiest way out. Though this appears to bear some resemblance to the familiar division between "good" and "bad" girls, the analogy breaks down because the "good" girls, the women athletes, may have a permissive sexual code in relationships with other men.

This analysis of the status-set conflicts with the "jocks" came from several women athletes. A somewhat different picture was presented by a freshman nonathlete who did socialize with college male athletes. But the "defense" in the following excerpt from her diary indirectly supports the existence of the stereotype and, beyond this, some residual ambivalence of her own.

Many is the time I have to defend myself for having "jocks" as friends. People say they are dumb, troublemakers, and too "macho." But they are basically nice guys. In fact, they are often preferable to female friends. I don't have to compete with them; I get along well with them, and they are very dependable. I don't understand why they have such a bad reputation. Prejudice against a race of people is considered bad, stereotyping is considered unjust, and yet this is, in essence, what people do to "jocks." (I'm doing it now just by calling them that.) People should try to treat them as individuals, because they would be amazed at what they would find on an individual basis. Very often it is a sensitive and kind young man, looking for an identity, and finding security in a bunch of guys similar to him.

Having defended having football players as friends, the diary continues:

> This morning my girlfriend called me to inform me of what happened last night after I left a party at the [male] dorm. She left with a certain guy at the party. As it turned out, he wanted a little more out of their encounter than she did. She told him that she was just fooling around and wasn't into any big physical experiences. He became annoyed and said he couldn't understand what was wrong with women here. "Why can't women deal with adult situations?" My girlfriend got very angry, and they didn't part on very good terms.
>
> We talked for a while about how sick and tired we were of the guys' attitudes here. We both ran into situations like this many times. We agreed that we didn't think it was right for us to be put upon this way. Later, as always, I tried to see things from the guys' point of view. I wonder how they feel trying time and time again only to be turned down. I'm sure it's very frustrating for them.

The cases just cited were chosen to exemplify analytically distinctive modes of role strain. In reality, individuals are likely to experience more than one of these modes, as the following case will illustrate. A senior, the daughter of Latin-American parents, went to a parochial school. She credited her new feminist consciousness to the impact of the college. It was only during college that she realized how unsatisfactory was her parents' traditional marriage. Her mother was totally dependent on her father: "He dishes out the money to her, demands his dinner, and generally puts her down. He makes her feel worthless. She is a nobody." As for herself, she was clear on one point:

"I couldn't live without working. I regard part-time work as a cop-out. When you work part-time, you have a job, not a career. When you take time off, you sacrifice too much of your career. I would feel cheated if I got married in my twenties. I would like to marry at thirty and have children in my mid-thirties. My college friends, whose values I share, have no plans for an early marriage. But my mother mentioned recently a couple of times, 'I can't wait until you get married.' All of a sudden, you feel like the odd man out. There is this tension that I feel."

She has been in a relationship for two years. Both of her parents would like to see them married. Her boyfriend is attending a professional school and they see each other twice a week.

He does not want marriage at this time in his life. She admits her ambivalence: "It's funny. If he wanted to get married now I would get all flipped out. But I do feel somewhat rejected when he says: 'If you're looking for marriage, don't look at me.' Intellectually and realistically I don't want to get married now, but there is this gut feeling that I can't ignore. We had a serious argument and we broke up for a month. The argument was about dating other people. We had agreed that we were free to do so, but I never did and I don't think he dated. But then one day he reminded me of this agreement and I just flipped out: 'No, you can't see anybody else.' Then I decided to date others to see if I could be attractive to other guys and to make him jealous. Whether he realizes it or not, he became much more attentive. He calls me every night now and I can tell he is concerned: 'What have I done? I could lose her.' So there is this constant tension back and forth."

She wondered whether it was possible to live up to her ideal of "being oneself," that is, being independent, and at the same time be really close to her boyfriend: "I mean, if you start calling someone every night, can you do it without becoming dependent?" She noticed that when she was feeling good about herself, she could do anything without worrying about being dependent. She and her boyfriend have discussed their occupational plans, about which both are uncertain. She was equally uncertain about the future of this relationship.

The interview with this senior demonstrates a variety of modes of strain. Cross-pressures from her traditional Latin-American family and the college was one of them. Equally conflict-ridden was her relationship with her boyfriend. His opposition to an early marriage would appear to fit her own preference not to sacrifice her strong career ambition to family life. But, at the same time, she was troubled by an intrapsychic conflict. Their ostensibly similar objection to marriage in the near future could not allay her fear of losing the man she loved.

SOME ADJUSTED COUPLES

Were we to stop with the foregoing description of role strains in female-male relationships, the portrayal would distort reality. Some couples were adjusted and happy. The theoretical problem of this section is to discover factors that have prevented the typical strains from arising or that minimized their severity. The cases to be analyzed do not include the traditional women. This exclusion says nothing about the relative adjustment of traditional women as against their career-salient classmates. But the focus of this chapter is on strains linked to transitional gender roles; whatever problems the traditional women experienced in relationships with men were more likely to stem from other sources.

The first case to be analyzed is instructive because, as a sophomore, this student saw her future as a series of irreconcilable dilemmas. By the end of the senior year, she was engaged and planning to get married soon after graduation from college. C. was an upwardly mobile daughter of a Jewish skilled worker and a homemaker-mother. In her sophomore interview she spoke of her family and her own plans:

> My family pushed me to be a professional. My mother got married at eighteen and had two babies before she was twenty. She would have a fit if I got married before I had established myself in a career. Ever since I was little, I can remember my mother telling me: "If you get engaged before you make something of yourself, I'll have your head." It's extremely important to me to make some mark in the world.

C. was something of a tomboy as a youngster, good with machinery and a good athlete. She entered college intending to prepare for a profession, one attraction of which was that it would enable her to be a pioneer in a traditionally male field.

It soon became apparent that she was neither interested nor good in the required courses for mathematics. Her determination to pursue a career had not weakened, but she realized that both her strengths and her interests were in working with people. Thus she began to explore other kinds of programs and graduate schools.

From the standpoint of social life, the freshman year was an awakening. Although a tomboyish misfit among her affluent, clothes-conscious high-school classmates, C. discovered more congenial intellectual classmates upon arrival at college. Above all, she was gregarious enough to initiate conversations with males in classes and on campus and discovered that she could be very popular with men: "I could have a date every night." This was so exhilarating a development that, as she put it, "I had a smile on my face all the time."

In her sophomore year, she and a graduate student fell in love. Her turmoil during that time was described in her own words (see p. 254): "Every two months or so I have a crisis and want to break up with him. He just sits back and waits and I'm back knocking at his door."

C. credited the college with strengthening her determination to achieve academic excellence:

> You are surrounded by bright women. Women who are working hard to do their very best. You sit in classes with all women and you come to respect their abilities and pit yourself against real bright people. You suddenly find yourself respecting women more. I'm glad I came to a women's college. You see things here that you wouldn't see at another school.

All in all, the college developed in C. a new kind of feeling of self-worth. As for the women's movement, C. became a little more sympathetic to it but she did not see the need for "yelling and screaming." She was not a feminist. "I am not angry. I have personally never encountered discrimination."

In the spring of 1983 she and her boyfriend decided to get married after her graduation from college, a decision their families would have to accept.

What happened to the crises of C.'s sophomore year, when an early marriage and a career appeared irreconcilable? One somewhat fortuitous circumstance precipitated a decision to get married and provided one way out of her dilemma. Her boyfriend accepted a well-paying job for one year in a foreign country—a country C. knew and loved. Working hours in the country are eight to two, the pace is slower than in the United States, and C. was already promised an interesting volunteer job. After the year abroad, C.'s husband would work and support her through graduate school, after which she too would begin her professional life.

C.'s confidence in the happy outcome of their plans is based on other factors. To begin with, her fiancé has, for her, a congenial combination of values. He is both ambitious for himself and fully respectful of her own professional aspirations. In this sense he is a new, egalitarian partner. But, as the interviewer concluded, another fact worked to allay C.'s misgivings about an early marriage. C. apparently felt strong enough in the relationship to expect that she could change her fiancé's residual traditional habits to accommodate her career requirements. Two illustrations point to that conclusion. Because he was a superior student, at first he did not understand C.'s need to study so hard. She was strong enough to make him accept her time schedule, even when it conflicted with his leisure plans for them. The other testimonial to her assertiveness is described in this excerpt from the interview: "He spends a lot of time in my room and leaves an awful mess. I find it mindboggling that at his home he had never wiped dishes or vacuumed. I hit the roof and explained to him what I expect."

The adjustment of this couple may be attributed to this man's admiring acceptance of C.'s professional plans. To that extent, he has incorporated new, egalitarian values. But C.'s sense of power in this relationship helped to instill confidence that he will be amenable to other reasonable concessions to her preferred life style.

By comparison with C., the next case illustrates an

adjusted relationship with a man by a much more politicized feminist. N. is a daughter of second-generation Catholic parents who are proud to have their daughter attend an Ivy League college. Her mother went to a vocational school and had no special professional aspirations for her daughter: "She simply wants me to be happy and hasn't the vaguest notion what college is like." Her father wanted her to take something practical, like accounting. N. herself wanted to be a professional writer and could not give up this hope even as she worried about the financial insecurity of such a choice.

N.'s feminist activism dates back to high school. Though she was in a group that ran school activities, she was not in the "rah-rah" set who "weren't aware of what was happening in the world and just wanted to party." Being excluded from that set, she felt something of an outsider.

In her senior interview she remained career steadfast, but, in contrast to the 1979 attitude, she felt that there *was* a chance of her being married in five years. Her conflicts about marriage, family, and career are described in her senior interview:

"I have a lot of political ideas about marriage and I could go through a whole three-hour discussion about why it's incorrect to be married, but I really want to be married or at least to live with the man I'm seeing now. It would be wonderful to have kids and live with this man and not be married, not go through all the traditional things, but I don't know if it can work. Everyone always says they got married for the kids, but I'm not sure you do have to get married for the kids—maybe you do." Although she's somewhat indecisive about the marriage issue, she does want to be living with someone in the next five years. "It goes back to my career and sacrifices I'll have to make. I'd love to have a job (freelance) where it wouldn't matter if I had kids, where

my home is my office. I don't at all feel that the
responsibility is the woman's when you have kids—and
I'd love to see changes, but I'm not sure how to change.
. . ." She doesn't foresee having children until she's in
her early thirties, and imagines working until then and
stopping. Although she cannot see herself doing childcare
full time, she has a gut feeling that she doesn't want
someone to take care of her kids for money—she would
ask her mother to help out. She and her boyfriend have
talked about this problem, but the solutions seem so
difficult that they have not come up with any answers.
"Ideally he would have a job with a flexible schedule
and we would both share childcare. . . . It's probably
not so open-minded to be a feminist pushing for day-
care centers and then want your mother to take care of
your kids."

This student was fully aware of how contradictory some
of her statements might sound, and pointed out what she
herself felt was "feminist heresy."

The happy relationship she enjoyed with her boyfriend
came after sifting out men who were not supportive of
her values. In her freshman and sophomore years, a
troublesome time for her because she was having serious
problems adjusting to college, she had an affair with a man
who felt so threatened by her being at an Ivy League
college that he kept sabotaging her by insisting that she
did not belong and should transfer to a public college.
When her life at college started to come together (her
very high grade-point average was but one sign of the
change), their relationship fell apart.

In contrast, this is how she described her current boyfriend:

"He's good-looking, and sure of himself without being
arrogant. He's giving and intelligent and understands

male/female stuff, which he talks about in concrete ways, not theoretically. There's a lot of give and take in the relationship." She claimed that there were no real conflict areas: "He feels so comfortable with himself that I don't feel responsible for his personality. He's just a separate person, and I've learned that you don't go into a relationship wanting to reform someone, so this just feels really good." She still has some difficulties imagining being out of school and having to make "permanent" decisions. "I want to live with him, but if a wonderful job came along somewhere else, I don't know what I'd do—he doesn't like to talk about it, but he knows it's a possibility that I might work outside of the city. I'd want to live with him, but if getting a job on a newspaper in the city is impossible and getting a job elsewhere would really help my portfolio, I have faith that he'd be here when I came back. I have to figure that out by June, and if nothing stunning presents itself by then I'll stay in the city for the next couple of years."

Although both of them would like kids, they still feel that this is a somewhat vague issue right now—they talk a lot about ideal relationships and, if it were feasible, they would definitely share childcare equally.

Whatever the residual uncertainties, N. is committed to a relationship that appears supportive and adult, with a man who understands and shares her feminist values and is apparently neither threatened by them nor overdependent upon her strengths.

What distinguishes the next case of A. is the fact that she was one of the most motivated and career-oriented students in the interviewed sample. By the beginning of her junior year, she had, after a purposeful and thoughtful exploration of the field and her own interests and abilities, decided on graduate training for a lifelong uninterrupted career in medical research. Her family had no direct influence on her occupational choice. Her parents were divorced and her relationship with both her mother and her father remained strained. "You aim too high" was her mother's warning.

At entrance to college, A. thought that she might never get married or want to have children. Her parents' unhappy marriage, she thought, must have turned her against the traditional feminine life.

What changed her attitudes toward both marriage and a family of her own so drastically?

In her junior year she met her boyfriend. The relationship got off to a good start when the two realized that they shared intellectual interests. They could and did discuss everything and were equally interested in each other's views and development. They started living together and intended to be married.

She felt that they were totally comfortable with each other, and neither intimidated or threatened the other. She found him attractive and his intelligence was an important element in this. In her own words:

> Any person with whom I feel close would have to be at least as intelligent or more intelligent than I, and I think he's more so. I'm very challenged by him and he can really argue me back at times. At the same time, he doesn't ever act superior and never puts me down. He thinks I'm more intelligent than he is, but he knows more science than I—here I should know all that stuff and he almost knows it better. Our interests are mutual, and the fact that we don't compete seems like the best part of our relationship.

Her boyfriend's mother is an M.D. and a remarkable woman—friendly, loving, and supportive of A.'s ambitions.

Her own son, A.'s boyfriend, was brought up by a "nanny" of whom he has fond memories. He has a good relationship with his mother and, consequently, the career-wife-and-mother combination is both familiar and unthreatening to him.

A. felt they had both become more mature during the course of their relationship. Their grades went up. The household tasks were shared naturally, depending on who had more work at a given time. They went through periods when he was more domestic, but everything always balanced out. Her boyfriend loves children and has changed her attitudes toward them by always pointing them out on the street and talking about them. Childcare would depend on when they had children. For A. it will be hard to have children until her internship and residency are over. But she knows that she will never be able to take a year or two off, so either her boyfriend would have to care for the children or, if they earn enough money, which they should because of her salary, then they would hire someone. "If I didn't feel that both things could be done, well, I would sacrifice having children," A. said, but her boyfriend's mother's example gives her hope. She has a fine medical career and has also done a good job with her children. "If my life could work out like hers, it would be terrific."

This case illustrates that some of the young men the career-salient women encounter are offspring of "new" egalitarian marriages. If their parents' marriages were successful and their relationships with their parents satisfactory, these youths are ready to reproduce this model in their own relationships with potential mates. The general feeling of the career-salient seniors was that these "new" men, both self-respecting and giving, are all too scarce.

9

Sexual Relationships

SOCIAL CHANGES that produced the ambiguous psychological relationships described in the last chapter also had consequences for social norms and behavior in the sexual sphere. In this regard, our most extensive data were collected through the sophomore interviews. The topic of sex was approached indirectly, in the discussion of the ethos of the college. The students were asked whether they believed the college could be characterized by some dominant values in several specified realms. This general question was followed by probing further, for example: "Who, in your opinion, would be more on the defensive on this campus, a student who looked forward to full-time homemaking (circumstances permitting) or a career-oriented woman?" On this issue, as was indicated in preceding chapters, the overwhelming majority perceived the homemaker to be more on the defensive because the climate of opinion favored, indeed demanded, achievement outside the home. In other realms, a frequent response was that the college stood for tolerance of diversity, with each individual free to live by her own values.

As for sex, the interviewer raised a similar question: "Who, in your opinion, is more on the defensive in this college—a virgin or sexually experienced student?" A frequent initial response to this question stressed the tolerance of diversity of sexual norms: "Sex is a personal decision. Even in suites people don't tell you to lead a particular life style. It is the attitude of 'live and let live.' No one is ostracized." This tolerance appeared in itself to be an ideal value. Further probing revealed a good deal about the dominant ethic, the limits of tolerance, and considerable variations within the college community.

DOMINANT SEXUAL NORMS

What emerged as the dominant sexual ethic was captured in the following remark of a student:

> It is generally assumed that women at this college will have some sexual experience in their four years of college. Ideally, what is desired is a relationship based on friendship and love, though not necessarily involving a commitment to marriage. One-night stands and sleeping around are disapproved as are the sleazy teasers who are out to collect men.

Concerning virginity, another student voiced a not uncommon view:

> I heard women, mostly very religious Jews and Catholics, say that they intended to remain virgins until they're married. Most people won't jump on someone whose reasons are religious. But if a woman expressed just a moral compunction, then other women will most likely

argue and attempt to convince her that sexual relations with a boyfriend are not immoral.

Another student, herself a virgin, indirectly confirmed these dominant values: "Students on my floor are quite open about sex, especially those who have had one or two affairs. Virgins don't talk about being virgins in a group, nor do women who are promiscuous." The prevailing censure of "sleeping around" was evident in the reported gossip about "sluts" and also in the anxiety about their reputation expressed by some women who in fact engaged in "casual" sex.

These were the prevailing sexual norms, but variations within the college community were wide. For some, the religious or moral prohibition of premarital sex was so deeply internalized that no conflict as to behavior arose. Contrast such a position with the attitudes expressed in the following excerpts from interviews:

Someone who was a virgin would definitely be on the defensive. You would never want to admit it, you'd be in a really bad social situation if you did. But sex somehow is not as important here as it was in high school. Sure, everyone talks about it, it's nice, but it's casual. When you have sex with a guy, it's just not that weighty, it doesn't mean that you're indebted to see him for the next four years. But you have to have a certain amount of sex in order to have a good social and self-image. Too much sex, on the other hand, is bad, because then people look at you as just being after sex, and perhaps you could be called a "sex object." There is such a thing as too much. It's a nice, casual attitude, though. They don't brag about it, as in high school, it's just part of life. It's a normal thing.

And, again:

Girls who don't believe in premarital sex have it somewhat rough on this campus because most girls have had
or plan to have sexual experiences so that the virgins
are the odd ones out. By and large, having a boyfriend
bestows prestige. When you are sleeping with someone,
it does give you a slight edge. You are somehow
considered a little tougher, a little better.

The variation of sexual norms confronted the individual
with moral choices. Those fully integrated into a group of
like-minded friends enjoyed the security of such a consensus.
But this did not solve the problems for the majority. For
one thing, most students had some friends outside their
own "crowds" who may have espoused different values.
Furthermore, few could be so insulated as not to be aware
of the variety of moral options. For some, this confusion
created a tormenting problem of choice. Even the degree
of sanctioned communication about sex varied enough to
generate stress.

At one extreme were only a few students who claimed
that they had never heard anyone voice an opinion for or
against premarital sex. One of these, a resident student,
"wouldn't think of discussing this even with my girlfriend.
So private a matter shouldn't be discussed by anyone but
the couple involved." The topic of sex had been completely
taboo in her family and apparently remained so for her in
college. In view of the reports of dorm discussions, this
student may have expressed her ideal of reserve and some
denial of reality. At the other extreme were experienced
women who, as one unsympathetic roommate put it,
discussed their own affairs and the performance of their
lovers in such "graphic detail" as to make her feel uncomfortable. The majority fell between the two poles. "How
open you are about your sexual activities depends on what
group you are in," observed one student, perceiving accu-

rately the variations in norms of self-disclosure about sex.

Given the desire for peer approval, each student had to test the operative norms of her new associates at college. Even this caution, occasionally, generated guilt: "Did I keep quiet about myself because I am ashamed of my behavior?," reflected one student. "What surprised me about my freshman roommate," recollected a sophomore, "was her blunt questions about sex life. She was a virgin and so were all of us in the suite. But she wanted to know where everyone stood on this issue. I was shocked because I would never ask such a question, nor would anyone in my high school."

"Generally people are open," remarked one sexually experienced sophomore, "but there's a lot of discretion too. For example, if I'm just starting a relationship, I won't talk about it until it's developed. On the other hand, if someone has the guts to ask me right away how it's going, I'll be gutsy in my response and tell them right off the bat."

Several students testified to a sense of liberation and general growth upon the discovery that sex was not a tabooed topic in college: "It was a good experience for me to be able to talk to someone frankly about sexuality because this topic was never broached in my home."

The uncertainty concerning acceptable limits of self-disclosure was, of course, much less of a problem than issues of actual sexual behavior. On this score the study's estimates are that 51 percent of the interviewed sophomores were virgins and 40 percent had had one or more lovers. The remaining 9 percent of the interviews did not contain conclusive information.

MALE PRESSURE FOR "CASUAL SEX"

This pressure was a frequently expressed grievance of the students interviewed in the fall of 1980. It was deemed one of the major barriers to social life with male students of the affiliate college. One freshman was confronted with this problem on her second day in school. She described the still-vivid memory:

> A guy came over to me during freshman orientation and we clicked at once. I fell for him and we spent three days and evenings together. Beginning with the second day, he started to pressure me to hop into bed. I tried to explain that I was a virgin and that this was too soon. "I understand," he'd say, "but you are seventeen years old, you can't be a virgin all your life, it's time to grow up." After four days he dropped me. Just like that. I cried for several days. He said how much he cared for me, that he loved me and I believed him. I guess he was on a big ego trip.

In a more lighthearted vein, another student recounted an incident from the freshman orientation week. She met a freshman entering the affiliate college.

> He was kind of rumpled, cute, innocent-looking, and very friendly. He was fun to be with until he made it known that his agenda for the first month of college was "to get himself a woman," a sexual partner and one, he hinted at it a lot, who would do his laundry and bake cookies for him. . . . I hate cookies, and I told him that he is really barking up the wrong tree with that one.

This friendship was short-lived.

Another student was more critical:

Social life with the guys is pitiful. The guys are basically interested in just one thing—sex, unless they are "nerds" and "jerks" who just study and are altogether incapable of socializing. As far as I'm concerned, the guys who are just out to sleep with the woman can go to the moon.

A similar grievance was expressed by another student:

Some girls go to the two pubs on the campus to meet men, but those are just "meat markets." The pubs attract guys who are into drinking and into the macho image and who are out for one thing—sex. If they walk you home, they think they've done you such a favor that you can't get rid of them.

Here is an account of a student's first evening with a male undergraduate whom she met at the campus pub:

After some dancing, he told her that he wanted her to go back to his room with him and meet his roommate, but as soon as he got there the roommate left. Then he turned on the music and started dancing and trying to get her into bed. She told him that she was a prude, that a kiss on the first date was about all that she was used to. She confessed she was exaggerating a bit in order to stop him. But "he couldn't believe that his charm was not enough for me to go lie on the floor for him. He was telling me that I'm nineteen years old and it's time I did something about it." She stopped seeing him soon thereafter.

The greater sexual permissiveness in recent years presents a new problem to young men whose seduction strategems have failed. They cannot, as easily as in the past, explain their failure by the norm of chastity but are apt to experience some sense of inadequacy or rejection. A salve to hurt egos is chiding women about their alleged sexual hangups or lesbianism. These were tactics of a good many frustrated young men.

One interviewed sophomore shared the feeling of her female classmates that the college males were under greater pressure to lose their virginity than were women. Although she had had sexual intercourse, she would not tolerate being pressured by a man because of his own ego needs. She abruptly ended her contacts with an "obnoxious" college man who wanted her to jump into bed on their second date. Some men have the reputation of being "one-nighters." She was invited to go out by one "jock" and was about to accept when she was warned by two girlfriends that he was interested in one-night stands and that he'd never call her again. She refused his invitation.

The male pressure for sex on the first encounter or soon thereafter would not be so pervasive did it not occasionally succeed. But despite the increase in sexual permissiveness, the interviewed women were still more likely than male undergraduates to reject casual sex and, upon their own testimony, were more eager for friendship with men, either as an end in itself or as a condition for eventual physical intimacy. Several sophomores observed ruefully that it was only after they acquired a "steady" and were recognized as part of a couple that they also succeeded in having close male friends who accepted the limits "just friendship" imposed.

Some interviewed women felt that the male pseudo-sophisticated stance—"I am out to experience life"—was a cover for using women:

On the whole, my impression of the college men is

very poor. Their philosophy of life as a series of experiences masks a self-centered, self-involved use of others to further their own ends. Perhaps they are still immature. But I believe that women in general are readier to give something of themselves in a relationship even as they try to receive something in return. I know this is true of me.

The male pressure for casual sex created an obstacle to social relationships even when it was not limited to the first or second encounters. One sophomore had dated a man who had "all the qualities I looked for" for about three months. He was the one to terminate the relationship, and she felt hurt and rejected. She explains:

> Part of the problem was sex. I liked him, but I wanted to know something more about him before I had sex with him. Someone tells me I'm living in the Victorian era when it comes to sex, but I feel there has to be something more established in a relationship before I have sex with a guy. If you just jump into bed, someone will get the shitty end of things, and it probably will be me.
> But this guy, for his part, probably would have been happier if I had slept with him right away, but I refused.

At the time of the interview she had not succumbed to this pressure, but she added: "After you've been rejected by enough guys because you won't sleep with them, you may decide that this is what you'll have to do in order to establish a relationship with them."

The final instance of grievance against male sexual pressure characterized a more lasting relationship. One freshman fell deeply in love with a male classmate, and they saw each other frequently for several months. She describes her painful disappointment:

Our relationship was mainly sexual because *he* wanted it that way. I was afraid to talk to him about my feelings because I felt he didn't want any emotional commitment. He treated me well only when he wanted me sexually. If things had been going badly for several weeks, he would take me out to a nice restaurant, pay for me, and treat me like a lady. Then he expected that when we went home we would go to bed together. I was very sexually attracted to him and didn't fight his sexual pressure.

Over the summer the student talked at length with her mother about this relationship:

My mother knew how much I invested in this relationship, but she explained that sometimes we just have to give up on people we're in love with because they're not very good people. I thought about it and took my mother's advice.

When I returned to college in the fall, I was angry at him but no longer felt any attraction. Later in the year the anger dissipated and I felt glad that I was able to end this relationship.

The repeated grievances that male insistence on sexual relations frustrates the longing for friendship require two qualifications. A few freshmen, whose high schools were characterized by sexual permissiveness, traditional male dominance, and lower intellectual and cultural standards, faced a different problem of adjustment to the college. One such student described her surprising discoveries:

The college men treat women as equals. They are really pretty liberated. In my high school, a one-to-one relationship implied sex and the guys sort of dominated. At college here, it's more of a dating scene, you're not obliged to have sex, it's more equal. Here, if a guy calls, I can honestly say I have to study and give him a rain check. In high school, if you give a guy a rain check, that's it, he won't see you any more.

During the first semester of college she met a young man in a class. They would sit on the building steps, smoke pot, and talk. But he was more into school activities, more liberated: "I wasn't ready for such friendship with a guy in my freshman year. If I had met him this year, we would have had more in common."

There was another and a more significant exception to the grievances of the majority that their longing for male friendship was unfulfilled. Members of some religious cliques, both female and male, upheld the ideal of premarital chastity and enjoyed a lively social life from the outset. One religious Jewish freshman described her close clique as consisting of four young women and five young men who ate together and participated in joint weekend activities. She "felt very comfortable with the guys, they were very good friends." In fact, she and another young woman went on a ski trip with four male friends, with full approval of her parents. If romantic relationships developed under such circumstances, she explained, a couple may "make out," but both sexes believed that "intercourse should be between married people." Whatever changes these religious students may undergo in college, their stricter moral code, somewhat paradoxically, contributed to an exceptionally active companionship with male classmates during the first year of college.

FEMALE PRESSURE TO BECOME SEXUALLY EXPERIENCED

Some students felt that the general cultural climate exerted a considerable pressure upon college women to lose their virginity, and in fact there were several indirect indications that such pressures did exist. These consisted of reports of bragging—that is, women claiming more experience than in reality they had—the speculations about sexual hangups of virgins, and the attitudes expressed by some students about their first sexual encounters. "I know," remarked one student, "that some girls in my dorm pretend to have had more sexual experiences than they had. I know for a fact that some are bragging." "In my crowd," said a sexually experienced sophomore, "if a girl is a virgin, one almost wonders why."

Other students also expressed the view that virginity is a problematic status to be accounted for. A sophomore who confessed that her own sexual encounters were disappointing, both physically and emotionally, commented on virginity: "The virgins I have known are afraid of men; they are holding on to their virginity as a cloak to keep them from having relationships with men." As for herself, she was happy that she lost her virginity even if her affairs fell below her expectations. She came to feel "more expanded, able to express my sexuality, not in a blatant way, but in subtle ways through my clothing, my walk, in the way I interact with people." She claimed that she could always tell which classmate was a virgin because "virgins are closed, girlish, and they don't express their sexuality."

These remarks by a relatively small number of interviewees reveal the readiness to attribute sexual hangups to virginity, almost in the manner in which rejected male seducers have been known to seek to account for their failures.

There is other indirect evidence of the prestige attached to sexual experience. A few freshmen, who first had intercourse very soon upon initial encounters with men and who found the experience unsatisfactory both physically and emotionally, expressed relatively little guilt or regret. The following excerpts from interviews suggest that in some cases the prestige attached to this initiation into adulthood offset the admitted disappointment and emotional hurt.

"In high school I had never had a boyfriend," said a student who met a male freshman during freshman orientation. They spent the three days together: "It was lots of fun. I really thought he liked me, that maybe he would be into having a relationship. We played Frisbee, we went to cocktail parties. We talked an awful lot. We went to a party in his room. At first he just kissed me and I wouldn't let him do anything more. I was inexperienced and very shy. He didn't force me but eventually we did have sex. But after that he was very casual. He just seemed to forget about the whole thing, and I would see him with other girls. It was very disappointing." This student may have concealed the depth of her disappointment when she added that she didn't regret her experience but explained in her own words: "I said to myself: 'Wow, now I understand what a one-night stand is. Now I know what it all means.'"

Another student reminisced:

When I first came here, I was ready for sexual experiences. I developed several relationships at the same time. It was horrible. I felt torn apart. When I met J. [her current boyfriend], I realized that it was important to me to give my love to just one person. I now know that I am happy only in a monogamous relationship, sexually and emotionally." "Horrible" as she felt her previous chaotic affairs to be, they helped her, she informed the interviewer, to acquire a deeper understanding of her own personality and to "get those desires out of my system."

As seen in the preceding cases, for some virgins the prestige attached to initiation into sexual intercourse served to allay the disappointment with the experience. This was not, of course, the reaction of all such students. Bitterness toward her sexual partners was described by a sophomore:

> I used to feel pressured to give in to sexual demands and that made me dislike men. They never wanted to experience me as a person and that used to make me real angry. All they wanted to do was to go to bed. Even if I wanted to sleep with them too, I always felt that I was rushed into it and there was always a core of resentment afterward. I'm still angry but it has diminished because I know now that I don't have to put up with that kind of pressure.

VIRGINITY: ADJUSTMENT AND CONFLICT

As noted earlier, there were some virgins whose strong religious and moral convictions called for premarital chastity. Those who belonged to organized groups with males who shared the same values frequently enjoyed cross-sex friendships in which sexual intercourse was not an issue.

But there were some others who, without these organizational ties, also enjoyed an active social life.

> A Catholic student described her close girlfriends as sharing her own intention not to have sex outside of marriage. These were exceptionally attractive women, popular with a group of athletes on the male campus who divided women into those "they would get serious with and others whom they see for sex." She and her friends tease the guys; if they see one of them at a party, they'll ask the next day: "Did you get lucky [meaning, did you get her into bed?]?" These guys all boast about their conquests. Yes, sex was quite a big topic of conversation among women. If anyone would ask her directly whether she was a virgin, she would tell; in fact, she did just that on one occasion without any feeling of defensiveness. A freshman roommate, who was her good friend, lost her virginity and now sleeps around. They became estranged.

The attractiveness of these conservative women combined with their selective association with men who also adhered to the traditional "double standard" seemed to account for their adjustment.

In one case the student's adherence to the norm of premarital chastity was not directly linked to religious affiliations, and she maintained her standards without the support of a subculture. Her boyfriend, she explained, "did not put any sexual pressure on me. We pet and are very passionate with one another, but we do not go all the way." She was not troubled about sexuality, she pointed out, because she has made her decision and her boyfriend respected it. Sex might become an issue were she to date several men, but she was satisfied with her life and had no desire for a wider range of dating partners.

These women did not appear to be in conflict about

their virginity because of their moral defenses and their selective association with others who shared their values. Another type of adjusted virgin is represented by a student whose self-esteem was so enhanced by other developments during the first year of college as to diminish the importance of sexual experience. These compensating interests and rewards derive from various sources: academic achievement, involvement in social causes, various extracurricular activities, a sense of personal development. In one case, an unhappy relationship with her boyfriend, paradoxically, contributed to a student's sense of growth.

> This girl had a high-school boyfriend who went to a different college. All through their relationship she was dependent on him and allowed herself to be at his beck and call. She wrote to him four or five letters a week and lived for vacations when they could see one another. But he "dumped her," telling her about a new girl he had at college. "I was hysterical for weeks, I lost weight. Then I started going out with one of his best friends, and this upset him a lot and he told me he wished he had never broken up with me."
>
> Gradually, she began to have an active social life with female and male classmates and felt an immense sense of liberation and pride. When the interviewer commented on her relief, she responded: "Oh, yeah, I feel great and I am happy with school this year. I even broke up with someone I was going with at the beginning of my sophomore year. Everyone's always broken up with me and now I actually decided that it wasn't a good relationship for me, so I left the person and I'm going out with someone else now. It is really nice."

This student felt that she was somewhat ambivalent about her virginity but her newly acquired sense of personal independence and self-esteem, her active social life, and an interest in the Equal Rights Amendment put the issue of sex temporarily into the background.

The virgins whose views have just been reported appeared relatively free of conflict. Some attained this serenity at the price of a high degree of selective association with women and men who shared their values in isolation from the larger college community. Others were attractive and flirtatious enough to enjoy social life with men who still accepted the double standard of morality and for whom they were the "nice" girls. Still others found compensatory sources of ego enhancement in the course of their freshman year so as to make the sexual questions relatively less pressing.

What about the virgins feeling conflict? Some of them were unwavering in their adherence to the norm of premarital chastity, but uncomfortable and defensive, while others were tormented by indecision.

The following case describes a student who felt herself to be a deviant at college and among her friends. But she was both critical about the prevailing code and quite defensive about herself.

> "Well," she said, "I'm a virgin and I'm going to stay a virgin until I get married. I don't think my friends are. My roommate is pretty free with what she gives. She disgusts me but my friends say that what she does is her own business. I guess that's true, but I still feel very uncomfortable around her."
>
> The student surmised that she is uncomfortable with her experienced suitemates because "it makes me odd, I'm the only one who wasn't having any sexual experience."

She went on to explain her attitude toward sex:

> It isn't a matter of religion with me. It is morality. I'd

like to be sure that I was in love with the guy before I went to bed with him. I'm not going to jump into bed with just anybody. I would feel used and somewhat dirty. I don't believe that sex is something that's dirty, but I'd feel that if I just jumped into bed with someone that I wasn't in love with, I would feel that I had compromised my own moral values. Also, although it was never explicitly said in my house, I think I was brought up to believe that you should wait until marriage, that you just shouldn't go to bed with the first guy that you meet. My parents never really said that I had to wait until marriage, but I always felt that they would be disappointed in me if I wasn't in a very serious relationship that was tending toward marriage and I went to bed with a guy.

This student was not embarrassed to talk with her close friends about her attitudes toward sex, but she never spoke up in a group. She reported that in the dormitory women discussed their sexual adventures quite freely, but that it embarrassed her. She never said anything, and if she became too embarrassed by the explicit talk, she left and returned to her room. There was one student on her dorm floor who frequented the college pub, picked up men, and went to bed with them. She was not only casual about her sex life, she was up front about it and did not seem to be embarrassed that she was the most talked-about girl on the floor. Sometimes she came into this student's room to exchange her sexual adventures with the student's equally promiscuous roommate. The student, who was too embarrassed to listen to their talk, left and was very resentful to be "kicked out of my own room."

The male students, this student felt, were able to spot virgins and were out to "get them," because this was deemed a special kind of conquest.

This student herself defined the crux of her stress: She

considered the sexual freedom of her classmates immoral and disgusting and yet they made her feel odd. Her plight might have been the result of fortuitous circumstances of room assignments in the freshman year or of her failure to seek out friends with more congenial values.

Another student, a virgin who believed that premarital sex was wrong, felt that virgins were made to feel on the defensive in the college. Her deep resentment of this attitude is apparent in the following comments:

> One of her three girlfriends at college did have sex with her boyfriend, but then the relationship went sour. "It would crush me to give myself to someone and have it not work out." No, she doesn't judge girls who have had intercourse badly: "Everybody has failings." She was told about another girl who met a guy and they were sexually attracted to each other and had sex. "The way I understood it, it wasn't love, just animal attraction. Guys will just get it from who they can." Another girlfriend was seeing a guy for a while and when she wouldn't have sex with him, he stopped seeing her.
>
> The student met some guys who were "mostly decent," but she was not dating.

For the next sophomore, the decision whether or not to have sexual intercourse was a major conflict.

> I'm pretty happy with myself. There is only one conflict I have and that's a really big thing in my life now. It is sex. I don't know what's the right thing to do. How old do you have to be before you decide when to do it? I am so confused and there's no one I can talk to about it. My two girlfriends who are still virgins are intending to marry their boyfriends in a couple of years, so they don't have to wait that long. They are doing it with the guys they are going to marry. Then there is another

friend who is a "free, liberated woman" who has been having sex for a long time. Her mother is so liberal that she doesn't mind if a guy sleeps over in the house. All of these friends wouldn't understand my confusion.

She went on to explain that she lost a boyfriend because she refused to have sex with him. "I'm just afraid of pregnancy, or that the guy won't want to marry me then." She'd "die" if she had to walk into the student health services to ask for advice. She certainly didn't want to wait forever, but she hated to be pressured by men. She explained that "I don't have firm standards to fall back upon. I sort of apologize when I refuse sex and I really don't know why I am saying 'I'm sorry,' but this only gets the guys aggravated. There's just no one to talk this whole business over with."

These are examples of both adjusted and conflict-ridden virgins. A few others could not be classified because the interviews suggested that some deeper conflicts may have been hidden despite the apparent adjustment. One such student admitted that though she was "somewhat uneasy" about sexual relations, she was not troubled because she had no desire to engage in sexual activities while still in college.

The student did not disapprove of premarital sex in principle. Some of her friends had and others did not have any sexual experiences, and that's a personal decision. She would never discuss sex in a mixed group. She intended to remain a virgin until she found someone that she wanted to spend her life with. She wasn't even sure that she would ever meet a man that she wanted to spend her life with, but she certainly wasn't going to have casual sexual relationships. She does not feel ashamed to talk with her girlfriend about the fact that she's a virgin. She talks to her closest friends about her lack of sexual experience and her lack of desire for sexual experience. One of her girlfriends feels that she's missing a great deal, but she knows for a fact that this friend herself is also a virgin.

While thus far the focus has been upon pressures operating within the college community, there are also other factors at work. Women in late adolescence have close and often ambivalent relationships with their parents, which play a major part in their sexual development. The research did not pursue this problem systematically, but the interviewed students had a good deal to say on the subject when parental relationships were especially supportive or especially tense over the issue of sex. The young women's conflicts were exacerbated when parental attitudes mattered and at the same time ran counter to those of significant peers. Concealment of an affair was a more or less satisfactory method of coping only when parental values did not generate excessive guilt. This is illustrated by a student who explained:

"I get a lot of pressure from my mother about not sleeping with the guys. One time I was staying over at my boyfriend's and my mother tried to phone me at eleven o'clock, at one, three, five, seven. When she finally reached me in the morning, she was hysterical and accused me of sleeping with my boyfriend and of neglecting my work. She offered to buy me a car if I were willing to stay home and commute. My father is a lot more open-minded about sex." He tells her that he was glad that her mother was a virgin but that it's up to her to make her own decision. This student expressed little anxiety over this conflict with her mother.

Although the issue of parent-child relationships as a

factor in the daughter's sexual development falls outside the scope of this research, there are references to this relationship throughout the book.

CASUAL SEX: DEVIANCE OR LIBERATION

Young women who "slept around" were the subject of unfavorable gossip. Whatever rewards they derived from such a life style, they were aware of their deviant status. Interviews with this small minority brought to light either anxiety about their reputation or an angry defiance.

One case illustrates the use of sex as desperate reassurance in the course of a disappointing freshman year. For this student the college turned out to be too pressured an environment, with classmates reacting too intensely to success and failure in academic performance. She explained:

> I would have preferred a more laid-back atmosphere. Worst of all, I had such a strong feeling of not fitting in socially that I went to see a psychiatrist. I expect people to respond warmly to me and I get upset when they don't.
>
> I had relationships with, perhaps, a dozen men in my freshman year—a few one-night stands, some lasting longer. Sometimes, when I just may be in the mood for a one-night stand, it can be okay, it can help you feel good. It can also make you feel lousy about yourself, if you don't understand what's happening from the beginning. You always hope you might enjoy a future with a guy. There is this strong emotional wish for stability with just one guy. But most guys are just interested in running around. One, I remember, was very blunt: "Are you a free bird?" he asked.

This student's attitude toward her sexual behavior is revealed in her own final remark: "I am paranoid about guys telling others about me. I never really told my best girlfriend about any of my sexual relationships. She found out by accident only once when it happened in my room."

But not all promiscuous women felt on the defensive. Some, apparently few in number, viewed themselves as the avant-garde of true sexual liberation, as the "cutting edge" of the new order. Echoes of their ideology were heard now and then beyond their ranks.

For example, one sophomore had a sexual relationship since her senior year in high school with a man attending another college. They discussed the possibility of a future marriage in a lighthearted way, neither one being ready to make a commitment. Because they were separated geographically, this gregarious young woman often accompanied female classmates to parties or to the college pub where, on occasion, some male student made a play for her. She confided a conflict to the interviewer. It was not the temptation to respond to some advances but the lack of her responsiveness that worried her. "Am I denying my sexuality," she wondered, "by refusing a one-night stand? I love my boyfriend but I wonder, is there anything wrong with me that I find a one-night pickup so distasteful, so alarming?"

Another sexually experienced sophomore discussed her current affairs freely with her equally experienced female friends. She expressed great admiration for one of them who was "very active sexually." The latter was determined to experience everything possible, and to learn about her body and its responses. Not particularly popular on her dormitory floor, she nevertheless enjoyed a certain measure of respect because others came to her with their sexual problems. The reporting student felt that this woman made a genuine search for a variety of experiences rather than regarding sex as a series of conquests. She added:

> Unfortunately, I believe that most women at this college have not had really satisfying sexual experiences and are engaging in sex out of competition, to prove to themselves and to their friends that they are sexually attractive. To treat sex as a conquest, the view that another man is an additional notch in her belt—this is a sick attitude, not liberation.

The values of the ideological subculture were described in a diary kept for us by a sophomore:

> What I have noticed in my own friends is the adoption of the traditionally male role of the hunter or the cruiser. I have done it myself to an extent but I have seen it carried too far, to the point where women pick up the very traits that they criticize in men. The behavior is an extension of what might once have been called the "tease." You make sure that you look very good but you don't wait for anyone to notice you. *You* do the eyeing up and down and make sure it's obvious that you are checking them all out. It's carried to an extreme when women will talk to or dance with several men just for the sake of rejecting them soon after. What differentiates these women from the traditional flirt or coquette is that they feel that what they are doing is all part of the greater feminist plan or at least of some sense of liberation, sexual or otherwise.
>
> This attitude comes out even more strongly in conversations about men—with or without men present. I think it's great that women don't feel inhibited about discussing their sexuality or what they like about a man's body. I don't feel a need, however, to discuss the male anatomy with the cold, "macho" eye of a prospective cattle buyer. Such reverse discrimination is inevitable up to a point, but I don't think it's particularly construc-

tive to assume the very characteristics that we are trying to rid men of. I know that some women feel they must do a lot of "catching up" on certain rights and privileges that have traditionally been an exclusively male prerogative. I tend to think there is a difference between "catching up" and running backward.

In rereading yesterday's installment I was reminded of an incident in high school that seemed to shed some light on the topic of women adopting men's attitudes. In the locker room after gym one day several of the girls were describing the evening they had spent at a male strip show the night before. We were all quite fascinated and made immediate plans to go. To prove your success with *all* men was one way to demonstrate your independence from men in general (or your steady boyfriend in particular). I think we all felt that watching men perform erotically for us was as good a way to assert our independence as any.

This account revealed a small group of women who prided themselves on having a string of lovers. The admired goal was to make a conscious decision to pick up an attractive college man, not to be picked up by him. "The ideal is to have the guy end up in your room the next morning, rather than ending up in his." The "superwomen" are those who engage in such freely chosen sex (and a lot of it) and still keep up with academic work. If such reports are to be trusted, there exists a small subculture in which equality is defined as a victory in the male model of sexual behavior: the decision when to have sex, the choice of a partner, the casual attitude toward intercourse, the position of power symbolized by both the initiative and the place of sexual activity.

LESBIANS

With what was perhaps undue caution, the interviewers did not raise the issue of sexual preference, and only two seniors described themselves as lesbians. The lesbian club at the college does not announce the size of its membership, and the questionnaires and interviews provide no way of estimating the number of lesbians on the campus, both members and those unaffiliated with the club. To be sure, this book is primarily a study of the heterosexual majority, but some material on lesbian students was drawn from scattered references in interviews, from two lengthy articles in the college newspaper based on a series of discussions with members of the lesbian club, and from the 1979, 1980, and 1983 interviews with a lesbian student in our sample.

The consensus of the club members, as reported in the college newspaper, was that the college (administration, faculty, and students) has a long way to go to convey full acceptance of lesbianism. (This was also the feeling of male homosexuals in the affiliate college.) The club members said that, despite repeated requests, the single course on the topic of the lesbian in literature is offered only sporadically. Moreover, they felt that many course syllabi could introduce topics dealing with various aspects of lesbianism and that the omission of these issues could not be justified on intellectual grounds. Not only the curriculum closed off avenues of study, but even when students occasionally proposed topics for term papers or research that had any connection with lesbianism, they reported discouragement by professors.

The lesbian club members complained that posters about club activities were sometimes removed from the bulletin boards soon after they were posted and unpleasant graffiti sometimes was found in the college rest rooms. "The kind of discrimination we face," summed up one member, "is not generally blatant; people don't go around carrying signs, 'No Lesbians at This College,' but our daily life is full of incidents that combine to give one a pervasive feeling of being an outsider, of not belonging in one's own college."

In view of the hostile attitudes, the problem of "coming out" is in itself a source of conflict. Of the few who "came out" publicly, one student was interviewed. The majority, if they do "come out" at all, do so very selectively, unwilling to pay the price that such disclosure allegedly entails. One member of the club who revealed her sexual preference to her "straight" friend received this chilling response: "That's fine, but what am I going to say when people see me with you?" The attitudes of the heterosexual interviewees toward lesbian classmates were not systematically explored, but the numerous references made in the course of the interviews ranged from marked hostility to calm acceptance and close friendship.

At the hostile pole was a student who in four years of college never stepped into the women's center on the campus because it had the reputation of radical feminism, which she opposed. She reported her assumption that radical feminism is linked to lesbianism. "I can tell them at a glance," she remarked. "No makeup, no nail polish, very short hair, army fatigue pants, green jacket. My girlfriends and I say to each other: 'There goes one of *them.*' " In contrast, another student's only misgiving about lesbianism was that it inhibited her generally affectionate nature out of fear of transmitting misleading cues.

Socialization into the Lesbian Subculture

The lesbian student K., interviewed in 1979, 1980, and 1983, had her first lesbian experience in high school with a friend of long standing. As a freshman in college, this exceptionally attractive young woman was very popular with socially elite male classmates of the affiliate college, but found dating them unsatisfactory. "Maybe I attract the wrong kind," she observed in her freshman year, "the kind of guys who think of me as merely a decoration, who aren't intelligent enough and don't want friendship with a date." In the beginning of her sophomore year, she had a romantic relationship with a man that was a "complete disaster" because her love for him was not reciprocated. Eventually she stopped dating men completely and by her senior year she "hardly even look[ed] at men."

The interviews with K. throw light on the process of socialization into the lesbian subculture, some of the distinguishing features of this subculture, and the residual conflicts with the family and the "straight" world.

In the second semester of her freshman year K. became friendly with a dedicated and forceful feminist classmate who played a major role in introducing K. to equally committed feminists and, thereby, involved her in feminist activism on the campus. It is likely, but not conclusive, that the two eventually became lovers; but the influence this friend exerted on her outlook was profound. She learned a lot about the E.R.A. and began reading feminist literature apart from requirements in women's studies courses. Her friend also helped her to formulate rebuttals for arguments with conservative friends who opposed feminism. The influence of this friend went beyond strictly intellectual issues to symbolic matters. K. began to understand the objection to tight jeans, which placed women in the role of an object defined as "sexy" by men. Again, K. used to feel that hair on women's legs and underarms was very ugly, but her friend explained the politics behind the decision not to shave. She explained that women allowed men to control what is "beautiful" and "fashionable." The latent dysfunction of this patriarchal control is that women begin to distrust themselves, striving to comply with male standards that they didn't create but have to live up to. K. was in some conflict because her brother and friends at home found women who do not shave "disgusting," but she eventually decided to change her early conceptions and concentrate on the "naturalness" of hair. In the fall of her sophomore year, she stopped shaving and wearing makeup and found that she was saving herself a lot of time and money.

"Some of my friends," she remarked, "thought that it was very ugly, and just one of my 'radical ideas,' but these friends were no longer an important reference group for me. I didn't really care what they thought."

The Lesbian Subculture

K. joined the lesbian club only in her junior year because she had previously not liked the dogmatic people who ran the organization. When they graduated and left, she joined her friends. Since not everyone in the club had "come out," confidentiality was important. Whatever the degree of congeniality, and "not everybody liked everybody else," members could count on mutual support in case of any emergencies and, in general, share the struggle for complete acceptance of gays in society. Some members associate with "straight" classmates, others do not.

K. apparently had two women lovers. The most recent relationship lasted over two years.

K. claims that women pair up and, while the relationship lasts, it is monogamous. "It is a very stable community as a whole, but periodic shifts in alliances do occur. Another difference from dating is that people don't necessarily do things or go places in pairs, just as often in small groups."

For gays, K. thinks, social life is more integrated with academic and college life. Heterosexual social life does take one away looking for and becoming involved with new people outside the college.

"The group has many intellectual interests in common and, whatever the differences in future plans, it is very supportive of all choices—except marriage."

Conflicts

The sophomore year, when K. "came out" to her family and some college classmates, was so full of conflict that she saw a therapist. She suspects that her serious ill health during the year was psychosomatic in origin and was traceable to these conflicts.

K.'s relationship with her mother has always been very strained. Her mother's pressure to achieve was coupled with a lack of confidence in her daughter's abilities to reach these high goals. Her mother told her that she chose to be a lesbian only because heterosexual relationships are harder to maintain. K. remarked that any relationship calls for hard work. Her current female lover is very religious and K. is an agnostic; this is only one of the differences they have to contend with.

K.'s father is generally more passive than her controlling mother. She would like to think he is more sympathetic, but she suspects that he too would prefer a heterosexual life for his daughter.

This case merely suggests the complex interplay of lesbianism and feminism. Much fuller study would be required to ascertain whether or not K.'s is a case of "pseudohomosexuality" in her struggle to resolve ideological and sexual elements (Defries 1976). On the one hand, she had had a lesbian experience in high school (even then she was sympathetic to feminism). On the other hand, she began her college life dating men and acknowledged in her sophomore year a sexual attraction and love for a male classmate who did not reciprocate her sentiments.

Although the psychodynamics of the origins of K.'s lesbianism could not be explored, the case throws some light on gradual stages of socialization into the lesbian subculture. At first, the new ideology was referred back to her brother and her heterosexual friends. Finally, the integration into the new social situation was so complete that, in K.'s own diagnosis, the "straight" associates no longer constituted a significant reference group for her. Hence their divergent views ceased to cause conflict. A major role played by her forceful classmate in the final outcome and some features of the lesbian subculture are other instructive findings of this case.

In conclusion, two findings as to sexual relationships of female undergraduates confirm the results of several studies. The first is the greater sexual permissiveness of women over the past decade or two. The second is the women's yearning for sex in the context of friendship as against casual sex. The difference between males and females on this score is supported by the 1980 Brown University questionnaire study of some 2,000 women and 1,000 men in six eastern colleges. Twice as many women as men "agreed strongly" that "two people should know each other really well before becoming involved in a sexual relationship"—42 percent of women and 19 percent of men.

The author wondered about the emotional wrenching felt by seniors involved in sustained sexual relationships who faced separation from their boyfriends caused by their attending different graduate schools or by accidents of job location. Some found compromise solutions, such as the sacrifice of the graduate school of first choice in order to avoid separation. Many, having found no compromise solutions, did suffer the pangs of impending separation. But other interviewed students did not appear as devastated as one might have expected. Perhaps for those women who had several sexual partners, their relationships were not necessarily more charged with intense affect than steady dating and "making out" short of intercourse was for an earlier generation. The breakup or separation of a relationship that included sexual intercourse need not inevitably be more painful than a termination of a dating relationship was in the past.

10

Conclusion

Dᴵᴰ COLLEGE make a difference? In one form or another, this is the question underlying the multitude of studies of college impacts. To be sure, each of these studies selects only some particular effects, and the present study is no exception. Earlier research focused on intellectual abilities, values, political philosophies, aesthetic and emotional development, or achievement goals; this study examines the role of one college as an agent of socialization of female undergraduates for gender roles. This focus accounts for what might appear to be neglect of other significant aspects of the college experience.

The concern of this book was to examine the impact of college on life-style preferences—specifically, the relative salience of career, marriage, and motherhood in the students' aspirations. We also examined students' attitudes toward the women's movement and the impact of college on occupational decision making.

The logic of such an inquiry requires a threefold structure. The first is, of course, an estimate of the extent and nature of the outcome, both change and persistence in the dependent variables—that is, the effects we set out to discover. Second is the identification of the features of the college experience that were decisive in either stimulating or hindering the changes in question. Finally, there are the initial predispositions, social and psychosocial, that made some students accessible to the operative features of the institution and shielded others from their impact.

MAJOR IMPACTS

Disregarding, for the present, the variations described in chapters 5 to 7, for the sample as a whole the general trend was toward increased career salience combined with family life and toward greater certainty of occupational choice. In comparison with the freshmen, the seniors were more committed in attitudes and behavior to the goals of the women's movement. Concerning their educational plans upon graduation from college, three changes are noteworthy. The percent of students planning to continue to obtain a master's or a doctoral degree declined by the end of the senior year. This is explained in part by the relative increase in the number of students who intended to enter professional schools. Finally, the percentage of those who did not plan to continue, at least not in the immediate future, increased. Some seniors charted a career that did not require a graduate degree. Others had no resources or no desire to continue their education.

Regarding occupational decision making, our major finding is the diversity of patterns. Angrist and Almquist (1975) pointed out that theories generally based on studies of male undergraduates (such as the narrowing down from a general field of interest to a specific occupation) did not fit their data. For example, such an orderly progression of narrowing down of choices described by Ginsberg and associates (1951) was true only of a minority of our students. In contrast to Angrist and Almquist, however, we found that women in our samples were more highly motivated to seek occupations with high status and high income. In general, our identification of six distinct patterns suggests that future research may show that the current emphasis on two or three theories of occupational choice does not do justice to the complexity of the problem.[1]

INSTITUTIONAL STIMULI AND INITIAL PREDISPOSITIONS

Several institutional factors were found to be associated with the dominant changes: the ethos of the college, which not only views the professional aspirations of women seriously but emphasizes their value; the relatively high degree of student-faculty contacts outside the lecture room; the initial openness to diversity in social contacts with classmates and the reinforcing influence of career-committed friends; academic and work experiences such as internships, assistantships, and part-time jobs. The effect of the college's metropolitan setting was not examined systematically, although references to it were frequent in the interviews with students who came from other areas. The more direct consideration of the influence of the metropolis is found in the sections dealing with its rich variety of internships and work experiences.

[1] In this respect our results confirm the conclusion of Titley, Titley, and Wolff (1976) that "an age-related linear progression in the process of career selection for all people in all [college] environments should not be assumed" (p. 110).

These institutional features were singled out because they were associated with differences in outcomes. The closer interaction with the faculty of the career-salient seniors, whether steadfast or converts, was discussed in chapters 5 and 6. These closer contacts were also related to occupational decision making. The constants and the crystallizers—that is, all those who by the end of the senior year were certain of their occupational choices—reported more frequent contacts with the faculty than did the undecided students. The career-salient students referred to female faculty members as role models more frequently than did the traditional seniors. Moreover, the noncareer students exhibited more homogeneity in clique member-ships in the freshman year, had fewer positive work experiences, and manifested a greater resistance to feminist ideology.

These findings present a complex problem of interpre-tation. For example, frequent contacts with the faculty may stimulate and raise the student's professional aspira-tions. But it is also likely that students who enter college with high aspirations initiate such contacts more frequently. The study by Pascarella et al. (1978) is one of several that have attempted to disentangle the causal links. They controlled a sample of freshmen for sex, racial/ethnic origins, high-school achievement, academic aptitude, several personality traits, and the level of parents' education. Holding these factors constant, they still found that the frequency of nonclassroom interaction with the faculty was significantly related to the freshmen's academic per-formance. Higher interaction focused on intellectual and course-related matters had the most pronounced association with a high level of student performance.[2]

Our interview data, lacking such measurements, never-

---

[2] Pascarella and Terenzini (1977) found an inverse correlation between informal student-faculty contacts and voluntary freshman withdrawal from college.

theless strongly suggest a circular and cumulative process, which might be described in more technical terms as feedback loops. Indeed, one of the most striking findings is the ubiquity of these circular and cumulative interactions between the students' initial characteristics and the institutional stimuli. It is in this fashion that seemingly minor initial differences were found to propel these students into ever-widening trajectories over the college years.

The initiative for student-faculty interaction came most frequently by far from the student, not the professors.[3] The factors that made some students reach out to professors are no doubt both social and psychological. Those who attended secondary schools that encouraged such contacts found it natural to follow familiar practices. Psychological motives (be they intellectual curiosity, need for reassurance, or desire to raise a grade) tended to evoke a faculty response that, in turn, strengthened the student's integration into the academic life of the institution. Constructive contacts with the faculty outside of class lectures can benefit the student in a variety of ways. Intellectual development may be furthered by an interchange in which academic problems are clarified, critical skills honed, and intellectual interests inspired. In the capacity of a mentor, the teacher may offer information and opportunities for assistantships and internships, thus reinforcing or lifting occupational aspirations. In the role of an adult counselor, the professor may raise the student's self-confidence to cope with academic and personal problems. The administrative concern with student-faculty ratio and size of classes reflects the recognition of the benefits that accrue from close contacts with the faculty.

When it comes to relationships with female versus male

---

[3] Wilson, Wood, and Gaff (1974) concluded that those teachers who were frequently sought out by students beyond the classroom tended to provide clear cues about their accessibility through their class teaching styles.

faculty, the interview materials can be supplemented with some quantitative results based on questionnaires filled out by our sample of 154 seniors. Women constituted about one-half of the faculty at this college. But since students took courses in other divisions of the university, the questionnaires distributed to seniors did not attempt to ascertain the total numbers of female and male professors who taught them over four years of college. What we did learn was the differences in the students' evaluation of the attributes of the female versus male professors whom they judged to be the most influential in their college career.

The questionnaire filled out by the seniors began with the question: "Think back to the professors you have had since entering college and up to the current semester. Which three stand out as most influential in your development? No names are required, but indicate the sex of the professor." The questionnaire also listed three types of influence, instructing the students to check, if applicable, more than one influence for any professor. The three modes of influence included were: (1) "Has been one of the most intellectually stimulating"; (2) "Provided a model to emulate through other qualities (e.g., drive, compassion, social concern, and others)"; (3) "Has given me encouragement, through personal interest shown in my development."

The senior sample listed 409 female and male professors (some seniors listed fewer than three). The male professors had a slight edge over the female with regard to "intellectual stimulation." Seventy-two percent of the 199 women professors listed were noted as providing intellectual stimulation, whereas 81 percent of the 210 male professors were singled out for this function.

Sex differences become more pronounced with regard to the two other types of valued attributes. Only 44 percent of the "most influential" male, compared to 67 percent of female, professors were appreciated for providing a model to emulate. Finally, 44 percent of male, in comparison with 57 percent of female, professors were cited as encouraging the students through personal concern in their development. When these quantitative results are added to the interview data cited for career-salient students, the conclusion is inescapable that female professors did function as role models, reaffirming or stimulating achievement aspirations and solidifying occupational choices.

Other recent studies shed some additional light on this issue. The Brown University study (1980) does not consider the sex of the professor in its chapter on student-faculty interaction. Nonetheless, it supports our findings indirectly. Women were found to have consistently higher faculty contacts than men in coeducational institutions. The highest levels of faculty contacts, however, were reported by women in single-sex schools. This advantage held across all majors and at all grade-point average levels. Since the proportion of women faculty is highest in women's colleges, students in such institutions enjoy a considerable advantage, as our findings suggest, in contacts with faculty that provide models to emulate and encouragement through personal interest in student development.

The same cyclical interplay between the predispositions the student brings to college and institutional features was observed in differential utilization of other resources of the college, apart from faculty, such as the placement office, the women's center, the counseling services, and the like. The flow of printed material, the announcements that fill the bulletin boards with news of forthcoming conferences, speeches, and workshops, the articles in the college newspapers would almost seem to be invisible to a segment of a student body, whereas others make maximum use of these resources with subsequent influence upon their development.

A repeated theme in the interviews was the role played by a classmate in drawing others into some particular activity. It would appear that some students serve as catalysts, engaging a previously indifferent classmate in the cycle of participation. Students already involved and self-directive serve, much as do opinion leaders in the mass media, as intermediaries between the individual and the college resources. A certain segment of the student body appears to require a primary or personal relationship to serve as a link to existing services.

This brings us to another illustration of the circular process of college impacts, the interaction with peers. The importance of friendships and peer groups in relation to gender role perspectives, as well as other personality development, was noted throughout the book. Many of the early studies of peer groups were based on the assumption that characteristics of the peers have a direct influence upon the subjects of the study. The most recent careful challenge to this assumption is found in the study by Cohen (1983) of peer influence on the decision of high-school students whether to attend college. Peer similarity in aspirations is not a reliable measure of peer influence because it does not control for the initial similarity in aspirations at the time of friendship selection. Cohen concurs with several recent studies in believing that, without controls for initial similarity, the influence of peers is overestimated. He concludes: "High school peer influence on college aspirations is a weak effect with a path coefficient between .10 and .15" (p. 728).

Our interviews confirmed the selective process in the formation of friendships. Occasionally, external circumstances of physical proximity in the dormitories or similar academic programs facilitated initial contacts. One of the most striking differences among freshmen was the degree of ethnic, religious, class, and other value homogeneity of their friends and social cliques. Some, at the outset, sought out like-minded friends, who in turn reinforced their original predispositions. Others did not so restrict their associates and, indeed, were attracted to classmates who differed from them. This degree of openness to heterogeneous groups had further implications. As a result, the students' preconceptions were challenged and their identities sometimes seriously disturbed or broadened or, in any event, modified. This pattern in selection of friends varied not only with individual students but, for some, continued to change at different stages of the college career. Some career-salient students shifted their closest friends from traditional to career salient by their senior year.

Thus the circular process of college influences is again illustrated. Whatever this initial selectivity, the friends, in turn, affected the student's attitudes toward traditional or egalitarian roles or toward other choices and values. Nearly every chapter of this book includes some testimony of a student attributing a change in herself to a classmate, the changes ranging from methods of study to major shifts in outlook on life.

The findings on the effect of the demographic background variables were reported in chapters 4 through 7. Some are, at first glance, surprisingly unrelated to the outcomes. Neither religious nor ethnic affiliations of parental families were related to the outcome variables of the total sample. But the interviews indicated that the decisive feature was the nature of the parents' ideology regarding women's roles. The traditional definition of women's roles differentiated Orthodox from Reformed Jews, unassimilated Asian families from more assimilated ones, and the like. This greater precision in using religion as the independent variable is the likely explanation of the differences between our results and those of studies that did find positive correlations between formal religious affiliations and career salience (for example, Angrist and Almquist 1975: 154). The equally negative results with regard to parental class backgrounds are possibly explained by the original selectivity of daughters from various strata choosing and being admitted to this college. Marital and parental relationships as factors in career salience were discussed at length in part II and do not require recapitulation. The most suggestive findings bear upon the conditions that determine whether the student's mother serves as a positive or a negative role model for her daughter.

I have emphasized the circular process between the "input" variables—that is, the characteristics of the student at entrance—and the impact of the college. The interviews describe the complexity of the process of socialization. The process is far from constituting the student's passive internalization of the dominant values of the institution. The student emerges as an active agent in her development. For one thing, the dominant ethos does not rule out all diversity, and the different subcultures create for the individual pressures and opportunities for choice. The most vivid feature of the interviews is the extent to which the student actively searches or is relatively passive, rejects or feels rejected, is repelled or inspired. She tries on for fit with her initial predispositions one possible reference group after another among her classmates and her teachers.

Another finding of the study deserves mention among these more general conclusions. In chapter 4 I set forth a hypothesis concerning psychological and social correlates of career commitment in women. Contrary to the orthodox psychoanalytic views of Helene Deutsch, I claimed that the correlates of career salience are not constant but vary with the social context. In our society, achieving women are not necessarily the pathological deviants they have been portrayed to be by Deutsch. Neither the frequency of dating in high school, nor the extent of college social life, nor yet the scores on the Adjective Check List for interaction with the opposite sex differentiated career-salient students from their traditional counterparts in this study. Significantly, however, L. R. Young (1976), in reexamining survey data gathered at the University of Michigan in the 1960s, did find that for women—but not for men—career commitment in college was associated with being lonely and friendless. The explanation of the differences between the two studies requires further analysis, but greater social acceptance of careers for women over the past two decades is likely to be one of the explanatory factors.

The study's findings, the author believes, carry some implications for college policy. The problems of transition to college would likely be eased by administrative and educational reforms, such as a drastic increase in number of freshman advisers, greater opportunities for out-of-classroom contacts with the faculty, and required freshman seminars. These changes were just being instituted at the college, too late for this study to investigate their results.

There remains one large and more difficult problem of educational reform. To be sure, a small minority of interviewed students (who were too psychologically disturbed, too poorly prepared for the required level of academic performance, or too serenely committed to other than academic values) could hardly be reached by any feasible changes in educational policy. But another group of students, it would appear, could be helped to benefit more from their college experience. These include students who were either too passive or too vulnerable to some initial blow to their self-esteem to utilize the resources of the college without some faculty intervention. It was not sufficient for the faculty to announce weekly office hours—these students needed a more active "outreach" on the part of the college. Possibly, they required adults who were gifted in facilitating the development of young students. The latter appeared especially sensitive to perfunctory questions or formal didactic pronouncements and even to what they perceived as a teacher's or a counselor's "putting on an act" of concern.

Although the intellectually involved and the relatively passive students differed in the extent of interaction with the faculty, the interviews failed to study whether laboratory courses or seminars provided greater opportunities than lectures for such interaction. There are, of course, teachers whose talents to stimulate the mind and broaden the vision are so extraordinary that they leave a lifelong imprint upon the student in large lectures, with a minimum of personal interaction. But such talents are rare.

Indeed, the capacity to engender intellectual involvement in a potentially able but alienated youth may, generally, be a rare attribute. Unfortunately, the reward system of institutions of higher learning does not encourage either the development or the expression of such gifts on the part of the faculty. The institutional rhetoric may proclaim the ideal of a teacher-scholar, but the publications, as the more visible accomplishments, yield much higher rewards. For college teachers this institutional ambivalence creates an ever-present tension in allocation of time to competing goals. Yet few would challenge the fact that the college might attain its educational goal more fully for a larger proportion of its graduates by increasing the relative rewards of teaching in comparison with publication.

In turning from intellectual to other values, the agenda is more problematic. The revolution of the past fifteen years that freed students from rigid institutional controls, symbolized by the philosophy of *in loco parentis,* was the product of several historical developments. One of these was the fact that many students found more restrictive codes at college than they had experienced in their own families. Inevitably they demanded change. But one by-product of the relinquishment of rigid controls of students' social life appears to be an excessive generational separation. As the varied problems confronting the students were reviewed, the extent of their dependence on their peers for understanding and guidance was especially apparent. But the peers themselves were equally perplexed by the current confusion in gender roles. No institutional reforms, such as live-in faculty advisers in residences and mentoring systems in which faculty members meet students in informal social settings, would guarantee magic solutions. Here, also, adults gifted in establishing productive contacts with the young are needed. In productive relationships, the adult evokes trust, but not a blind following. The aim is to give the young student a better chance to find her own way amid the welter of conflicting pressures and develop to the full her individual potential.

AFTERWORD

For the great majority of the women in this study, relationships with men were a significant concern during college years. Chapters 8 and 9 describe the strains in these relationships that are directly linked to current social changes in gender roles. These chapters are not intended to evaluate recent changes or point in the direction of public policies that might alleviate current problems. Such assessments inescapably reflect the values of the observer. Some reflections on these matters are presented in these concluding pages.

To conceive of a society completely free of human

suffering—painful dilemmas, frustrated goals, conflict, regret, guilt, or unrequited love—defies reality. But the interpersonal and intrapsychic conflicts emphasized in chapters 8 and 9 do not, in the author's opinion, fall into the category of problems intrinsic in the human condition. They stem from the rapid—but not rapid enough—transition from one social system of gender roles to another. At the root is the familiar lead-lag pattern of social transformation: some elements of an interrelated complex have changed while others resist the adaptations necessary to ensure a new social equilibrium.

Before a fuller development of this theme the emphasis on personal problems in chapters 8 and 9 should be qualified. The very conflicts in which the students were embroiled may be viewed as a measure of the progress made toward more egalitarian roles. They often reflect the challenge to the traditional patriarchal system and constitute the cost of change in the direction of greater equality for women. Intellectual rivalry and power contests are signs of this trend. And, to cite a well-known general proposition, anomie, or lack of consensus about norms, creates confusion and conflict. The dating problems generated by this kind of ambiguity have been described. Anomie often leaves the situation open to an unregulated play of self-interest. But the obverse side of ambiguity is the greater freedom of choices it provides. Under favorable conditions it creates a new flexibility, more conducive to harmonious adjustment of the two personalities. For example, the formerly rigid imperative that the man pays the dating expenses is now modified by the relative economic resources of each partner, the circumstances of the occasion, and the character of the relationship. The traditional male financial obligation was, after all, linked to the privileges this bestowed. The obstacles to reaping the advantages of the emerging, more flexible and differentiated set of dating norms stem, generally, from the resistance of one or the other partner to change or from the selfish claim of either to the double dose of privileges, those of the old and those of the new roles.

In calling attention to the positive side in female-male relationships, the author does not intend to minimize the persistent severity of the reported conflicts. In stressing inconsistent mutual expectations of men and women and their anxiety about the future, the interviewed students reiterated a dominant theme of all current literature on the subject. In one of the most recent books, Doyle (1983) claims that women's expectations of both expressive and instrumental qualities in men have "caused many men to become confused or even angered over what they see as a 'no-win' situation" (p. 17). Clearly, despite the positive changes in the status of women and whatever their life-style aspirations, students are bound to face serious problems. The majority of the seniors who hoped to combine careers with motherhood will be forced to depend on makeshift arrangements that will fall far short of what social reorganization *could* provide.

This restates the opening thesis that the problems depicted in this study are, in the author's view, amenable to social control. For one thing, very few of the so-called inconsistent or contradictory mutual expectations that plague female-male relationships today are intrinsically irreconcilable. Many values of a given society create the illusion of contradictions when they are viewed in the abstract. But in reality, in a given social status the actor is called upon to bring into play only those values appropriate to the role. Ideally, the father is nurturant to his child, and the soldier aggressive and destructive in battle.

Gender roles, however, are especially resistant to change precisely because they are linked to gender and not to the particular status or situation of the actor. To return to

Doyle, there is nothing intrinsically contradictory in the woman's wish for both expressive and instrumental qualities in a male partner (or, for that matter, the same wish of a male in a female). Are courage and warmth, competence and tenderness, compassion and self-confidence, and similar alleged dualities really incompatible attributes of human personality? It is much more likely that we have been trapped on the horns of false dilemmas by the traditional stereotypes of femininity and masculinity. If men continue to be socialized to suppress emotional expressiveness at the threat of appearing "sissified," they will be deprived of the capacity for emotional intimacy. If women are made to feel that self-confidence and ambition to succeed in work are "abrasive" and "castrating," they will continue to fail to develop their full human potential.

Must we not abandon these false dilemmas and try to rear both little boys and little girls to be warm and strong, creative and sensitive, able to accept responsibility for themselves and for others? Ideally these are the attributes that in various degrees must be combined in all human beings, played out at different times as the situation demands. We need to present to both sexes more vivid models of egalitarian relationships in order to replace the traditional beliefs so deeply etched in social consciousness.

The changes in psychological sex stereotypes will continue to be resistant to change as long as society maintains the traditional ideology concerning role segregation of the sexes within the family. Such changes are needed for many reasons, including the huge increase in the proportion of working mothers that generally places upon women the triple burden of working, child rearing, and homemaking.

In essence, the equality that the women in this study claim as their due in the public spheres—economic, political, cultural—will not be realized for the vast majority as long as we maintain gender-role segregation within the family, with no alternative *real* options.

There is no profit in minimizing the radical transformations in contemporary value systems and in several social institutions that the realization of the goal of sex equality would require. Real options for men and women will be available only when our society includes—along with economic success, creative professional achievement, athletic prowess, and political power—esteem for nurturant socialization of children not as a task for women only. If men believed for a moment that building bridges, or managing a corporation, or writing books was no more essential to society than helping to shape the personality of a child, they would demand more of a hand in this endeavor too. A recent newspaper article described the plight of several male kindergarten teachers. When they were asked by strangers what they did, they found it expedient to reply that they taught elementary school. One touchstone of the humane society would be their willingness to give an honest answer, unafraid that it would arouse the scorn and suspicion it does in most circles today.

But a society's basic values do not change without institutional reorganization. If we are to translate pious egalitarian proclamations into reality, we shall have to overhaul several institutions in a profound way. Americans are vociferous about the sanctity and centrality of the family, even as they grant every other major institution a prior claim to pursue its interest without the slightest concession to family welfare. For example, the public takes it for granted that the industrial time clock is not to be tampered with, whatever the consequences are for children and families. A recent survey of a large number of American companies showed that only about 33 percent offer some flexible work hours, only 4 percent have policies aimed at helping the spouse of a relocating employee in finding a job, and only 19 percent offer monetary support for childcare facilities.

Strong social movements are necessary to mediate between intolerable conditions and social remedies. On this score, a comparison with Britain and Sweden is revealing. The unprecedented increase in paid employment of mothers with young children in Britain failed to generate enlightened policies with regard to nursery schools, parental leaves of absence, or job sharing. By contrast, in Sweden, a coalition of government, business, and labor resulted in the commitment of the state to cope with the consequences of the entry of women into the labor force (Ruggie 1984).

We are shortsighted if we view these projected reforms as gains for women at the total expense of men. The most poignant regret expressed by male college seniors about parental relationships in an earlier study by the author (Komarovsky 1976) was the distance most experienced in their relationships with their fathers. They were determined to be involved in more active parenting with their own sons. Many voices are heard in favor of such double parenting by mothers and fathers in the interest of a more fully realized potential of human personality.

Once such real options exist, whether more women than men will continue to be involved in nurturant socialization of young children is still an open question, although some writers feel that science has already closed this case. In any event, those who will choose this path will enjoy an honored cultural alternative. High-powered, exceptionally creative individuals, male or female, ambitious to reach peak positions, will choose a single-minded dedication to their careers. Such persons may choose to remain childless or to find mates willing to play complementary roles.

The majority of the college seniors whose views are

reported in this study dreamed of a society in which the father's role in child rearing is given its due importance. They envisioned a world in which the demands of work and family life are balanced by institutional reorganization and social innovations—a world with more symmetrical and egalitarian gender roles.

Appendix

PROFILE OF THE COLLEGE

OF the freshmen who entered the college in 1979, 66 percent came from the Middle Atlantic states and 11 percent from New England. The southern and western states each represented about 6 or 7 percent, with foreign students comprising 4 percent of the entering class. Self-identified minorities included thirty-seven Blacks, forty Latins, fifty-five Asians, and six Chicanos.

The median Scholastic Aptitude Test scores were Verbal 620 and Mathematics 600. With 10.2 percent of the class scoring over 700 on the Verbal section of the SAT, 83.4 percent of the entering class ranked in the top fifth of their secondary schools.

Annual family income reported by students exceeded $26,000 in 55 percent of the cases, with 21 percent under $15,000. Fathers' occupations were either business executives (30 percent) or professional. Only 26 percent of the mothers were full-time homemakers; others were employed in a variety of jobs, with teachers making up the largest proportion (16 percent).

When compared with college freshmen nationally,[1] this class was slightly younger, more liberal, wealthier, and more academically and professionally oriented. It included more Jewish, Catholic, and "no religion" members, fewer

[1] Based on data from Cooperative Institutional Research Program, *The National Freshman Norms for Fall 1979*, Graduate School of Education, University of California at Los Angeles.

Protestants, and more students from small families. They valued the academic reputation of the college, but its connection with the university and location in the metropolis were valued even more positively. Thus, the fact that it was a women's college was not the decisive factor in their choice.

The research strategy of the study is described in the Introduction; the major research tool was the interview, discussed in detail below.

THE INTERVIEW

The twenty-two-page guide provided by the author for the 1980 interviews contained both an inventory of the topics to be covered and suggestions on the techniques for obtaining the data.

Prior to the interview, the interviewers had on hand the following materials for each student: the sets of completed questionnaires for 1979 and 1980 and the transcribed 1979 interview. Therefore, they could initiate the questioning by observing: "I see that in 1979 you checked this item and in 1980 your response was (identical, different)." The interviewer's task was twofold: to ascertain the nature of the changes, if any, in respect to the question under discussion, and to probe the factors accounting for the change or stability of the response.

One of the main impediments in such voluntary interviews is not so much the deliberate refusal of the student to disclose the requested information as her inability to do so. Direct questions often put excessive demands on the student's self-awareness and reflectiveness. Approaches must be devised to stimulate reflection.

A recurrent concern of the study was to scrutinize the influences exerted upon the student's attitudes and development by "significant others," including professors, classmates, and other college personnel as well as persons outside of the institution, especially family members and boyfriends.

The first step in ascertaining the influence of some associate (or role partner) was to seek the latter's own values, beliefs, and attitudes in the given area. For example, with regard to the Life-Style Index, the interviewer asked: "If your boyfriend (mother, father, sister, a particular professor, etc.) saw this schedule, which answer do you think he or she would hope you would check?" Another probe proved useful when the student, initially unsure of the attitude of some associate, was asked to compare it with the views of another. "Well," the student might realize, "A is more (or less) sympathetic to the women's movement than B." Comparisons often brought to a student's awareness some latent observations. Our standard instruction requested the interviewer to follow up such general replies with specific illustrations. This call for specification served two purposes: as a safeguard against perfunctory answers and to convey the precise meaning some general response carried for the student.

Still another procedure was used in probing some sensitive areas. The interviewer generally introduced such lines of questioning with these words: "Students whom we have interviewed varied greatly in their responses to this question, as you can see from these quotes (drawn from the diaries and other interviews). Which of these, if any, are similar or different from your own feelings or thoughts? Is there any response you personally would add to these quotes?" This approach helped some students voice sentiments they might otherwise have been embarrassed to express. Their initial responses were followed by our standard request for concrete illustrations.

The reference made in the introduction to the procedure of "discerning" causal relations within a single case is derived from this author's earlier work (1940: 135–146). The keynote of the procedure is the insistence on specificity and concreteness in conducting the interviews. No general testimony is accepted without understanding its meaning in terms of concrete experience. The application of procedure in this study calls for three steps: the checking of evidence on the possible influence of college in a given area by eliciting specific and concrete illustrations; checking the evidence for its consistency with other situations in the life of the respondent; and testing the possible alternative explanations of the change in question.

OTHER RESEARCH INSTRUMENTS

Of the total questionnaires used in the study, the appendix reproduces only the more complex and those adapted from previous studies in order to add a comparative perspective to our findings. For example, the Gough and Heilbrun Adjective Check List (1965) is a well-known personality test. The Life-Style Index was adapted with one minor change from Angrist and Almquist (1975: 227ff). The Attitudes Toward Sex Roles scale was developed by Spence and Helmreich (1978: 237).

One conclusion emerges from this replication of previous research measures. In the case of our students (and, I suspect, more generally) the shift from traditional to more egalitarian attitudes was so strong that the measures tend to lose their discriminative power. Their continued use forces the researcher to contrast minorities at the extreme poles of the sample and delays the development of new measures, more appropriate to emerging attitudes.

MASCULINE AND FEMININE
PERSONALITY TRAITS

The purpose of this page is to find out your beliefs about average feminine and masculine personality traits in contemporary society (whatever nature or nurture had to do with these traits).

Please check the statement expressing most closely your opinions:

1. Women are more sympathetic than men.
   ____Agree   ____Agree somewhat   ____Uncertain
   ____Disagree somewhat ____Disagree

2. Women are more emotional than men.
   ____Agree   ____Agree somewhat   ____Uncertain
   ____Disagree somewhat ____Disagree

3. Women are more sensitive than men.
   ____Agree   ____Agree somewhat   ____Uncertain
   ____Disagree somewhat ____Disagree

4. Men are more aggressive than women.
   ____Agree   ____Agree somewhat   ____Uncertain
   ____Disagree somewhat ____Disagree

5. Men are more ambitious than women.
   ____Agree   ____Agree somewhat   ____Uncertain
   ____Disagree somewhat ____Disagree

6. Women have a higher moral character than men.
   ____Agree   ____Agree somewhat   ____Uncertain
   ____Disagree somewhat ____Disagree

7. The reasoning ability of men is greater than that of women.
   ____Agree   ____Agree somewhat   ____Uncertain
   ____Disagree somewhat ____Disagree

8. Women are more artistically inclined than men.
   ____Agree   ____Agree somewhat   ____Uncertain
   ____Disagree somewhat ____Disagree

9. It probably goes against basic needs of men and women to place women in a position of authority over men.
   ____Agree   ____Agree somewhat   ____Uncertain
   ____Disagree somewhat ____Disagree

10. Men are more straightforward, less devious, than women.
    ____Agree   ____Agree somewhat   ____Uncertain
    ____Disagree somewhat ____Disagree

11. Women tend to be pettier than men.
    ____Agree   ____Agree somewhat   ____Uncertain
    ____Disagree somewhat ____Disagree

12.   Men are more original than women.

_____Agree   _____Agree somewhat   _____Uncertain
_____Disagree somewhat _____Disagree

13.   Women are more insecure than men.

_____Agree   _____Agree somewhat   _____Uncertain
_____Disagree somewhat _____Disagree

14.   Women are more superficial than men.

_____Agree   _____Agree somewhat   _____Uncertain
_____Disagree somewhat _____Disagree

15.   Women are more artificial than men.

_____Agree   _____Agree somewhat   _____Uncertain
_____Disagree somewhat _____Disagree

16.   Women are more easily offended than men.

_____Agree   _____Agree somewhat   _____Uncertain
_____Disagree somewhat _____Disagree

SOURCE: See K. Kammeyer, "The Feminine Role: An Analysis of Attitudes Consistency," *Journal of Marriage and the Family* (August 1964): 295–305; and K. P. Johnson, "A Progress Report on a Study of Factors Associated with the Male's Tendency to Negatively Stereotype the Female," *Sociological Focus* (1969): 21–35. Reprinted by permission.

ATTITUDES TOWARD SEX ROLES

The statements listed below describe attitudes toward the roles of women in society which different people have. There are no right or wrong answers, only opinions. You are asked to express your feelings about each statement by indicating whether you (A) agree strongly, (B) agree mildly, (C) disagree mildly, or (D) disagree strongly.

1.   Swearing and obscenity are more repulsive in the speech of a woman than a man.

A	B	C	D
Agree strongly	Agree mildly	Disagree mildly	Disagree strongly

2. Under modern economic conditions with women being active outside the home, men should share in household tasks such as washing dishes and doing the laundry.

A	B	C	D
Agree strongly	Agree mildly	Disagree mildly	Disagree strongly

3. It is insulting to women to have the "obey" clause remain in the marriage service.

A	B	C	D
Agree strongly	Agree mildly	Disagree mildly	Disagree strongly

4. A woman should be as free as a man to propose marriage.

A	B	C	D
Agree strongly	Agree mildly	Disagree mildly	Disagree strongly

5. Women should worry less about their rights and more about becoming good wives and mothers.

A	B	C	D
Agree strongly	Agree mildly	Disagree mildly	Disagree strongly

6. Women should assume their rightful place in business and all the professions along with men.

A	B	C	D
Agree strongly	Agree mildly	Disagree mildly	Disagree strongly

7. A woman should not expect to go to exactly the same places or to have quite the same freedom of action as a man.

A	B	C	D
Agree strongly	Agree mildly	Disagree mildly	Disagree strongly

8. It is ridiculous for a woman to run a locomotive and for a man to darn socks.

A	B	C	D
Agree strongly	Agree mildly	Disagree mildly	Disagree strongly

9. The intellectual leadership of a community should be largely in the hands of men.

A	B	C	D
Agree strongly	Agree mildly	Disagree mildly	Disagree strongly

10. Women should be given equal opportunity with men for apprenticeship in the various trades.

A	B	C	D
Agree strongly	Agree mildly	Disagree mildly	Disagree strongly

11. Women earning as much as their dates should bear equally the expense when they go out together.

A	B	C	D
Agree strongly	Agree mildly	Disagree mildly	Disagree strongly

12. Sons in a family should be given more encouragement to go to college than daughters.

A	B	C	D
Agree strongly	Agree mildly	Disagree mildly	Disagree strongly

13. In general, the father should have greater authority than the mother in the bringing up of children.

A	B	C	D
Agree strongly	Agree mildly	Disagree mildly	Disagree strongly

14. Economic and social freedom is worth far more to women than acceptance of the ideal of femininity which has been set up by men.

A	B	C	D
Agree strongly	Agree mildly	Disagree mildly	Disagree strongly

15. There are many jobs in which men should be given preference over women in being hired or promoted.

A	B	C	D
Agree strongly	Agree mildly	Disagree mildly	Disagree strongly

SOURCE: Adapted from J. T. Spence and R. L. Helmreich, *Masculinity and Femininity: Their Psychological Dimensions, Correlates, and Antecedents* (Austin: University of Texas Press, 1978), p. 237.

THE LIFE-STYLE INDEX

I. As far as you can tell now, do you plan to continue your education after receiving a bachelor's degree? Please circle the appropriate number:

       Yes, graduate school   1

       Yes, professional school   2

Yes, other training   3
No, I do not plan to continue   4

II. Below are some conditions under which women work. Rate yourself on these by speculating how you might feel about holding a job after marriage and graduation from college. Circle 1, 2, 3, 4, or 5 according to *whether you would want to work under each condition.* (Be sure to rate yourself on all 7 conditions.)

		Definitely Not	Probably Not	Unde-cided	Probably Would	Definitely Would
1.	No children; husband's salary adequate.	1	2	3	4	5
2.	One child of preschool age; husband's salary adequate.	1	2	3	4	5
3.	One child of preschool age; husband's salary not adequate.	1	2	3	4	5
4.	Two or more children of preschool age; husband's salary not adequate.	1	2	3	4	5
5.	Two or more children of school age; husband's salary adequate.	1	2	3	4	5
6.	Two or more children of school age; husbands salary not adequate.	1	2	3	4	5
7.	Children have grown up and left home; husband's salary adequate.	1	2	3	4	5

III.   Assume that you are trained for the occupation of
       your choice, that you will marry and have children,
       and that your husband will earn enough so that you
       will never have to work unless you want to. Under
       these conditions, which of the following would you
       prefer (circle one):

To participate in clubs or volunteer work   1
To spend time on hobbies, sports, or
   other activities   2
To work part-time in your chosen
   occupation
   Please check 3a, 3b, or 3c
   To work part-time with preschool
   children   3a
   To work part-time as long as children
   are of school age   3b
   To work part-time whatever the age of
   the children   3c
To work full-time in your chosen
   occupation   4
To concentrate on home and family   5
Other (explain briefly)   6

IV.   Fifteen years from now, would you like to be:

A housewife with no children   1
A housewife with one or more children   2
An unmarried career woman   3
A married career woman without children   4
A married career woman with children   5
Other: what?   6

SOURCE: Adapted, with revision of part III, from S. S. Angrist and E. M.
Almquist, *Careers and Contingencies: How College Women Juggle with Gender* (New
York: Dunelen, 1975), pp. 237 ff. Reprinted by permission.

RELATIONSHIP TO MOTHER
IN CHILDHOOD

1. She made me feel wanted and needed
   ____very true   ____tended to   ____tended to   ____very
                        be true   be untrue   untrue

2. She set very few rules for me
   ____very true   ____tended to   ____tended to   ____very
                        be true   be untrue   untrue

3. She praised me when I deserved it
   ____very true   ____tended to   ____tended to   ____very
                        be true   be untrue   untrue

4. She never let me get away with breaking a rule
   ____very true   ____tended to   ____tended to   ____very
                        be true   be untrue   untrue

5. She ridiculed me and made fun of me
   ____very true   ____tended to   ____tended to   ____very
                        be true   be untrue   untrue

6. She wanted me to have complete control of my actions
   ____very true   ____tended to   ____tended to   ____very
                        be true   be untrue   untrue

7. She acted as if I didn't exist
   ____very true   ____tended to   ____tended to   ____very
                        be true   be untrue   untrue

8. She pushed me to do well in school
   ____very true   ____tended to   ____tended to   ____very
                        be true   be untrue   untrue

9. She was overprotective of me
   ____very true   ____tended to   ____tended to   ____very
                        be true   be untrue   untrue

10. She tended to keep out of and withdraw from family situations
    that might be unpleasant
    ____very true   ____tended to   ____tended to   ____very
                         be true   be untrue   untrue

SOURCE: Adapted with permission from A. Roe and M. Siegelman, "A Parent-Child Relationship Questionnaire," *Child Development* 34(1963):355–369.

RELATIONSHIP TO FATHER
IN CHILDHOOD

1. He made me feel wanted and needed
____very true   ____tended to   ____tended to   ____very
    be true   be untrue   untrue

2. He set very few rules for me
____very true   ____tended to   ____tended to   ____very
    be true   be untrue   untrue

3. He praised me when I deserved it
____very true   ____tended to   ____tended to   ____very
    be true   be untrue   untrue

4. He never let me get away with breaking a rule
____very true   ____tended to   ____tended to   ____very
    be true   be untrue   untrue

5. He ridiculed me and made fun of me
____very true   ____tended to   ____tended to   ____very
    be true   be untrue   untrue

6. He wanted to have complete control of my actions
____very true   ____tended to   ____tended to   ____very
    be true   be untrue   untrue

7. He acted as if I didn't exist
____very true   ____tended to   ____tended to   ____very
    be true   be untrue   untrue

8. He pushed me to do well in school
____very true   ____tended to   ____tended to   ____very
    be true   be untrue   untrue

9. He was overprotective of me
____very true   ____tended to   ____tended to   ____very
    be true   be untrue   untrue

10. He tended to keep out of and withdraw from family situations
that might be unpleasant
____very true   ____tended to   ____tended to   ____very
    be true   be untrue   untrue

SOURCE: See note, page 332.

FAMILY RELATIONSHIPS

Every family is not only a whole unit, but a number of twosomes. For each of the following twosomes in the family in which you grew up, check the category which best describes the relationship.

	Very tense and strained	Somewhat tense and strained	Neutral	Somewhat close and intimate	Very close and intimate	No such twosome
Mother and father						
Mother and me						
Father and me						
An older brother and me						
A younger brother and me						
An older sister and me						
A younger sister and me						

Which of your parents do you take after in A. personality and temperament; B. intelligence; and C. outlook on life?

	A. Personality and temperament	B. Intelligence	C. Outlook on life
Neither parent			
Mother only			
Father only			
Both parents, but mother more			
Both parents, but father more			
Both parents equally			
Don't know			

SOURCE: This questionnaire was used in the first follow-up of 1961 seniors by the National Opinion Research Center Study, conducted in 1964 (Chicago: N.O.R.C.). Reprinted by permission.

FAMILY BACKGROUND

1. What is your father's occupation (or, if he is retired or deceased, what was his occupation)? Please give a detailed answer, such as "welder in an automobile factory," "high school English teacher," "accountant in a large insurance company."

2. Does he (or did he) work for himself or for someone else?

   1 _____ for himself   2 _____ for someone else

3. About how much was your father's income last year as far as you know? (If your father is not the chief breadwinner in the family, indicate income of main earner.)

1 _____ less than $3,000	5 _____ $10,000 to $15,000
2 _____ $3,000 to $5,000	6 _____ $15,000 to $20,000
3 _____ $5,000 to $7,500	7 _____ $20,000 to $30,000
4 _____ $7,500 to $10,000	8 _____ over $30,000

4. How certain are you about this income?

   1 _____ I am quite certain about it
   2 _____ I know it approximately
   3 _____ I am mostly guessing

5. How much formal education did your father have? Your mother?

Father		Mother
1 _____	Some grade school	_____ 1
2 _____	Finished grade school	_____ 2
3 _____	Some high school	_____ 3
4 _____	Finished high school	_____ 4
5 _____	Some college	_____ 5
6 _____	Finished college	_____ 6
7 _____	Graduate or professional school after college	_____ 7

6. How old are your parents? (Guess if you are not sure):
    Father's age _____   Mother's age _____

7. Do you have any sisters or brothers?
    1 _____ yes   2 _____ no
    If yes: List them in order of their ages:

Sisters' Ages	Brothers' Ages
1 _____	1 _____
2 _____	2 _____
3 _____	3 _____
4 _____	4 _____
5 _____	5 _____
6 _____	6 _____

8. How many of your sisters will probably go or have gone to college? _____

9. How many of your brothers will probably go or have gone to college? _____

10. In what country were your parents born?
    Father's country of birth _____
    Mother's country of birth _____

11. What is your parents' religious background?

Mother		Father
1 _____	Protestant	_____ 1
2 _____	Catholic	_____ 2
3 _____	Jewish	_____ 3
4 _____	Other (What?)	_____ 4

12. Do your parents belong to a church, synagogue or temple?
    Mother 1 _____ yes   2 _____ no
    Father 1 _____ yes   2 _____ no

13. How old are you? _____

14. Where were you born? (Give city, state and country)

    _____

15. Does your mother now hold a paying job or has she ever worked during your lifetime? (Including managing her own business or working in a family business.)

    1 _____ yes, she works now full-time

    2 _____ yes, she works now part-time

    3 _____ yes, she worked previously but not now

    4 _____ no, she never worked during my lifetime

16. If she has worked during your lifetime, what different jobs has she held? (Describe as precisely as you can):

    1 _____

    2 _____

    3 _____

    4 _____

17. Did your mother ever receive special occupational or professional training?

    1 _____ yes   2 _____ no

    If yes, describe briefly _____

    _____

18. As far as you know, did your mother ever work for pay before you were born?

    1 _____ yes   2 _____ no   3 _____ not certain

    If yes, what work did she do? _____

19. In the past few years, has your mother been active in any of the following? (check one or more):

    1 _____ clubs or organizations

2 _____ community or volunteer work

3 _____ sports

4 _____ hobbies . . . Which ones? _____

5 _____ other . . . What? _____

6 _____ no, she has not been active in these ways

SOURCE: The author is indebted to S. S. Angrist and E. M. Almquist for permission to use this schedule (private communication).

Bibliography

Angrist, S. S., and Almquist, E. M. "Role Model Influence on College Women's Career Aspirations." Paper presented at the 65th annual meeting of the American Sociological Association, 1970.
———. *Careers and Contingencies: How College Women Juggle with Gender.* New York: Dunelen, 1975.
Astin, A. A. *Four Critical Years.* San Francisco: Jossey-Bass, 1978.
Astin, H. S., et al. *Women: A Bibliography on Their Education and Careers.* Washington, D.C.: Human Service Press, 1971.
Auster, C. J., and Auster, Donald. "Factors Influencing Women's Choice of Nontraditional Careers: The Role of Family Peers and Counselors." *Vocational Guidance Quarterly* 29, no. 3 (1980): 253–256.

Bakan, D. *The Duality of Human Existence.* Chicago: Rand McNally, 1966.
Baruch, G. K. "Maternal Influence Upon College Women's Attitudes Towards Women and Work." *Developmental Psychology* 6, no. 1 (1972): 32–37.
Bose, C. E., and Priest-Jones, J. *The Relationship Between Women's Studies Career Development and Vocational Choice.* Washington, D.C.: National Institute of Education, 1980.
Brim, O., and Wheeler, S. *Socialization After Childhood.* New York: John Wiley, 1966.
Broverman, I. K., et al. "Sex-role Stereotypes and Clinical Judgments of Mental Health." *Journal of Consulting and Clinical Psychology* 34, no. 1 (1970): 1–7.
———. "Sex-role Stereotypes: A Current Appraisal." *Journal of Social Issues* 28, no. 2 (1972): 59–78.
Brown, M. D. "Career Plans of College Women: Patterns and Influences." In P. J. Perun, ed., *The Undergraduate Woman: Issues in Educational Equity.* Lexington, Mass.: Lexington Books, 1982.
Brown University. "Men and Women Learning Together: A Study of College Students in the Late 70's." Report of *Brown Project*, 1980.

Cherlin, A. "Postponing Marriage: The Influence of Young Women's Work Expectations." *Journal of Marriage and the Family* 42, no. 2 (1980): 355–365.
Clark, B. R., et al. *Students and Colleges: Interaction and Change.* Berkeley:

Center for Research and Development in Higher Education, University of California at Berkeley, 1972.

Cohen, J. "Peer Influence on College Aspirations with the Initial Aspirations Controlled." *American Sociological Review* 48 (1983): 728–734.

Cooperative Institutional Research Program. *The National Freshman Norms for Fall 1979.* Graduate School of Education. Los Angeles: University of California.

Cross, P. *Beyond the Open Door.* San Francisco: Jossey-Bass, 1971.

Davis, J. A. "The Campus as a Frog Pond." *American Journal of Sociology* 72 (1966): 17–31.

Defries, Z. "Pseudohomosexuality in Feminist Students." *American Journal of Psychiatry* 133, no. 4 (1976): 400–404.

Der-Karabetian, A., and Smith, A. "Sex-role Stereotyping in the United States: Is it Changing?" *Sex Roles* 3, no. 2 (1977): 193–198.

Deutsch, H. *The Psychology of Women: A Psychoanalytic Interpretation.* New York: Grune & Stratton, 1945.

Doyle, J. A. *The Male Experience.* Dubuque, Iowa: Wm. C Brown Publishing, 1983.

Drew, D. E., and Astin, A. W. "Undergraduate Aspirations: A Test of Several Theories." *American Journal of Sociology* 77, no. 6 (1972): 1151–1164.

Epstein, G. F., and Bronzaft, A. L. "Female Freshmen View Their Roles." *Journal of Marriage and the Family* 34, no. 4 (1974): 671–672.

Feldman, R. A., and Newcomb, T. M. *The Impact of College on Students,* vol. 1, *An Analysis of Four Decades of Research.* San Francisco: Jossey-Bass, 1969.

Fernberger, S. W. "Persistence of Stereotypes Concerning Sex Differences." *Journal of Abnormal and Social Psychology* 43 (1948): 97–101.

Fitzgerald, L. F., and Crites, J. O. "Towards a Career Psychology of Women." *Journal of Counseling Psychology* 27, no. 1 (1980): 44–62.

Foote, N. N. "Changing Concepts of Masculinity and Femininity." In *The Individual, Sex and Society,* edited by C. P. Broderick and J. Bernard. Baltimore: Johns Hopkins University Press, 1969.

Freeman, H. R. "Sex-role Stereotypes: Self-Concepts and Measured Personality Characteristics in College Women and Men." *Sex Roles* 5, no. 1 (1979): 99–103.

Gallup Opinion Index. *Report 128.* March 1976, p. 30. Princeton: Gallup International, Inc.

Ginsburg, E.; Ginsberg, S. W.; Axelrod, S.; and Herma, J. L. *Occupational*

Choice: An Approach to General Theory. New York: Columbia University Press, 1951.

Goldsen, R. K.; Rosenberg, M.; and Williams, R. M., Jr. *What College Students Think.* Princeton: Van Nostrandt, 1960.

Gough, H. G., and Heilbrun, A. B. *Adjective Check List Manual.* Palo Alto, Calif.: Consulting Psychologists Press, 1965.

Haber, S. "Cognitive Support for the Career Choices of College Women." *Sex Roles* 6, no. 1 (1980): 129–138.

Holland, D. C., and Eisenhart, M. A. "Women's Peer Group and Choice of Career." N. I. E. Final Report (unpublished). Chapel Hill, N.C.: Policy Research and Learning Group Inc., 1981.

Jacob, P. E. *Changing Values in College: An Exploratory Study of Impact of College Teaching.* New York: Harper Bros., 1957.

Johnson, K. P. "A Progress Report on a Study of Factors Associated with the Male's Tendency to Negatively Stereotype the Female." *Sociological Focus* 3 (1969): 21–35.

Johnson, M. M. "Sex Learning in the Nuclear Family." *Child Development* 34 (1963): 319–333.

Kammeyer, K. "The Feminine Role: An Analysis of Attitudes Consistency." *Journal of Marriage and the Family* 26 (August 1964): 295–305.

Kaufman, D. R.; and Richardson, B. L. *Achievement and Women.* New York: The Free Press, 1982.

Kirkpatrick, C. "The Measurement of Ethical Inconsistency in Marriage." *International Journal of Ethics* 48 (1936): 444–460.

Komarovsky, M. *The Unemployed Man and His Family.* New York: Farrar, Straus & Giroux, Inc., 1940.

———. "The Class of '44 Considers our Family Patterns." *Barnard Quarterly* (Spring 1943): 12–20.

———. "Cultural Contradictions and Sex Roles." *American Journal of Sociology* 52 (1946): 182–189.

———. *Women in the Modern World: Their Education and Their Dilemmas.* New York: Irvington Publications, 1953.

———. *Dilemmas of Masculinity: A Study of College Youth.* New York: Norton, 1976.

Korn, H. A. "Career: Choice, Chance and Inertia." In *Growth and Constraint in College Students,* edited by J. Katz. Stanford, Calif.: Stanford Institute for the Study of Human Problems, 1967.

Lipman-Blumen, J. "How Ideology Shapes Women's Lives." *Scientific American* (January 1972): 34–42.

Lipman-Blumen, J.; and Thompson, P. G. "Maternal Employment and

Adult Role Orientations of Young Married Women." Paper presented at the 71st annual meeting of the American Sociological Association, 1976.

Lueptow, L. B. "Stability in Sex-role Orientations." *Sociological Focus* 13 (1980): 125–141.

McKee, J. P.; and Sherriffs, A. C. "The Differential Evaluation of Males and Females." *Journal of Personality* 25 (1957): 356–371.

———. "Men's and Women's Beliefs: Ideals and Self Concepts." *American Journal of Sociology* 64, no. 4 (1959): 356–363.

Mason, K. O.; and Bumpass, L. L. "U.S. Women's Sex-Role Ideology, 1970." *American Journal of Sociology* 80, no. 5 (1975): 1212–1219.

Mason, K. O., et al. "Change in U.S. Women's Sex-Role Attitudes, 1964–74." *American Sociological Review* (August 1976): 573–596.

Mattfeld, J.; and Van Aken, C., eds. *Women in the Scientific Profession.* Cambridge, Mass.: MIT Press, 1965.

Merton, R. K. *Social Theory and Social Structure.* New York: The Free Press, 1968.

Monteiro, L. "The College Academic Environment. Student-Faculty Interaction." In Report of *Brown Project.* Brown University, 1980.

Newcomb, T. M. *Personality and Social Change.* New York: Holt, Rinehart & Winston, 1943.

Newcomb, T. M., et al. *Persistence and Change.* New York: Wiley, 1967.

Newcomb, T. M., and Wilson, E. K., eds. *College Peer Groups.* National Opinion Research Center. Chicago: Aldine, 1966. (Several important articles.)

Nielsen, J. M., and Doyle, P. T. "Sex-Role Stereotypes of Feminists and Non-feminists." *Sex Roles* 1, no. 1 (1975): 83–95.

Nye, F. L., and Hoffman, L. W. *The Employed Mothers in America.* Chicago: Rand McNally, 1963.

Oates, M. J., and Williamson, S. "Women's Colleges and Women Achievers." *Signs* 3 (Summer 1978): 795–806.

Parelius, A. P. "Change and Stability in Women's Orientation Towards Education, Family and Work." *Social Problems* 22 (1975): 420–431.

———. "Emerging Sex-Role Attitudes and Strains Among College Women." *Journal of Marriage and the Family* 37, no. 1 (1975): 146–153.

Parish, S., and Powell, E. M. "A Comparison of Adult Women's and Men's Ascriptions of Negative Traits to the Same and Opposite Sex." *Sex Roles* 6, no. 3 (1980): 457–462.

Parsons, J. E., et al. "Intrapsychic Factors Influencing Career Aspirations of College Women." *Sex Roles* (1978).

Pascarella, E. T., and Terenzini, P. T. "Patterns of Student-Faculty Informal Interaction Beyond the Classroom and Voluntary Freshman Attrition." *Journal of Educational Research* 71 (September/October 1977): 21–26.

Pascarella, E. T., et al. "Student-Faculty Interactional Settings and Their Relationship to Predicted Academic Performance." *Journal of Higher Education* 49, no. 5 (1978): 450–463.

Petro, C. S., and Putnam, B. A. "Sex-Role Stereotypes: Issues of Attitudinal Change." *Sex Roles* 5, no. 1 (1979): 29–39.

Rapin, L. S., and Cooper, M. A. "Images of Men and Women." *Psychology of Women Quarterly* 5, no. 2 (1980): 186–195.

Ridgeway, C. L. "Predicting College Women's Aspirations from Evaluations of the Housewife and Work Role." *Sociological Quarterly* 19 (Spring 1978): 281–291.

Roe, A., and Siegelman, M. "A Parent-Child Relationship Questionnaire." *Child Development* 34 (1963): 355–369.

Rosenkrantz, P. S.; Vogel, S. R.; and Broverman, D. M. "Sex-role Stereotypes and Self-Concepts in College Students." *Journal of Consulting and Clinical Psychology* 32 (1968): 287–295.

Rossi, A. S. "The Roots of Ambivalence in American Women." Paper presented at Continuing Education Conference, Oakland University, Michigan, 1967.

Ruggie, M. *The State and Working Women: A Comparative Study of Britain and Sweden.* Princeton, N.J.: Princeton University Press, 1984.

Sanford, N., ed. *The American College.* New York: John Wiley, 1962. (Some individual contributions stimulating for hypotheses.)

Schlossberg, N. K. "The Right to Be Wrong Is Gone: Women in Academe." *Educational Record* 55 (Fall 1974).

Sherriffs, A. C., and McKee, J. P. "Qualitative Aspects of Beliefs About Men and Women." *Journal of Personality* 25 (1957): 451–464.

Simpson, R. L., and Simpson, G. H. "Occupational Choice Among Career Oriented College Women." *Journal of Marriage and the Family* 23 (1961): 377–383.

Spence, J. T., and Helmreich, R. L. "The Attitude Towards Women Scale." *JSAS Catalog of Selected Documents in Psychology* 2 (1972): 667–668 (ms. no. 153).

———. *Masculinity and Femininity: Their Psychological Dimensions, Correlates, and Antecedents.* Austin: University of Texas Press, 1978.

Tangri, S. S. "Determinants of Occupational Role Innovation Among College Women." *Journal of Social Issues* 28, no. 2 (1972): 177–99.

Thornton, A., and Freedman, D. *Consistency of Sex Role Attitudes of Women, 1962–1977* (Working Paper Series). Ann Arbor: Institute for

Social Research, University of Michigan, August 1979.

————. "Changes in Sex Role Attitudes of Women, 1962–1977: Evidence from a Panel Study." *American Sociological Review* 44 (1979): 832–842.

Tidball, M. E. "Perspective on Academic Women and Affirmative Action." *Educational Record* 54 (Spring 1973): 130–135.

————, and Kistiakowsky, V. "Baccalaureate Origins of American Scientists and Scholars." Science 193 (1976): 646–652.

Titley, W.; Titley, B.; and Wolff, M. "The Major Changers: Continuity or Discontinuity in the Career Decision Process." *Vocational Behavior* 8 (1976): 105–111.

Wallace, W. L. "Peer Groups and Student Achievement: The College Campus and Its Students." Chicago: Report 91, National Opinion Research Center, 1963.

————. "Institutional and Life-Cycle Socialization of College Freshmen." *American Journal of Sociology* 70 (1964): 303–318.

————. *Student Culture: Social Structure and Continuity in a Liberal Arts College.* Chicago: Aldine, 1966.

White, B. J. "The Relationship of Self-Concept and Parental Identification to Women's Vocational Interests." *Journal of Counseling* 2 (1959): 202–206.

Wilson, R.; Wood, L.; and Gaff, J. "Social-Psychological Accessibility and Faculty-Student Interaction Beyond the Classroom." *Sociology of Education* 47 (1974): 74–93.

Woloch, N. *Women and the American Experience.* New York: Alfred A. Knopf, 1984.

The Women's College Coalition. "The 1980 Profile of Women's Colleges." Washington, D.C., 1980.

Yankelovich, D. *The New Morality.* New York: McGraw-Hill, 1974.

Young, L. R. "Career Commitment, Sex Roles, and College Education." Ph.D. diss., State University of New York at Stony Brook, 1976.

Index

academic performance, 31, 107; and career choice, 207; and career salience, 132–33, 152–53, 175–77, 197; coping with setbacks in, 203–4; expectations of, at entrance, 107; poor, 218, 219; and self-concept, 30–40, 81–82; of shifters, 209

"achieving woman," Deutsch's theory of, challenged, 110–11, 310–11

administrative reform, 311

administrators, 142

adolescence, 30, 73

affiliated male college (this study), 18, 35, 226, 274, 294

affiliation score on ACL and career salience, 112

aggression score on ACL and career salience, 112

alienation, 19, 21–22, 23, 27; from academic program, 209; from parents, 59

Almquist, E. M., 90, 108n11, 120n1, 123n2, 200n1, 205n2, 220–21, 302–3, 324

ambivalence: about feminism, 183–84; parental, 40, 147, 159–60, 170–71; in separation from family, 65–66, 69; toward work, 136–37; institutional ambivalence, 312

American Civil Liberties Union, 180–81

androgynous ideal, 96, 97, 103, 104

Angrist, S. S., 90, 108n11, 120n1, 123n2, 200n1, 205n2, 220–21, 302–3, 324

anomie, 229–34, 248, 314

anxiety: in career choice, 201, 211, 219; about grades, 203

architecture students, 207

Asian-American students, 24, 309; career salience of, 108–9, 128–29, 130, 166, 196

Asian Students' Club, 130

athletes, status-set conflict, 255–60

attitude change, freshman to senior, 117–62

Attitudes Toward Sex Roles scale, 89, 324, 326–29

autonomy score on ACL and career salience, 112, 114; work and, 92

beliefs about psychological sex differences of career and noncareer students, 115; consistency of beliefs and other elements of gender perspective, 99–106

Black students, 24; career salience, 108–9, 129, 166–67

boarding school, 59

boyfriend(s), 40, 272; and career salience, 193; role in independence from parents, 64–65; separation from, 299–300; traditional, 228, 234–38